The Best American
Travel Writing 2000

The Best American Travel Writing 2000

Edited and with an Introduction
by **Bill Bryson**

Jason Wilson, *Series Editor*

HOUGHTON MIFFLIN COMPANY
BOSTON · NEW YORK   2000

ISSN 1530-1516
ISBN 0-618-07466-X
ISBN 0-618-07467-8 (pbk.)

Printed in the United States of America

QUM 10 9 8 7 6 5 4 3 2 1

Contents

Foreword: Why Travel Stories Matter

WHEN I WAS still in school, I spent a summer in a small Italian village named Pieve San Giacomo. I lived with a family on a farm, with chickens and pigs walking outside my window. Every day I took the train into the city of Cremona for school or played soccer with the local boys or rode my bicycle through the village, and every night I ate vegetables and meat from the farm and drank homemade wine. I learned the dialect. By summer's end, I had become an adopted part of *la famiglia.*

A few days before I left, the family's recently widowed aunt put on a tremendous Sunday feast, just for me. Her whitewashed courtyard was jammed with tables of breads and pastries and cheeses and Coca-Cola, bought especially for me. At the end of the meal, which lasted four hours, she presented me with a gift: her dead husband's huge yellow floral-print bathrobe.

"You'll promise to wear this?" she asked, tears welling up in her eyes. Here I was, a teenager with an already filled backpack getting ready to shove off for the rest of Europe. What the hell was I going to do with a gigantic ugly bathrobe? What could I do? I smashed down what clothes I could and left the rest behind. I carried the heavy bathrobe. I still have that ugly robe hanging in my bathroom today. I've carried it through a dozen moves, from dorms to apartments to houses.

When I came home from Italy, I was prepared to tell people about the many cathedrals I'd visited, *David,* the mosaics at Ravenna, sipping cappuccinos in cafés, the beautiful women in Milan, Mama saying "*Mangia, mangia*" — any variation of *la dolce vita* they wanted. But all anybody wanted to hear about was that one feast in one widow's courtyard. And about that bathrobe.

"The more we know of particular things," Spinoza wrote long ago, "the more we know of God." This is perhaps never truer than with travel writing. Having a travel writer report on particular things, small things, the specific ways in which people act and interact, is perhaps our best way of getting beyond the clichés that we tell each other about different places and cultures, and about ourselves.

In his essay "Why We Travel," Pico Iyer writes, "Travel is the best way we have of rescuing the humanity of places, and saving them from abstraction or ideology." Abstraction is what has given rise to one of the biggest myths going: the supposed "globalization" of the world. The idea that we all share one insidious monoculture. That very soon the world will all be the same.

For sure, the influence our exported American consumer products and values has had on the world is undeniable: there is a T.G.I. Friday's in Tegucigalpa, there is a McDonald's in Ulan Bator, and there are children on the streets of Hanoi singing songs recorded by Britney Spears. But things are rarely as simple and clearcut as we would like to believe. Though information has never been easier to find — everyone can find Web sites about Madagascar, or flip to the Discovery Channel and see Masai warriors or to ESPN and see Australian rules football or to MTV and see Tibetan monks — we, as Americans, understand less and less about the world.

Just because our American pop culture has spread like a virus doesn't mean the world is suddenly turning monochromatic. Look closely at the specific ways in which various cultures adopt American icons and ideas and see how quickly your notion of globalization becomes confounded.

A taxi driver in Managua and I almost came to blows over a misunderstanding about a fare. When the misunderstanding was finally cleared up (it was mainly the fault of my horrible Spanish), the driver turned off the meter and shook my hand. "Now we are friends," he said with a warm smile. "To show you there are no bad feelings, I will now play some American music for you." He popped in a cassette, and Kenny Rogers's "The Gambler" soon emanated from the speakers.

Saintíl, my guide in Haiti, told me that his favorite actor was Shaquille O'Neal. He particularly loved O'Neal's work in the movie *Steel*. Saintíl's two-room home in Port-au-Prince, where he lived with his wife and eight children, was powered by a rusty generator. This allowed, if he was lucky, about four hours of electricity each day. For almost two of those four hours, Saintíl would use the generator to power his VCR and his television so that he could watch American movies — some, he hoped, starring Shaquille O'Neal.

No, though we've been told otherwise, the world never quits growing on us. It's just as vast as ever, and it reinvents itself every day. The job of the travel writer in the twenty-first century is the same job that it was in the time of Herodotus or Marco Polo or James Boswell or Charles Darwin: to chart this new world in all its rich detail, then report back. This is why travel writing remains as popular as ever with readers.

One of the beauties of travel writing lies in its simplicity. What other genre has a premise that's so straightforward? Pick a place. Tell about it. It's the most basic of writing exercises, one we can all remember from school. What fourth-grader hasn't written an essay called "What I Did on My Summer Vacation"?

All of us have gone somewhere. It matters little whether we've gone to visit Aunt Bea's in Sheboygan via Greyhound, schussed down the log flume at Great Adventure, renovated a home in Provence or at the Jersey shore, been pinned down by a blizzard on Everest, or performed some peddling-across-Uzbekistan-on-a-BigWheel kind of stunt. Face it: these days, we've all got a travel story to tell. Lots of people keep travel diaries. Almost everybody has written a postcard at one time or another. Traveling, after all, is what most of us like to do for fun, so writing about the experiences we have wherever we go can't possibly be work, right?

But since I've already laid out how important travel writing is, I must stress that it should be left in the hands of skilled professionals, people who've spent years of toil and struggle getting advanced degrees from Travel Writing School, people who have kneeled and kissed the ring of elder travel writers, people who . . .

Okay, okay. Of course I'm kidding. No one has to spend any

amount of money or time to call himself a travel writer. There's no secret handshake. No initiation ritual. No ceremonial gowns or fezzes. And just as everyone can imagine, it's a pretty damn enjoyable way to make a buck.

But be warned. Just because traveling is fun and everyone can tell a travel story, not everyone should do it. Think about that bore who explains the floorplan of each museum he set foot in and every meal he ate during his twelve-cities-in-nine-days bus tour through Europe. Think about that teenage friend of yours who returns from trekking in Nepal or Sedona or the Green Mountains and begins and ends his description of the trip with "Duuuude." Think about that blowhard next to you in the airport who, after the flight is pronounced late, tells you in excruciating detail about each and every time she's ever experienced a flight delay.

When I was maybe seven, my parents took me to dinner at the home of some family friends. The friends, whom we'll call Mr. and Mrs. Dwyer, had just returned from their honeymoon in Acapulco. As luck would have it, Mr. and Mrs. Dwyer had taken one of those Super 8 movie cameras with them.

After dinner we were escorted into the Dwyers' rec room. Little did we know of the documentary surprises that awaited us. A little canvas screen had been set up, and a card table, on which a small film projector sat. Next to the projector stood a five-foot stack of little blue plastic film canisters. Mr. Dwyer proudly threaded the first reel into the projector, and the lights were dimmed.

In living, grainy, hand-held Technicolor, the Dwyers' honeymoon trip passed before us: Mr. and Mrs. Dwyer getting off the plane; Mr. and Mrs. Dwyer serenaded by a brass band in sombreros; Mr. and Mrs. Dwyer settling into their well-appointed suite; Mr. and Mrs. Dwyer getting a little tipsy on margaritas at poolside.

My father and mother exchanged exasperated glances and eyed the stack of little blue canisters. The next reel opened with Mr. and Mrs. Dwyer bobbing on a deep-sea fishing boat. For several minutes there was lots of high-speed waving by the Dwyers and their crew. Then Mr. Dwyer suddenly had a strike and started reeling in his fishing line.

At that point, all we saw was choppy, out-of-focus ocean, with the occasional bobbing white of the boat along the bottom. Every few minutes a little speck of black appeared in the distance. "See!

That's a marlin," said Mr. Dwyer, pointing at the screen. My parents looked at Mr. Dwyer with dazed smiles plastered on their faces. We all soon learned that it can take nearly an hour to land a marlin in the open ocean.

As our rear ends fell asleep on the Dwyers' couch, my parents continued to sit and nod politely in the darkened rec room. All of us counted the stack of little blue canisters as it slowly shrank, canister by canister. Mr. Dwyer finally landed his fish. But then there was Mrs. Dwyer waving, getting a strike, and the first mate helping her to reel it in. Two, three more blue canisters down. And then an unknown man was reeling in a marlin. "This is a guy we met on the boat. Great guy" was Mr. Dwyer's explanation.

Several hours later, the stack of blue canisters was exhausted. When we finally escaped and staggered to our car, my parents heaved a sigh of relief. And then they chuckled. And then they playfully cursed their hosts the whole way home. From the back seat, I listened, then asked, "Why did we stay?" "To teach you a lesson," my father said, still laughing. "What lesson?" I asked. My father, most likely at an utter loss for words over, let alone a lesson from, what had just transpired, simply said, "If you go somewhere and you feel you have to tell people about it, pick out a few interesting things and leave the rest alone. Don't just tell people everything. Don't ever do that to people."

Like the Dwyers, a great deal of contemporary travel writing tries to tell us too much, as if one magazine article could entirely sum up what Quebec or Antwerp or Cape Town means. Why would anyone attempt to tell us everything about San Juan or Cairo or Helsinki in 2,500 words (or more likely 2,300 words, once the story is trimmed to fit between the pretty pictures)? In those cases, San Juan or Cairo or Helsinki comes into focus no more than a blurry ocean sporadically interrupted by a little black speck in the distance that's identified, somehow, as a marlin.

The travel stories selected for this anthology, however, represent just the opposite experience. Though their topics are diverse — drinking the first drink of the day, breaking down in the middle of the desert, picking up hitchhikers in Cuba, playing golf in Greenland, smuggling cheese from France, witnessing the birth of a new state — they share common traits. The writers here are all keen observers who bring places to life by honing in on particular, human details. Their writing also pulsates with true emotion — love, desire, humor, fear, despair. They give us just a slice of the world, but in that slice they teach us a great deal.

"The misperception is that the travel book is about a country," Paul Theroux once told me. "It's really about the person who's traveling." Travel stories are necessarily told in the first person. This point of view is one of their strengths, and where the importance always lies. Great travel writing is guided by a strong voice that is not afraid to take a stand. The writer's biases and misperceptions are also paraded before the reader, for they create a context for the writer's hard-won insights about a place. There's little attempt at a supposed objectivity. One of the important messages of a good travel piece is, This is my trip and no one else's.

Travel writing is always about a specific moment in time. The writer imbues that moment with everything that he or she has experienced, observed, read, lived, bringing all of his or her talent to bear on it. When focused on that one moment, great travel writing can teach us something about the world that no other genre can. Perhaps travel writing's foremost lesson is this: we may never walk this way again, and even if we do, we will never be the same people as we are right now. Most important, the world we move through will never be the same place again. This is why travel writing matters today.

A few words about how the following stories came to be included in the inaugural edition of *The Best American Travel Writing*. I surveyed nearly three hundred publications that publish travel material, from Sunday newspaper travel sections to niche publications to literary journals to in-flight magazines. My eyes are far from perfect. But I have done my best to be fair, and in my opinion the best one hundred stories were forwarded to Bill Bryson, our outstanding guest editor. Mr. Bryson has been a pleasure to work with, and I greatly appreciate the care with which he has chosen the twenty-five selections for this anthology. I believe that as you read, you will see that he has put together an excellent collection that will stand the test of time very well.

And so, as this anthology is being published, I have begun anew by reading hundreds of travel essays and articles published this year. I am once again asking editors to submit the best of whatever it is they define as "travel writing." These submissions must be nonfiction pieces published in the United States during the year 2000. Reprints and excerpts from published books are not accepted. Each submission must include the author's name, the date of publication, and the publication's name, and must be submitted as tearsheets, a copy of the whole publication, or a clear photocopy of the piece as it originally appeared.

All submissions must be received by February 1, 2001, if they are to be considered for the next volume. Publications that want to make certain that their contributions will be considered should be sure to include this anthology on their subscription list. Submissions or subscriptions should be sent to Jason Wilson, *The Best American Travel Writing*, P.O. Box 260, Haddonfield, NJ 08033.

I want to thank Don Hymans and Ryan Boyle at Houghton Mifflin for all their support in making *The Best American Travel Writing 2000* happen. The staff at the Haddonfield Public Library was most helpful with this project, as were all the editors who sent nominations, which made this task less stressful. Of course Jennifer and the rest of my family were instrumental in helping me keep my sanity. But the writers deserve the greatest credit, both for this series and for continuing to make travel writing a vital enterprise. *The Best American Travel Writing 2000* is their book, and I promise you will enjoy it.

Jason Wilson

Introduction

Travel writing, as I once observed elsewhere, is the most accommodating — one might almost say the most promiscuous — of genres. Write a book or essay that might otherwise be catalogued under memoir, humor, anthropology, or natural history, and as long as you leave the property at some point, you can call it travel writing.

With luck or persistence, you might even find a publisher willing to underwrite the cost of the trip. I remember the moment it occurred to me that this was an unusually agreeable way to make a living. It was in the early 1980s, when I was living in London. In those days I had a desk job for the London *Times*, but to supplement my income I began in my spare time to write small articles for newspapers and magazines. Usually these were features on some aspect of British life or culture, but once, more or less out of the blue, I was asked by an editor of the in-flight magazine of Trans World Airlines if I would go to Copenhagen, where the airline was about to inaugurate flights, and write of its attractions.

Well, Copenhagen is a splendid city, and I had the most marvelous time. It was while dawdling over a coffee on Strøget, the city's principal pedestrian thoroughfare, that the giddy if somewhat tardy realization dawned on me that I was spending five days in a European capital at someone else's expense, having an awfully good time, and that all that was required of me in return was to write down a thousand words or so of observation on what I saw and did. And for this I was to be paid real money — pretty good money, as I recall. It was then it occurred to me that this was a pretty well unbeatable way to make a living.

So I began to write travel books. The problem was that in the 1980s there wasn't any real market for them in the United States. Travel books at that time meant guidebooks and almost nothing more. Occasionally someone would write a travel narrative that would attract critical attention and sell well — Paul Theroux with *The Great Railway Bazaar,* William Least Heat-Moon with *Blue Highways* — but for some reason they weren't allowed into the travel section. Once a travel narrative was published and had finished its time on the "New Releases" shelves (which in my case seemed to be something in the region of three or four hours), there wasn't any place to put it. On those occasions when I dropped into bookstores to visit my old titles and helpfully move them to positions where they might catch the eye of someone less than eight feet tall or not lying supine in the aisle, I would generally find them in the oddest places, shelved under current affairs or social commentary or geography — anywhere, in short, but near the travel section, where Fodor, Frommer, and *Let's Go* reigned supreme.

How happy I am to report that all that has changed, though it took an amazingly long time when you consider how big the travel literature market has been in other countries for years. The first time I can recall seeing travel books (by which I mean real books with chapters and a story to tell) gathered together in their own section anywhere in the United States was only in about 1990, in San Francisco. But little by little the practice has spread until now it is customary, if not quite universal, for bookstores to offer an assortment of literary travel titles among the more conventional guides. It is telling, I think, that while anthologies comprising the year's best essays, short stories, sports writing, and plays, among goodness knows what else, have been around for years, and sometimes decades, it is only now, thanks to the dear and enlightened folks at Houghton Mifflin, that travel writing is being accorded equal standing. It feels like a genre whose time has come.

The question that naturally arises is why all this has taken so long. The United States is, after all, a nation predicated on the idea of movement — the movement that brought people to the country in the first place and then kept them spreading out from east to west. There is still a restlessness in the American character — a willingness to up sticks and move elsewhere without much in the way of a backward glance — that would strike many people in more settled countries as at the very least unusual, perhaps even just a trifle shiftless. In any case, if anyone ought to be predisposed by nature and history to an interest in the excitement and possibility presented by the unfamiliar and far-flung, then surely it would be us. Yet with a few exceptions — Mark Twain and S. J. Perelman from time to time, the tireless Paul Theroux more regularly — few American writers of a literary bent have been tempted into the field. Insofar as the exotic features in American letters, it is nearly always as a backdrop for fiction. What a pity we haven't got Dorothy Parker traveling through Weimar Germany, say, or William Faulkner in Africa, or Robert Benchley bemusedly scrutinizing the Orient, or John Updike anywhere at all.

It's a curious omission when you consider just how durable and popular the field has been elsewhere. In Britain, travel writing has long been a mainstay of publishing. Since at least *Smollett's Travels Through France and Italy,* published in 1766, scarcely a writer of note in British literature has not at some time turned his hand to travel writing. Johnson and Boswell, Sterne, Dickens, Darwin (with *The Voyage of the Beagle* — a travel book par excellence), Anthony and Frances Trollope, Robert Louis Stevenson, D. H. Lawrence, E. M. Forster, Evelyn Waugh, George Orwell, Graham Greene, Winston Churchill, and others well beyond enumerating all produced travel books, often very good ones. Moreover, many of Britain's most gifted writers — Redmond O'Hanlon, Jonathan Raban, Norman Lewis, Jan Morris, Eric Newby, Bruce Chatwin, and Colin Thubron — have built successful careers largely, sometimes all but exclusively, on the idea of traveling to a place and writing about it.

It seems entirely possible that something like that may be happening in the United States now. As the pages that follow amply demonstrate, many of the sharpest minds and freshest voices in journalism are drawn to foreign subjects these days — increasingly (and encouragingly) to places far beyond the trampled paths of tourism. A generation ago, I daresay a book of this sort would have been dominated by European and American destinations — Capri and Pamplona and the Florida Keys. Today instead we get places of a far more diverse and challenging nature: Zanzibar, Cambodia, the Atlas Mountains of Morocco, the forbidding Cape York Peninsula in Australia. That the geographical spread of this collection is so largely exotic pleases me no end, but I should note that it is less a reflection of my own predispositions than those of the publications from which these selections were culled.

All this, it goes without saying, is heartening to see. One of the first things that struck me when I first ventured abroad in the early 1970s was how much more attention, compared with America, the rest of the world paid to the rest of the world; and one of the first things that struck me when I returned to the States to live twenty years later was how much less attention we paid now than we had before. Though there are some commendable exceptions — notably that great underappreciated asset National Public Radio and some of our larger daily newspapers, as well as many of the magazines whose contributors are represented in this volume — most of our popular media seem to be much less drawn to foreign matters than formerly. I urge you sometime to go to a library and look at *Time* or *Newsweek* magazines from the 1950s or early 1960s. You will find that they are dense with reports from abroad — of tottering governments in Italy or corruption scandals in South America and so on — and their covers were as often graced with portraits of foreign notables as of domestic ones. There seemed then to be a genuine and natural interest in the politics and culture of foreign societies, a presumption that what people were up to in Paris and Rio and Capetown was worth knowing. In those days too, if you are old enough to recall, the evening news on television would always have at least a sprinkling of reports each showing a serious-looking correspondent in a trenchcoat standing with a microphone in front of a foreign stock exchange or flotilla of bobbing sampans or Congress of the People's Revolution — something that was patently not North American. Even if you paid no attention to these dispatches, they at least reminded you that you existed in a wider world.

No longer. In 1997, for a column I was then writing for a British newspaper, I tracked *Time* for the first three months of the year. In that period, our most venerable news magazine offered its readers not one report from France, Italy, Spain, or even Japan, among many, many others not present. Britain attracted notice just once, for the cloning of a sheep in Scotland, and Germany likewise managed a single appearance, because of a dispute between its government and American Scientologists. As I write (in the early spring of 2000), this week's issue of *Newsweek* contains three articles filed from abroad. *Time* has none. Not one. (In fairness, it does have one article on the United States' troubled relationship with Colombia, but written in Washington.) For purposes of comparison, the current issue of Britain's *Economist* has sixty-four articles on foreign topics.

Television can hardly claim to be much better. During the same period that I was monitoring *Time* magazine I devoted five weeknights to watching CNN's main hour-long evening news program. In the course of that week it ran 112 news reports, of which just 8 concerned non-American topics — and this on a program that calls itself (with exquisite if unintended irony) *The World Today.*

I don't mean this as a criticism — at least, not exactly. There are all kinds of extenuating circumstances for our failure to follow the rest of the planet as keenly as we might. A very large part of what happens in the world — in politics, finance, entertainment, you name it — originates in the United States. All the world's news pages are disproportionately filled with happenings from America. Only for us, of course, it's domestic news, not foreign. Of those sixty-four foreign articles in *The Economist,* almost fifty concerned American affairs. It isn't that foreign news publications are inherently more devoted to foreign news coverage, more that they are merely as interested in America as we are.

There is also the consideration that we are lulled into complacency by the ubiquitousness of our culture. A Briton traveling abroad who craves a serving of steak and kidney pudding or news of how Leicester City fared in its soccer match on Saturday will, in most places, be out of luck. A Frenchman traveling abroad is unlikely to hear his favorite pop tunes playing in the background (and thank goodness, of course). An Australian or New Zealander knows that for the duration of any trip overseas he will almost certainly read or hear no news of home. A poor Canadian has only to step over the forty-ninth parallel into the United States to find his country disappearing even from weather maps. But for a traveling American, in most places America is there already — American foods, soft drinks, movies, songs, newspapers, stock market results. It is entirely possible for an American to travel abroad without, in a sense, actually leaving home.

One of the oddest travel experiences I have ever had — odd simply because I didn't realize this was what it was like for so many tourists — came early in my freelance career when I was invited as a guest lecturer on a Rhine cruise. I had recently written an article for *National Geographic* on the new Main–Danube Canal, a German engineering wonder, and I was thus somehow deemed to be an authority on European waterways.

The ship on which we cruised bore a complement of perhaps seventy or eighty passengers, all American, of late middle age or beyond, and clearly well heeled. (The week's trip was costing them something like $3,500 apiece.) It was a pleasant if somewhat low-key undertaking, in that each day we would sit on a deck or in the grand salon, watching Germany slide by in the background, rather as if we were watching it on a very large screen television. Late each afternoon the ship would tie up at some cheery and attractive Rhineland village. After hours of such untaxing confinement, I couldn't wait to get off, to stretch my legs and wander through the streets or browse in shop windows or have a cup of coffee — to be, in short, in Germany. And here was the odd thing that struck me. Each day, upon docking, all the other passengers would eagerly assemble by the gangway and wait for the tour guide to step up to escort them en masse, rolled umbrella held aloft, to the market square or Baroque church or whatever other attractions the community offered, sparing them the necessity of having to puzzle over German signs or fumble with marks and pfennigs. On most evenings we ate aboard the ship, but on a couple of occasions we were loaded onto buses and driven off to some restaurant or *Bierstube*, which we would entirely take over, and there over the perky cacophony of an oompah band we would sample German life without Germans. On the last day, as we stood on the quayside in Cologne waiting for our bags to be offloaded, I fell into conversation with a fellow passenger, who professed the trip a huge success. For no particular reason — just making conversation really — I asked him how he had found the Germans.

He thought hard for a minute. "I'm not sure we met any," he replied with a vaguely troubled expression.

I have since accompanied two other groups on similiar excursions in which the participants paid large sums to be transported to some distant place and then shielded from it. Seems very odd to me. To my mind, the greatest reward and luxury of travel is to be able to experience everyday things as if for the first time, to be in a position in which almost nothing is so familiar that it can be taken for granted.

I grew up in the middle of the country in a middle-income household in the middle of the century. As with most families of that time and place, we were not great adventurers. In our house, ketchup and Cool Whip were the most exotic sauces. Overseas travel was not remotely an option. So when, in 1972, I arrived as a gangly (for which read pimply and squinting) young backpacker in Europe, I was about as innocent as a traveler can be. In those days the only cheap flights to Europe were on Icelandic Airlines to Luxembourg, so it was in that endearingly diminutive country's equally small-scale capital that I had my first look at another world. I cannot tell you how exciting it was. I walked about for hours in a kind of vivid daze, astounded to discover that there were so many interesting ways to do fundamentally mundane things. Everything that came before me was novel. I hardly knew where to put my amazed and besotted gaze. As I wrote in a book called *Neither Here Nor There:*

> I had never seen a zebra crossing before, never seen a tram, never seen an unsliced loaf of bread (never even considered it an option), never seen anyone wearing a beret who expected to be taken seriously, never seen people go to a different shop for each item of dinner or pro- vide their own shopping bags, never seen feathered pheasants and un- skinned rabbits hanging in a butcher's window or a pig's head grinning on a platter. And the people — why, they were Luxembourgers. I don't know why this amazed me so, but it did. I kept thinking: "That man over there, he's a Luxembourger. And so is that girl. They don't know any- thing about the New York Yankees, they don't know the theme tune to the Mickey Mouse Club, they are from another world." It was just wonderful.

I regret to say that I have never advanced terribly far from that happy day. My own requirements for adventure are so easily achieved that a stroll around Luxembourg still gives me nearly all the buzz I need, I'm afraid. So I have long been fascinated by, and filled with admiration for, those people who really travel — people like Tim Cahill, Mark Hertsgaard, Isabel Hilton, and Jeffrey Tayler, whose contributions I am proud to see included here. I once did a reading in Birmingham, England, with the British travel writer Colin Thubron, long a hero of mine, and afterward rode with him on a train back to London. He had just returned from a long trip through the remote parts of western China, as I recall. Thubron is a modest and undemonstrative fellow, but he grew animated as he described for me the pleasures of spending weeks sleeping on hard floors, eating strange and stringy foods, being days beyond the reach of editors and friends. I had always thought of that kind of discomfort and dislocation as the price you paid to experience interesting places, but not part of the pleasure. For Thubron it was — he positively rejoiced in it — and to me it was the greatest revelation. I suppose we most admire what we cannot do, and I cannot be truly adventurous. For that reason, many of the articles collected here represent risky travel to challenging places. One in particular, "The Last Safari," by Mark Ross, is, I guarantee, one of the most harrowing reports you will read this year. It isn't strictly travel writing at all, but it was too good and too moving not to include.

Essentially, however, the pieces that follow are here simply because I liked them. In almost every instance I started off reading about some trip or experience that I had no certain expectation that I would find absorbing, and quickly found myself immersed and engaged, sometimes transported. Apart from the deftness of touch and originality of observation that you would naturally expect to find in any compilation of the year's best of anything, about all that the pieces that follow have in common is that their authors went somewhere, though as some of the contributions prove — notably Bill Buford's game and good-natured account of a night spent in Central Park and David Halberstam's fond survey of the changes that have overtaken his beloved Nantucket in a generation — you don't necessarily have to go far to achieve something memorable. You just have to be able to see things in a different way.

They share, I think, one other outstanding quality: a penetrating curiosity, an almost compulsive desire to experience and try to understand the world at some unfamiliar level. Even when matters are not proceeding smoothly, as in Ryszard Kapuscinski's brilliantly unsettling account of being stuck in the middle of nowhere in Africa or Patrick Symmes's no less gripping portrayal of a run-in with former Khmers Rouges in Cambodia, you have a sense that these authors would not have traded their experiences for anything. In nearly every case, you feel that if it were not for the mildly irksome need to return to civilization to file their stories, they would just have kept on going.

The fact is, of course, that there is an amazing world out there — full of interesting, delightful, unexpected, extraordinary stuff that most of us know little about and consider much too seldom. Turn the page and I promise you will begin to see what I mean.

BILL BRYSON

WILLIAM BOOTH

Boat Camp

FROM *The Washington Post Magazine*

IT MUST BE some old but stubborn gene that causes this odd stirring, this tug that pulls like a spring tide. Almost every sailor I know suffers the affliction. We dream the dream of boats on water.

With the night lamp on, I lie in landlocked bed and read the strangest things: instructions for winch disassembly, dense meteorological texts and detailed cruising guides to coral atolls I will never visit. My wife finds this sweetly nutty, the hours I can spend studying a dog-eared catalogue comparing knot meters. But she does not know this: when I cannot sleep, I close my eyes and remember days on water. And if I am lucky, if I can push away the dayplanner of ordinary life, then in that cusp before real sleep comes, my last conscious thought is of the ocean a mile from my home, a sea so blue it is purple, moving and alive beneath the clockwork of stars, and there, somewhere way out on the edge of the continental shelf, is a tight little ship, and what have I launched, but a dream?

Though I am not sure exactly why, I thought it a good idea to begin to race again. What I wanted to experience was not Sunday afternoon dinghy races around the buoys, but an overnight ocean race on a serious boat, with a serious captain and crew, a real race, with the vague intention of lending myself out as crew here and there around southern California, and then someday talking a skipper after a couple of drinks into letting me accompany him or her on a Transpac, the annual race from San Francisco to Honolulu. But you gotta crawl before you walk.

The biggest race in southern California yachting circles is the sprint from Newport Beach, California, to Ensenada, Mexico, one of the most popular and best attended sailing events in North America, which has been running every year since 1948. Some five hundred competitors race 125 nautical miles to Old Mexico at average speeds, depending on the wind and the boat, between the pace reached by a determined retiree with a walker and Ben Jonson stoked on steroids.

So I called Vic Stern.

Vic's name and number were listed under "race seminar chairman" in one of the local sailing rags, and a few minutes on the telephone revealed more: Vic had sailed his boat, the same boat, in thirty-five Newport–Ensenada races. Consecutively. Never missed a start. I told him I was looking for a ride. He suggested himself. It never occurred to me to ask, then, why a captain so experienced, so salty, would need a fresh, untested, and not entirely skilled hand he'd never met. It was not until much later, perhaps in Bahia Todos Santos, where the shouting began, that I had an idea.

Early on a Friday morning in April, I arrived at the dock at Alamitos Bay and got my first look at *Imi Loa* (Hawaiian for "distant wanderer"), the forty-two-foot ocean-racing catamaran that would be my home for the next four days. In a marina filled with yachts so well maintained they look like floating pieces of Louis XIV furniture, *Imi Loa* was a standout. Above decks, the peeling varnish on her wood had turned a sickly gray-orange, and the oldest spinnaker winches, dating to the 1950s, were oxidized with age. Below, in the main salon, the portholes were crazed and cloudy, so you could not see out the windows, and the cushions were a slimy green vinyl, the kind of pads you might see in Third World hospitals. I noticed that gear — huge shackles and snatch blocks and batteries swollen with rust — was stashed in the cubbyholes, and that in the panels where electronics and gauges once glowed with essential information, there were fistfuls of exposed wiring.

And now comes Vic.

A shore trim gent with a dapper mustache and battered tennis shoes, here he was, at a time in his life when many of his contemporaries are intimidated by a round of golf, marching around the docks with a nimble intensity.

Vic was seventy-five years old.

I would learn later that Vic was a retired Cold Warrior from the military-industrial complex, a Berkeley Ph.D. astrophysicist with a love for Wagner and Mahler, who had spent his career thinking about the cleverest ways to penetrate hardened silos with deep burrowing nuclear warheads.

Well met! Glad to be aboard!

But Vic did not have time for bonhomie.

"Yes, hello, we need to get going."

He handed me a large cardboard box filled with groceries and told me to stow it. The other six crew members were already busy, pulling lines out of lockers, dragging immense sail bags onto the deck. Two of the experienced hands — Harry, the leathery first mate, already stripped to his shorts, a marlinspike hanging from a lanyard tied to his waist, and quiet, bespectacled, polite Gordon — were grunting and swearing over the new cradle for the outboard motor with a finicky throttle that was supposed to get us out of the docks and to ward the starting line ten miles south off Newport Beach.

The two other new crew members and I, the cherries, sort of flailed around, looking for odd jobs to be helpful about without doing something horribly wrong. On came the beer (not nearly enough!) and then the bags of ice, and suddenly, the motor was gulping for air, then purring psychotically, and Harry pushed *Imi Loa* out of her slip beside the Crab Pot restaurant and flung himself aboard.

It was out into the channel, and we raised the mainsail and the genoa jib, but the winds were contrary, and the engine, with a smoker's hack, hiccuped, spat phlegm, rattled deep in its lungs, and died, and we drifted toward the rocks of the breakwater, and there were tense long seconds, one-Mississippi, two-Mississippi, but Harry revived the engine and we were free of rocks and shore. This is something elemental but I think quite philosophical, which takes new sailors time to understand: it is not the sea that one needs to fear. It is the land.

The start of any sailboat race appears, and often is, an unorganized and organic moment.

It is not a ballet.

It is a mosh pit.

This is because sailboats cannot be still, and do not start from a standing stop, but are constantly jockeying for position, motors forbidden, tacking and jibing, as the minutes and seconds are counted down, and blue, white, and red flags on the committee boat are raised and lowered, and finally a shotgun or a cannon blasts, and you're off, wondering what happened.

When there are 438 boats and two starting tines, as there were this day for the fifty-first running of the Newport–Ensenada race, it looks like a slow-motion pileup on an icy interstate. Total chaos. The person who does not feel the exhilaration and dread of a big start has given up the will to live.

Imi Loa was in the first group to start. There was great confusion because the committee boat failed to raise and lower certain flags when it should have, and the start was a snarl, and boats were called "over early" and had to return and start again, including *Imi Loa* and one of our competitors, the superfast catamaran *Stars & Stripes,* of America's Cup fame, which was skippered by adventurer-balloonist-sailor Steve Fossett. *Stars & Stripes* would win the race in a record-breaking 6 hours and 46 minutes, averaging 18.5 knots (a knot is the speed of one nautical mile per hour, equal to 1.15 miles per hour on land). As *Imi Loa* tacked to return to the line, *Stars & Stripes* streaked by, one hull out of the water. "This is gonna be a ride, dude!" shouted David, a twenty-something crewman on *Imi Loa* who spends summers racing boats and winters skiing mountains.

And the dude was right. In a few minutes, in a clean, fresh breeze of about 15 to 18 knots off the stern quarter, the spinnaker came out of the bag and was hoisted, and *BAMMM!* it snapped open and filled, this sail so monstro-powerful that you sensed it as an animate object, willful and dangerously conscious, and suddenly you could feel the acceleration, like giving a young horse that is still a little bit crazy its head, and *Imi Loa* went from walk to gallop, and Harry was yelling from the foredeck, gaddammit this and gaddammit that, and in the cockpit, I and the other cherries were working like monkeys on amphetamines, pulling in lines four turns around the winches, winches as big around as a pie tin, and the loads were so great, the lines stretched and pinged like piano wires.

It has been said so often, in such florid prose, that the observation has become banal. But: what a thing a boat is under sail. The power, every bit of it, provided by a force you cannot see, the invisible, infinite molecules of air, manipulated with ropes and cloth and muscle. And in its essence, for all the new space-age alloys, there is not a single important fact that is different now from when Juan Rodriguez Cabrillo, searching for the mythical Northwest Passage, sailed on these waters in his leaking caravels *San Salvador* and *Victoria* in 1542, stopping at Ensenada to replenish his leaky casks with sweet water.

The cosmetically challenged *Imi Loa* whose measure I took at the dock became herself on the ocean. With the spinnaker filled and pulling, I looked at the speed gauge. In my own boat, a twenty-eight-foot coastal cruiser, I am very pleased with 5 knots. At 7 knots, guests and crew get nervous, and I feel that rush at the wheel of being barely in control. *Imi Loa* was moving at 9 knots on average, but in the right puff, coming down a big swell, she would hit 14.

"That's pretty fast," Vic later admitted. "You could say that is faster than most people have ever been on a sailboat."

Just when you could not ask for more, on a warm, sunny day off southern California, surrounded by boats flying spinnakers as colorful as regal banners, in a beautiful breeze on blue waters covered with spilled sapphires, a gray whale surfaced, not one hundred meters off our port beam. And I thought, okay, okay, this is excellent. I do not deserve more. This is what you stash away and hope to remember when your time on the earth is just about over.

All that day we sailed, from Newport Beach down the coast a few miles offshore, just outside the kelp beds, following the rhumb line, the shortest distance a navigator plots between two points, start to finish. No need to tack or jibe, just steer the compass heading of 145 degrees southeast, making small adjustments to the sails. *Imi Loa* was so fast that we left the hundreds of boats behind and sailed alongside only our direct competitors, the other racing catamarans. Past Laguna Beach and the mission at San Juan Capistrano, past the point named for Richard Henry Dana, Jr., the author of *Two Years Before the Mast,* and the Camp Pendleton Marine Base, then La Jolla and the mouth of San Diego Bay at dusk. Vic was very meticulous, in his way. He spent little time at the helm, steering, but he ran the boat. We rotated in four-man watches, every three hours. We made log entries every hour, using the Loran to pinpoint our position with radio waves, writing with a stubby yellow pencil our heading, estimated average speed, wind direction, course heading. Lunch was served. Slabs of deli meat with a big glob of yellow mustard, hard-boiled eggs, salty chips, and cold soft drinks. You felt ravenous. Then at sunset, Vic went to the galley, and with a bottle of rum and mai tai mix concocted his British West Indian Painkillers, and doled them out, grog for the crew, the sailor's balm, and we toasted the day, our health, our comrades, and Captain Vic. The punch filled your veins like a truce, the cleanness of a good first drink, and all was sweet and just and true.

The sun set in a curtain call of orange.

Perhaps because I was a cherry, and perhaps because I deferred to others, and maybe because I was intimidated, I did not take my first turn at the helm until dusk, as we crossed the international border and saw the bullring and lighthouse in Tijuana. *Imi Loa* has two rudders in the water, one for each of the catamaran's two hulls, and the two tillers are connected with a pole. To steer *Imi Loa*, a new helmsman must creep out on the stern of the catamaran, inch around the safety nets that would catch you and keep you from falling into the ocean, if you were lucky, and sidle behind the helmsman you are to replace. Then you reach around him, in a moment of intimacy, your chest pressed against his back, and take the tiller on the boat's high and windward side, first with fingertips and then hands.

"Got it? You got it?" This was David asking quietly. You do not lose control of the tiller in a boat like this on a beam spinnaker run. There lies all hell breaking loose.

"Yeah, got it, got it. Okay." And David slipped from between my arms and crawled away, and the helm was mine.

I could now feel the whole boat in my two hands, and it was like a living thing. It reminded me of touching a wild animal.

You do not have to fight the tiller to keep *Imi Loa* on course; a ten-year-old child has the strength to control her, but you must constantly adjust, a little to port, a bit to starboard, because she always is just ready to bolt, to point toward the wind and get one of her hulls out of the water. This is not good.

Vic and another crew, years ago, turtled — actually flipped — *Imi Loa,* and had to be rescued by Coast Guard helicopter and have the boat towed to harbor. This story, which Vic told me that night, tended to focus the mind. That and Vic himself, who, down in the galley making Shrimp Sri Lanka for dinner, would pop his head out of the passageway and bark, "Keep her down!"

It took me a few minutes to get the feel of a new helm, but then she was mine. The stars rose above the Coronado Islands off Mexico, and then were blanketed by low, scudding clouds, and the wind freshened and filled, and rain fell in the dark, scattered in small microbursts around us, and *Imi Loa* surged, 11, 12, 13 knots, and my watchmates looked at the gauges and shouted, GO, GO, GO, and I was fatally one of the brotherhood.

Later that night, my watch long over, I stumbled down into the main cabin. Above decks, in the clean air, when I'm watching the horizon, doing chores, sailing can be invigorating. But below decks, at sea, I suddenly feel very strung out, like I'm pulling an all-nighter in a dorm room that keeps moving. I gulped a warm Coke and candy (the only meal that the Coast Guard informs its recruits tastes the same coming as going) and lurched down the ladder into the forward starboard hull, and, still wearing my foul-weather slicks, I crawled into the narrow bunk called aboard *Imi Loa* "the torpedo tube." I had a brief flash of a scene from the German submarine movie *Das Boot*, but I was exhausted, and I curled into a warm natal ball and found myself surrounded in the liquid darkness by sound: *shhhusssh*, crackle, ripple, bubble, *booom*, as the hull rose, shouldered, fell, and settled in the swells.

I passed into a coma of the innocent.

A few hours before dawn, Gordon was pulling on my leg. "Get up, get up, we need to jibe."

We had made Bahia Todos Santos, the bay that crooks around Ensenada. We took down the spinnaker, raised the jib, turned — and then the wind completely died, in the collision of air between land and sea breeze.

Stalled.

We had no forward motion, no motion at all. The boat was "in irons," it could not be tacked. We drifted. The other catamarans and the ultralight sleds were clustered around us. We were one hundred meters from the finish line off the Ensenada breakwater. Vic was at the helm. And then his seasoned crew and Vic began to shout at one another, and then, deprived of sleep and cranked with competitive juice, to *really* shout. It was not a pretty moment. It was, though, typical of sailboat racing, the minutes you regret later and never talk about. Finally, after dropping sails and raising them, after all the yelling, the boat began to inch forward and we crossed the line at 3:43 A.M., fifteen hours and forty-three minutes after our start. We had finished fourth in our class, but after being given a five-minute bonus because of errors made by the committee boat at the start, we placed in the money, at third. It was Vic's fastest run ever in *Imi Loa* in the Newport–Ensenada run, a race he had won three times.

Harry cranked up the phlegmatic engine and we motored into Ensenada. We all pulled cold early-morning beers out of the cooler and stood on the foredeck, the sails down, as we looked for a place to drop the anchor in the twinkle of harbor lights. We ran aground. We all fell down. We laughed and got *Imi Loa* off the mud and dropped the hook.

We had arrived.

About Ensenada itself, on race weekend, I can say only a few words. Vic and most of the crew went to sleep in the clammy air-conditioned motel rooms on shore. I took a hot, glorious shower there and returned to sleep in my torpedo tube as the sun began to rise.

For the weekend, the town was taken over by gringo sailors. We made the pilgrimage to the folkloric cantina Hussong's, to drink free-base margaritas with fresh lime and puff Cuban cigars, and then to the disco Papas & Beer, for more pleasures, to slap each other on the back and remember the ride, to flirt and dance, with faces flushed from the sun and drink, and then to the late-night stalls in the old market to eat warm, papery corn tortillas wrapped around grilled fish jacked with dimes of jalapeño. There were trophies and bikinis and collect calls home. It was all a bit frat-ratty.

But fun enough.

Yet what I will remember about the race is my hours at the helm, my fingertips not here on a keypad in a Dilbertian cubicle, but offshore on *Imi Loa*, the boat so fast and full of intent, and what have I stashed in my duffel but another dream for those nights when I cannot sleep?

BILL BUFORD

Lions and Tigers and Bears

FROM *The New Yorker*

So I THOUGHT I'd spend the night in Central Park, and, having stuffed my small rucksack with a sleeping bag, a big bottle of mineral water, a map, and a toothbrush, I arrived one heavy, muggy Friday evening in July to do just that: to walk around until I got so tired that I'd curl up under a tree and drop off to a peaceful, outdoorsy sleep. Of course, anybody who knows anything about New York knows the city's essential platitude — that you don't wander around Central Park at night — and in that, needless to say, was the appeal: it was the thing you don't do. And, from what I can tell, it has always been the thing you don't do, ever since the Park's founding commissioners, nearly a hundred and fifty years ago, decided that the place should be closed at night — a decision heartily endorsed by its coarchitect Frederick Law Olmsted, who said that once the Park was dark he'd "answer for no man's safety in it from bullies, garroters, or highway robbers." At the time, the commissioners were recovering from one of the Park's first fatalities: the result of a downtown lad's overturning his two-wheeler and snapping his neck in a brandy-inspired carriage race down the Mall. Most felons then were reckless carriage drivers. In modern times, they're distinctly more menacing, as Ogden Nash observed in 1961:

> If you should happen after dark
> To find yourself in Central Park,
> Ignore the paths that beckon you
> And hurry, hurry to the zoo,

And creep into the tiger's lair.
Frankly, you'll be safer there.

Even now, when every Park official, city administrator, and police
officer tells us (correctly) that the Park is safe during the day, they
all agree in this: only a fool goes there at night. Or a purse snatcher,
loon, prostitute, drug dealer, homophobic gay basher, murderer
— not to mention bully, garroter, highway robber.

I arrived at nine-fifteen and made for the only nocturnal spot I
knew: the Delacorte Theatre. Tonight's show was *The Taming of the
Shrew*. "Bonny Kate," Petruchio was saying, "she is my goods, my
chattel . . . my horse, my ox, my ass, my any thing." Lights out, applause, and the audience began exiting through the tunnels at the
bottom of the bleachers. So far, so normal, and this could have
been an outdoor summer-stock Shakespeare production anywhere
in America, except in one respect: a police car had pulled up just as
Petruchio began his soliloquy and was now parked conspicuously
in view, its roof light slowly rotating. The police were there to reas-
sure the audience that it was being protected; the rotating red light
was like a campfire in the wild, warning what's out there to stay
away.

The Park has had its own police precinct since the end of the
nineteenth century, and it is now staffed with what Police Commissioner Howard Safir, himself an evening-roller-blading Park enthusiast, describes as "people persons" — well-spoken, well-mannered
policemen whose first task is to make visitors feel happy. And, on
any normal visit, I, like anyone else, would actually be very happy to
see one of the men in blue. But not tonight. It's against the law to
spend the night in the Park, and at around eleven o'clock the police start their "sweep" — crisscrossing the place on foot and in unmarked cars, scooters, little three-wheeled vans, and helicopters.

During my first hour or so, I wandered around the Delacorte, reassured by the lights, the laughter, the lines of Shakespeare that
drifted out into the summer night. I was feeling a certain exhilaration, the euphoria that comes from doing the thing you're not
meant to be doing, climbing the steps of Belvedere Castle all alone,
peeking through the windows of the Henry Luce Nature Observa-
tory, identifying the herbs in the Shakespeare Garden, seeing no
one, when, after turning this way and that, I was on a winding trail
in impenetrable foliage, and, within minutes, I was lost.

There was a light ahead, and as I rounded the corner I came upon five men, all wearing white tank-top T-shirts, huddled around a bench. I walked past, avoiding eye contact, and turned down a path, a narrow one, black dark, going down a hill, getting darker, very dark. Is this a good idea? I asked myself, when, as if on cue, I heard a great shaking of the bushes beside me and froze. Animal? Mugger? Whatever I was hearing would surely stop making that noise, I thought. But it didn't. How can this be? I'm in the Park less than an hour and already I'm lost, on an unlighted path, facing an unknown thing shaking threateningly in the bushes. It was no small thing moving around in there, and, what's more, it was moving in my direction, and I thought, Shit! What *am* I doing here? And I bolted, not running, exactly, but no longer strolling — and certainly not looking back — turning left, turning right, all sense of direction obliterated, the crashing continuing behind me, louder even, *left,* another man in a tank-top T-shirt, *right,* another man, when finally I realized where I was — in the Ramble, stupid, where I'd been only once before (and got lost) — as I turned left again, and there was a lake, and the skyline of Central Park South, the Essex House Hotel, and the reassuring sign for A&E's *Biography,* announcing the temperature (eighty-two degrees), the time (ten-fifteen), and tonight's *Biography* special (William Shatner). I stopped. I breathed. Relax, I told myself. It's only darkness.

About fifteen feet into the lake, there was a large boulder, with a heap of branches leading to it. I tiptoed across and sat, enjoying the picture of the city again, the very reassuring city. I looked around. There was a warm breeze, and heavy clouds overhead, but it was still hot, and I was sweating. Far out in the lake, there was a light — someone rowing a boat, a lantern suspended above the stern. I got my bearings — the twin towers of the San Remo in view, a penthouse all lit up, a party. I was on the West Side, around Seventy-seventh. People use the cross streets, imaginatively projecting them across the Park, like latitude lines, as a way of imposing a New York grid on this bit of New York gridlessness. The far side of the lake must be near Strawberry Fields, around Seventy-second. Just where that boat was now, I realized, was where, two years ago, the police had found the body of Michael McMorrow, a forty-four-year-old man (my age), who was stabbed thirty-four times by a fifteen-year-old. It was possible, the thought occurred to me, to chart my progress through the Park via its recent murders (I entered at East

Seventy-second, where, two months ago, the police found the body of a publishing executive, inexplicably felled, the headphones of his Walkman still clamped to his ears, and later, as I headed for the Reservoir . . .), but no, this didn't seem like a fruitful way of organizing the evening. Even so, the menacing Central Park crime mystique lingered: the idea that here anything is possible. You enter the Park, you have sex in the bushes with a stranger, you leave. No memory, no trace. You find someone all alone, you rob him, you disappear. Unseen transgressions. After McMorrow was killed, he was disemboweled, his intestines ripped out so that his body would sink when rolled into the lake — a detail that I've compulsively reviewed in my mind since I first heard it. And then his killers, with time on their hands and no witnesses, just went home. Another feature of a Central Park crime: no one knows you're here.

One of the first events in the Park took place 140 years ago almost to the day: a band concert. The concert, pointedly, was held on a Saturday, still a working day, because the concert, like much of the Park then, was designed to keep the city's rougher elements out. The Park at night must have seemed luxurious and secluded — a giant evening garden party. There were no other entertainments. No rides, no playgrounds, no venders. The Park was to be strolled through, enjoyed as an aesthetic experience, like a walk inside a painting. George Templeton Strong, the indefatigable diarist, was an early Park user. On his first visit, on June 11, 1859, the place was a desolate landscape of mounds of compost and lakes without water. But even at that stage Strong recognized that the architects were building two different parks at once. One was the Romantic park, which included the Ramble, the thirty-seven-acre, carefully "designed" wilderness, wild nature re-created in the middle of the city, *rus in urbe,* an English notion — nature as surprising and unpredictable. The other, the southern end of the Park, was more French: ordered, and characterized by straight lines. Strong was unhappy with the straight lines, and could see that once the stunted elms were fully grown ("by A.D. 1950," he wrote) the place would look distinctly "Versailles-y." But by 1860 this section was tremendously popular, and paintings show a traffic jam of fancy carriages, all proceeding the wrong way up Fifth Avenue — "a broad torrent of vehicular gentility wherein profits shoddy and of petroleum were largely represented," Strong wrote in disgust.

I climbed back down from the rock. In the distance, I spotted a couple approaching. An uncomfortable thing: someone else in the Park. Your first thought is: nutcase? But then I noticed, even from a hundred feet, that the couple was panicking: the man was pulling the woman to the other side of him, so that he would be between her and me when we passed. The woman stopped, and the man jerked her forward authoritatively, and there was a muted exchange. I was surprised by how expressive their fear was — even in the way they were moving. As they got closer, I could see that he was tall and skinny, wearing a plaid shirt and black horn-rimmed glasses; she was a blonde, and looked determinedly at the ground, her face rigid. Both of them were now walking fast and stiffly. When they were within a few feet of me, he reached out and grabbed her arm. I couldn't resist: just as we were about to pass each other, I addressed them, forthrightly: "Hello, good people!" I said. "And how are you on this fine summer evening?" At first, silence, and then the woman started shrieking uncontrollably — "Oh, my God! Oh, my God!" — and they hurried away.

This was an interesting discovery. One of the most frightening things in the Park at night was a man on his own. One of the most frightening things tonight was me. I was emboldened by the realization, newly confident: I was no longer afraid; I was frightening. Another man approached, big and fat, wearing only shorts, with blubbery tits hanging over his swollen belly. Ah, well, I thought, someone who really is insane. No matter. I greeted him. He was very friendly. He had an aluminum container of food, and he was eating as he walked. He offered me some.

"What is it?" I asked.

"Pasta," he said. "Mmm, mmm. Would you like a bite?"

"No, thanks," I said. "I've eaten."

"You sure?" he said. "I got plenty."

"No, really," I said. "That's very kind, but I couldn't."

Not everyone likes the Park, but just about everyone feels he should. This was at the heart of Henry James's otherwise impressively incomprehensible observations when he visited the Park, in 1904. The Park, in James's eyes, was a failure. All the fake nature stuff, got up to be so many wild scenes, was not unlike "the effect of those old quaint prints which give in a single view the classic, gothic and other architectural wonders of the world." The Park was too

narrow, and too short, and was overwhelmed by an obligation to
"do." The most remarkable thing about it was simply that it existed,
and any person who didn't, as James put it, "keep patting the Park
on the back" was guilty of being seen as a social ingrate. By then,
the Park's founders had died, and the Park, no longer the domain
of the privileged, had been taken over by immigrants — a "polyglot
Hebraic crowd of pedestrians," in James's inelegantly revealing
phrase. In fact, between James's visit and the nineteen-thirties, the
Park might well have been at its most popular, visited by more people than today, when current estimates put the number of visitors
somewhere between ten and twenty million a year. The Park in
fact was being destroyed by overuse, until 1934, when the legendary Robert Moses, genius urban impresario and civic fascist, was
appointed parks commissioner. Moses was responsible for the third
design element in the Park — neither English nor French, neither Romantic nor classical, but efficient, purposeful, and un-
apologetically American. All that arty pretend-you're-in-a-painting-
of-the-Hudson-River-School: he had no time for it. He wanted baseball diamonds, shuffleboard, volleyball, and swimming pools. He
closed the Casino — originally the tea salon of the Park's other
architect, Calvert Vaux, but by the nineteen-thirties a dubious if
highly charismatic speakeasy of jazz, celebrities, and corrupt glam-
our — and replaced it, characteristically, with a playground. Even
the Ramble became a target: Moses tried to chop it down and in-
stall a fourteen-acre senior citizens' recreation center. He was
blocked by the protesting bird-watchers — one of the few times
Moses was stopped. The irony was that by the end of the Moses era
the Park — no longer a piece of nature but a piece of property, a
venue for recreation, not conservation — was dangerous.

In my new confidence I set out for the northern end of the Park.
Near the reservoir, a gang of kids on bicycles zoomed across the
Eighty-fifth Street Transverse, hooting with a sense of ominous
power. A little later, there was another gang, this one on foot —
about a dozen black kids, moving eastward, just by the running
track. I kept my head down and picked up my pace, but my mind
involuntarily called up the memory of the 1989 "wilding" incident,
in which a young investment banker was beaten and sexually assaulted by a group of kids on a rampage.

Around Ninety-fifth Street, I found a bench and stopped. I had taken one of the trails that run alongside the Park's West Drive, and the more northern apartments of Central Park West were in view. I sat as residents prepared for bed: someone watching television, a woman doing yoga, a man stepping into the shower. Who needs curtains when it's only the Park outside your window? Below me was the city, the top of the Empire State Building peeking over the skyline. George Templeton Strong discovered the beauty of Central Park at night on July 30, 1869, on a "starlit drive" with his wife. But what Strong saw was different from what I was looking at. The Park was darker then than now, genuinely empty, and something much closer to Olmsted's nature in the seeming wild. And, of course, you could see the stars. Tonight, even if it weren't clouding over, there'd be no stars. Too much glare. The Park is now framed, enveloped even, by the city in a way that Olmsted never imagined, but there was no escaping the recognition that this city — contrived, man-made, glaringly obtrusive, consuming wasteful and staggering quantities of electricity and water and energy — was very beautiful. I'm not sure why it should be so beautiful; I don't have the vocabulary to describe its appeal. But there it was: the city at night, viewed from what was meant to be an escape from it, shimmering.

Olmsted's son, also a landscape architect, was offended by the tall buildings that had begun crowding round his father's achievement. It was ruinous, the son said, "ugly, restless, and distressing," and there was talk of limiting the height of what greedy real estate developers could build. Young Olmsted did not understand the romance of what was taking form.

A policeman appeared. It was after midnight, and I thought that my visit was now terminated. But he could see that I was enjoying the view, so he found a bench not far away. He had a shaved head and a mild manner. He said nothing and took in the view himself. And that was what we did, sitting together, separated by twenty or thirty feet, in silence, for ten minutes, saying nothing, until finally I felt I could get up, and said good night, and resumed my journey.

I walked around the Harlem Meer, busy even at one in the morning — couples on benches, young men hunched over their girl-

friends like question marks. From the hill of Fort Clinton, where
the British drove Washington's troops north and took temporary
possession of Manhattan, I watched a slow seduction. I walked and
walked. Around one-thirty, I entered the North Woods, and made
my way down to what my map would later tell me was a stream
called the Loch. The stream was loud, sounding more like a river
than a stream. And for the first time that night the city disappeared: no buildings, no lights, no sirens.

I was tired. I had been walking for a long time. I wanted to unroll
my sleeping bag, out of view of the police, and fall asleep. I was
looking forward to dawn and being awakened by birds.

I made my way down a ravine. A dirt trail appeared on my left.
This looked promising. I followed it, and it wound its way down to
the stream. I looked back: I couldn't see the trail; it was blocked
by trees. This was good. Secluded. I walked on. It flattened out and
I could put a sleeping bag here. This was good, too. Yes: good.
There were fireflies, even at this hour, and the place was so dark
and so densely shrouded by the trees overhead that the light of the
fireflies was hugely magnified; their abdomens pulsed like great
yellow flashlights. There was also a smell: a dampness, a kind of rotting fecundity. And the stream was very loud: this was the sound of
nature, true, but it was all a bit too incongruous. Olmsted or not, I
knew I was in Harlem.

I spotted a white article on the ground. I stared at it for a while
before walking over to pick it up. It was a woman's blouse. Of
course. A woman had simply left it behind. Fifty yards from here, a
Brazilian jogger was killed — the murderer never found. (A week
later, a woman would be murdered nearby, at the Blockhouse, at
this very hour, her screams ignored by a resident who heard them.
When I returned here, at midnight two nights after that killing, I,
too, would hear a woman's screams — spooky, bleating screams,
which I then reported to a policeman, startling him in the dark
where I tracked him down.)

I eventually rolled out my sleeping bag atop a little rise beside
the bridle path by the North Meadow, and then I sat, cross-legged,
and asked myself questions: Why did I bring a little airline tube of
toothpaste but no flashlight? Why didn't I bring a cell phone?
Wouldn't a can of Mace have been prudent? I crawled inside my
bag and closed my eyes. And then: *snap!* A tremendous cracking

sound. I froze, then quickly whipped round to have a look: nothing. A forest is always full of noises. How did I manage to camp out as a kid? Finally, I fell asleep.

I know I fell asleep because I was awake again. Another branch snapping, but this sound was different — as if I could hear the tissue of the wood tearing. My eyes still closed, I was motionless. Another branch, and then a rustling of leaves. No doubt: someone was there. I could tell I was being stared at; I could feel the staring. I heard breathing.

I opened my eyes and was astonished by what I saw. I was surrounded by — what? Something. There were three of them, all within arm's reach. They looked very big. At first I didn't know what they were, except that they were animals. The only animal I'd seen in the Park was a rat. These were not rats — that was my first thought. Actually, that was my second thought; my first was: This is not the police. Maybe they were bears, small ones. Then I realized; they were — what do you call them? Those animals that Daniel Boone made his hat out of.

They weren't moving; I wasn't moving. They just stared, brown eyes looking blankly into my own. They were obviously very perplexed to find me here. Suddenly, I was very perplexed to find me here, too. "Imagine this," one of them seemed to be saying. "A grown man sleeping out in Central Park!"

"Obviously, not from New York."

"Hi, guys," I muttered. I said this very softly.

My voice startled them and they scurried up the tree in front of me. But only ten feet up. Then they stopped and resumed staring. And then, very slowly, they inched a little farther up. What should I do? If I ignored them and fell asleep, I faced the prospect of their coming down again. On the other hand, why would I want to frighten them? Besides, what if I frightened them and they *didn't* leave? After all, I was now in their way. They inched a little farther. They were about forty feet up, directly above me now, and the tree was swaying slightly with their weight.

It was starting to drizzle. I heard a helicopter, its searchlight crisscrossing the bridle path only ten feet away. So maybe there were bad guys.

I looked back at the raccoons. "Are there bad guys here?" I asked them. It was stupid to speak. My voice startled them and, directly overhead, one of them started peeing. And then, nature finding herself unable to resist, it started to pour.

But not for long. The rain stopped. The raccoons stared. And I fell asleep. I know I fell asleep because the next thing I heard was birds. A natural, naturally beautiful sound.

This Teeming Ark

FROM *Outside*

IT WAS LIKE trying to drink a beer on the subway at rush hour. Jostled from all sides, I stood hard against the flimsy railing of a makeshift stall and tried to hold my place against various swirling currents of humanity.

Several of the drunks I'd been cultivating peeled out of the crowd to greet me.

"You are my friend," said Maurice, who at nine o'clock in the morning was already in the condition I aspired to achieve. "Buy me a beer." It was his ritual greeting.

"No way in hell," I said, which had become my ritual reply.

It was my tenth excruciating day aboard the *Flueve Congo* — a conglomeration of eight flatbed barges cabled to a great throbbing riverboat motoring down the Congo River. During the endless hours on deck, I had discovered that only drunkards were intelligent enough to comprehend my hundred-word French vocabulary.

Maurice, a Congolese Bantu, like most of the other passengers, was a thin, gangly man with a goofy smile. He didn't really want a beer. He drank palm wine, which he carried about with him in a yellow plastic jug that looked like it had once contained motor oil.

The temperature was rising rapidly, the beer was warm, and I was wearing shorts. My skin was a sickly pale white. I felt like a couple of dozen gallons of raw milk. Maurice pointed out all the slowly healing insect bites, the welts, the scabs on my legs.

He wanted to know what had happened to me, and I told him, for the fourth or fifth time, that I had just completed a long walk through an uninhabited forest.

"What were the people like?" Maurice asked.

"There weren't any people. It was uninhabited."

I told Maurice that it was like Eden, this forest in the north of the Republic of the Congo, the former French Congo. The animals there hadn't been hunted, and they approached our party boldly: elephants and chimps and gorillas and antelope. I had been happy there. But here? On the barge? I was not happy.

"I don't like crowds, Maurice," I said.

I told him that my entire life to date had been an exercise in avoiding crowds. I didn't know how many more days I could bear aboard this Congo River barge, along with three thousand other human beings, all of us compressed into a space about the size of a football field. For me it was . . . what was the word I was looking for?

"Buy me a beer," said Maurice.

"No way in . . ." *L'enfer!* That was the word. This was my own personal hell.

I drained the beer and gave the bottle back to the man who'd sold it to me.

"Maurice," I said, "do you know God?"

"Yes."

"Have you seen him this morning?"

"No."

"Damn." I really needed to talk to God.

I was traveling with Michael Fay, a wildlife biologist, and Cynthia Moses, a filmmaker. The walk through Eden was Michael's project. His job was to inventory the flora and fauna of the forest and report back to the Congolese government with a recommendation about whether the area should be protected as a national forest. (He thought it should.)

Cynthia documented the walk on video, and my job was to write about it. We had traveled with several Bantus and about a dozen Pygmies, but it had been simple enough for me to drop back or plunge ahead of the line of march. By myself, it was possible to imagine that I was the only human being who had ever set foot in the forest. Chimps howled and screamed in the trees above, and they often came way too close — well within rifle range — because they felt it was necessary to throw feces and to piss on my head. I was just another primate, and not very special to boot. Even so, I was really quite content alone on the forest floor, ambling through the yellow, dung-studded rain.

Eventually we had stumbled out of the forest and made our way to Impfondo, on the Ubangi River, where several thousand people stood in an open courtyard while lightning ripped the sky apart and rain fell in sheets. Suddenly the rain stopped. Hours passed. People began fainting in the heat.

Michael, Cynthia, and I were the only whites, and we moved in line with the Congolese; with Habib, from the Ivory Coast; with Alphonse, from Gabon; with riverboat con artists and naive villagers on their first trip downriver. The bottleneck turned out to be the soldier who was checking everyone's papers. He wore a camouflage uniform and a brown beret and carried an automatic pistol in a white plastic holster. His name, stitched in red on his left breast, seemed faintly mocking: THERMOMETER.

A great wash of humanity carried us onto the corrugated metal deck of the barge, and eventually, engines thrumming, the *Flueve Congo* moved majestically out into the current and began floating down the Ubangi, toward the Congo and our destination, Brazzaville.

Cynthia, Michael, and I stood at the very back of the very last barge, watching Impfondo recede into the distance. On the bank to our left was a small village, and I saw a woman run down the dirt path to the river and begin screaming at us. She was in her late teens, I'd guess. Tall and angular, she flapped her arms like the black herons that rose occasionally along the shoreline. Her cries couldn't be heard above the noise of our diesels.

"Missed the boat," I said.

The woman dropped to her knees, turned her face to the sky, and howled soundlessly. She beat her palms on the rain-sodden red earth, raising splashes of mud that stained her orange dress.

"Seems disappointed," Michael observed.

Cynthia told us that we were like all men: cynical in the face of strong emotion. She felt sorry for the young woman.

We humped our gear through the crowds, looking for the first-class cabin we'd booked. The riverboat's three-story wheelhouse loomed above the eight barges lashed to the bow, the sides, and the stern; our cabin was behind the wheelhouse, in a high edifice that had once been the superstructure of another riverboat. The room was an olive-drab metal cubicle that felt distressingly like a jail cell; the three of us immediately escaped back onto the teeming decks.

Along the starboard railing, men and women dropped a bucket on a rope into the river, pulled it back up, and used the water to wash their clothes, their children, themselves. A harried mother asked us to watch Juliet, her toddler, while she bathed her baby. Juliet was four, and she held my index finger in her small hand.

As we were standing there baby-sitting Juliet, a man in clean khakis and a bushman's hat came by with a young chimpanzee that was clinging to him as if the man were its mother. The chimp had a rope around its waist, and the man put it down on the deck. It scampered about on its feet and hands, oofing and woofing. Juliet's mother swept her up in a single motion. People scattered in all directions. Chimps are strong, and they can bite.

Cynthia, who had once worked on a film with Jane Goodall and knew something about chimps, knelt in front of the animal. She held out her left palm and touched it with the bunched fingers of her right hand. A grooming gesture. The chimp took her left hand for a moment, then turned its back to her. Cynthia parted the hairs on the back of its head, grooming it, and the chimp seemed content.

The man who held the rope told us his name was Sarafin. He had bought the chimp in a village upriver for about eight dollars. It was an orphan. He thought he could sell it to the zoo in Brazzaville.

Michael told Sarafin that, in the Republic of the Congo, any traffic in primates was forbidden. He said that he consulted with the government on poaching issues, and warned Sarafin that he'd be arrested at the zoo. The thing to do, Michael advised, was to take the chimp to the primate orphanage in Brazzaville, where it would be rehabilitated, taught to hunt and forage, and released into the forest.

Later, in the cabin, we talked about the encounter. Michael said he wasn't really sure that Sarafin would have been arrested at the zoo. He thought that the chimp-and-gorilla orphanage was a feel-good solution and that what was important was to stop any kind of commerce in wildlife. Sarafin seemed like a bright young guy who had no intention of breaking the law. He'd help pass the word.

Cynthia said that while the chimp looked healthy enough, she still felt sorry for it.

I identified with it.

There are almost no roads in the northern Congo, and people travel by river. But the *Flueve Congo* wasn't truly about transportation. It was about commerce. Even at the smallest villages, the captain brought the engines to an idle and people paddled out in pirogues. They came to sell smoked fish, or oranges, or live dwarf crocodiles with their snouts wired shut, or chickens or goats. There was no refrigeration on the barges, and meat was kept alive until dinner.

Periodically one or more of the flat-topped barges would be uncabled at a village, and another two or three would be added as additional passengers poured aboard the *Flueve Congo*. Shopkeepers who maintained stalls on the barges sold batteries, lamps, soap, salt, shampoo, T-shirts, hard candy, and music cassettes. Bargaining was a high-volume affair. Folks shouted at one another in the way I might address someone who'd just shot my dog. But there was always a smile hidden somewhere very close behind the seeming abuse.

Eventually the Ubangi emptied into the Congo proper. At the town of Mossaka, we became deck passengers. A local politician had booked our cabin weeks before. The captain allowed us to pile our gear and cameras in the wheelhouse for safekeeping.

In the early-afternoon sun the metal decks of the barges were searingly hot. People sat on boards or bricks or rolls of foam padding. Sheets rigged on sticks provided some protection from the sun. At each stop, another 780,000 people boarded the barge. There was now such a crush of bodies aboard the *Flueve Congo* that no one could take a single step without bumping into someone else.

It was a world of constant apology, and my choice, as I saw it, was between passive acceptance or madness — despite the fact that everyone else seemed to be having a swell adventure. Cynthia obtained the captain's permission to stand on top of the wheelhouse and shoot crowd scenes along with sunrises and sunsets. Michael, already fluent in French, worked on his Lingala vocabulary. He underlined useful words in a dictionary and then strolled about looking for opportunities to work *ekila* ("abstinence") or *ezanga tina* ("crazy" or "absurd") into a conversation.

I, on the other hand, could not write my essay about heaven and hell, about the Edenic forest and the sweltering barge. Exquisitely uncomfortable and unable to finish a sentence, I spent many moping hours on one of the flat-topped barges devoted to livestock: goats and pigs and chickens and me all bunched together under a tarp that provided a little bit of shade. One of the goats fell in love with a pig, to the porker's great annoyance. It was entirely *ezanga tina,* a lesson, I thought, about all of us swirling down the drain of the behavioral sink. I longed to be back in the forest, in the monkey-shit rain.

After two days on deck I became disconsolate and sought the company of drunkards. One beer, maybe two, and then back to the goats, back through the general hubbub of too much humanity apologizing to itself. Excuse me. Pardon me. I imagined the future of the human race as an endless ride on the Congo barge, and shuddered in the heat.

Cynthia found me hunched up and brooding among the animals. "Can I do something for you?" she asked.

"Yeah," I said, "go away."

I met folks named George and Slava and Josephine and Enrique. Many of them were extremely attractive. God, however, was easily the most handsome man I'd ever met. He stood a couple of inches over six feet, a lean, well-muscled man of about twenty-five who seemed vastly amused by life in general.

God had just graduated from college and was going to Brazzaville, where he had secured a job teaching school. He apologized about the name. He'd grown up in a remote village where his father heard educated people talking with great respect about a person called God. It seemed a good name for a son, and young God lived half a dozen years before he realized that people other than his father found the name either offensive or amusing. "But I'm stuck with it," he said.

God had traveled often on the *Flueve Congo* and was our single best source of information. There was no set schedule. Some nights we'd anchor in the darkness; sometimes we'd run all night long. It depended a lot on the captain's mood and the heat of commerce conducted at various villages. God had a kind of sixth sense for the captain's humor. He'd predicted our arrival at the confluence of the Ubangi and the Congo to the hour.

Now, after ten days, I needed to know when we'd arrive in Brazzaville. My drinking buddies had varying opinions. Some thought two more days, some three.

"Who knows?" Maurice said.

God knows, I thought, and set off to find him.

I bumped into Cynthia on the way, and together we sought him out across the crowded expanse of the *Flueve Congo* universe. We found him waiting in a long line outside what was now the only functioning public toilet on the barge.

We stood with God, inching our way toward the toilet.

"Tim is going insane," Cynthia told him.

"How much longer?" I asked.

"Twenty-four hours," he said. "We should be in Brazzaville tomorrow morning at this time."

That, I thought, was acceptable. I could certainly bear it for one more day.

But now Cynthia had a problem. At the disembarkation, she wanted to get off first so she could turn around and film our arrival. It was going to be a madhouse. Everyone with something to sell would rush off in order to get the best prices or find the best corner to set up shop.

"Tim and Michael can carry the gear," Cynthia told God, "but could you help me get off and find a high spot to stand?"

God said it would be no problem. Cynthia was happy: she'd get her shot, with the help of God.

I spent the remainder of the last full day drinking beer with Maurice and maundering on, mostly in English, about the difference between Eden and the end of the world as we know it. Maurice agreed with everything I had to say and I finally bought him the beer he didn't really want.

We pulled into the port of Brazzaville at ten the next morning, just as God had foreseen. People began pouring off the barge, but God never showed, and I wasn't going to sit around waiting for him.

"Absenteeism," said Michael, trying to recall the word in Lingala. Cynthia, who'd put her faith in God, was bitterly disappointed.

"He helps those who help themselves," I muttered as I grabbed my share of the gear. And then — apologizing profusely all the way — I got the hell off that godforsaken barge.

TOM CLYNES

The Toughest Trucker in the World

FROM *National Geographic Adventure*

HIDDEN UNDER the rain-forest canopy of Australia's Cape York Peninsula, Pajinka Wilderness Lodge is a tropical retreat for wildlife lovers, bird-watchers, and fishermen. The lodge lies just short of the northernmost point in Australia, at the tip of a slender green finger that stretches up toward Papua New Guinea. Locals call this spot simply "The Top."

After a day in the sun deep-sea fishing with Pajinka's then manager, Alan Geary, a few guests cooled off at the lodge's outdoor bar. Someone brought over a round of XXXX (Queensland's beloved home-brewed beer, pronounced "Four-X") and asked Alan a question of essential interest: In a place where the temperature rarely dips below ninety degrees Fahrenheit in the dry season, a place far too remote for electrical lines, how is it that the beer at Pajinka is always cold?

Alan answered with a tropical syllogism. For good conversation, he said, you need cold beer. To get cold beer, you need electricity. To get electricity, you need fuel for the generator. To get fuel to The Top . . . you need Garry White.

Ten times a year, Alan told us, "this bloke Garry" pulls his full-size tractor-trailer rig out of Cairns and heads up the peninsula to the fuel depot at Weipa. There, he fills the tanker with diesel for the cattle stations and aboriginal settlements in the distant north, and for Pajinka. The two-thousand mile round-trip — not much of it on paved roads — takes him through the continent's most inaccessible wilderness. He has to ford jungle rivers, chainsaw downed trees, and shovel his way out of truck-gobbling mud holes. Every

time he stops to change a flat tire or replace an axle, he's bait for
leeches, wild boars, taipans, and giant crocs.

"It's a well-known fact," said Alan, "that he is the world's toughest
trucker."

I couldn't judge the roads because, like most of Pajinka's guests,
I had flown in via bush plane. So I called Trinity Petroleum, which
supplies fuel out of Cairns, and asked the owner if anyone else
brings big tankers up to The Top. "Well, other drivers have gotten
trucks in there," he said. "But aside from Garry, no one has managed to get 'em back out."

"So you want to ride up to The Top, eh?" I had expected a seven-
foot-tall hybrid of Mad Max and Crocodile Dundee. But the guy
who comes to the door looks a lot like . . . my dad. He's a burly five
feet nine inches tall, with a standard-issue trucker's belly and a
brushy cop mustache that nearly hides two missing front teeth.
With blotchy English skin and a perpetual squint, he looks altogether unsuited for the tropics.

It's late October, and Garry says he's running dangerously late
for his last far-north run before "The Dry" gives over to "The Wet,"
the northern Australian monsoon season. When The Wet arrives
— which could be any day now — it can deliver more rain in a
week than Seattle gets in a year. The big storms will push the rivers
up as much as twenty feet a day, devouring the land. Anything that
can't fly or float out will have to stay put for the next four months.

Garry and his wife, Kathy, live in a concrete-floor house outside Mareeba, a scruffy town in the tablelands above Cairns. Kathy
fires up some dinner for us, and talks about the trials of being a
"truckie's" wife. She misses Garry while he's gone, which can be for
up to a month at a time. Sometimes she'll ride with him on easier
trips; she likes to sit beside him and "watch his tummy bounce up
and down like a lump of jelly."

As we eat, a miniature pony clomps through the open door and
into the living room. It's joined by a slobbering cattle dog named
Diesel.

The next morning, Garry and I head to Mareeba's supermarket,
to pack some "tucker" into the truck's small fridge. He steers the
shopping cart directly toward the meat counter and picks out some
bacon for breakfast. Then some pork sausage for lunch. "We'll get

some sliced ham for sangers [sandwiches]," he says, "and we'll need something for tea tomorrow." He suddenly decides to cut me in on the decision-making process: "D'ya like pork cutlets?"

Since we've covered most of the pig, I propose some vegetables. Garry gives me a puzzled look.

"Veggies? Like — what?" he asks.

"Like, say, cucumbers."

"Nah," he says. "They return on me." I decide that I can live without a definition of this digestive condition, and we compromise on a couple of fat T-bone steaks.

For the first leg of the trip, we'll head up the peninsula with tandem trailers. At Weipa, we'll unhook the rear tanker and negotiate the narrow tracks to the far north with a single trailer. Over the course of the trip, which should take between six and eight days, we'll barrel through coastal mountains, scrub forests, heaths, rolling hills, swamps, deserts, jungles — some of the wildest terrain on the continent.

Garry's rig stretches 115 feet back from the headlights. Kenworths don't come off the line as ORVs, but this one has been fitted for serious off-road extremes. It has a 470-horsepower turbocharged Detroit Diesel, with eighteen forward speeds and four reverse. The prime mover rides on a Hendrickson air suspension.

"It takes a flogging," Garry says proudly.

Garry calls the tractor Pegasus and has had a winged horse painted on each door. The cab interior is spartan brown vinyl, embellished only by a set of evergreen air fresheners hanging from the sleeping compartment ceiling, just behind the seats.

The pavement ends and the outback begins about 120 miles from Garry's house. Crawling up and down the mountain ranges that make up the northern stretch of the Great Dividing Range, we roll past teams of jackaroos (Aussie cowboys) on horseback, driving their herds between giant termite mounds that bulge out of the rust-red earth.

The ranches, called stations, are too vast to fence, and animals roam freely across the road. Garry seems to know which bulls will interrupt a graze to bolt suddenly across our path. He tells me that he's "conked a few," and that he used to carry a gun under the seat so he could dispatch anything he hit quickly and humanely. But recently, a law was passed forbidding guns in Australian vehicles.

"Last brumby [wild horse] I hit, I had to finish 'im off with a piece of pipe." There's melancholy in his voice. "I didn't like that."

Around midnight, Garry pulls the rig under a silver gum tree and shuts down the engine. In the warm wind, the land seems to exhale magic. Garry pulls a camp stove and a dusty pan from the spare-parts cubbyhole, and we fry up some pork. Then he puts on the billy — a camp kettle that looks like a paint can — and makes some coffee.

We get to talking. He tells me that his grandparents came from England and settled near Cairns. Garry was raised on farms, and he likes to be around animals. He got into trucking "back when the money was good," and now, with his hazardous-cargo rating and years of experience, he can still "make a fair quid." But it's rough on the marriage and rough on the back.

When Garry retires into the truck's sleeper, I grab my swag — the Aussie bedroll, a pad and sheet wrapped in thick canvas — and climb up to the tanker's flat top. In the few minutes before I drift off, I see a dozen meteors shooting in and out of the unfamiliar constellations.

At dawn, I wake to the sound of a gong being struck next to my eardrum. Actually, it's a rock hitting the fuel cap I'm using for a pillow. I sit up and look over the side of the tanker. There's Garry, with a fistful of stones, grinning up at me.

"Wakey, wakey, hands off snakey!"

He tells me to go have a "dingo's breakfast" — a piss and a look around — as he inspects the truck. We hop in and press on into the interior, where the vibrant greens of the coast give way to dull olive and beige hues. The Dry shows no signs of abating. In fact, the landscape seems permanently blighted. Wildfires have carpeted the forests with black ash. For hours, there's no sign of human life. Then the Archer River Roadhouse comes into view.

"Go in for a feed?"

When we walk in, it's clear that Garry White is a celebrity in these parts. All the regulars drop what they're doing to find out what "Whitey" is up to. The cook, a cheerful, enthusiastic woman known as "Feral Cheryl," fires up an English-style breakfast of greasy fried eggs and heaps of undercooked bacon, and talk eventually gets around to where we're heading. "The Top," Garry says, raising eyebrows all around. Glen, who manages the roadhouse, speaks up.

"You're takin' a big risk goin' up this late, aren't you, Garry? One big storm and you'll be up there for the duration of The Wet."

Garry admits that he's procrastinated "about three weeks too long." Cheryl asks him about the longest he's been stranded in the bush. He mentions the time he was "bogged in tight" for five days near the Gulf of Carpentaria. He had to dig a ditch to drain the track, then cut down trees and lash them together, finally driving out over his makeshift wooden road.

"Ran low on tucker, so I made some crab traps and put 'em out in a billabong, not even thinkin' about the crocs. I made the mistake of going back there the same time three days in a row, wadin' right out into the tea. On the last day I had the boots off and was ready to go in when I got a feeling. Threw some rocks out and sure enough, a big saltie was out by the trap, waiting 'round for me. They're smart. They'll watch their prey for a few days; they'll learn your habits."

On the way out, Garry decides to call home. When he climbs back in the truck, he's perturbed. He tells me that Kathy "went crocadelic" on him for spending too much time and money in the pub-tent the other night. "It's getting to the point where a bloke can't even have a reasonable piss-up with the mates without getting an ear bashing."

The road, horrendously cut up after eight months of dry-season traffic, narrows into a track of sand and bare rock. It's a bone-jarring, ear-rattling ride. An hour out of Archer River, the air brakes on the rear trailer lock up. Garry finally finds the culprit, a valve fitting with its threads vibrated bare. There's no spare, but Garry rummages around in his "mobile workshop," pulling out boxes of tools and parts until he finds a couple of other fittings to cobble together, and we're on our way again.

A hot wind has come up, driving red dust into the air. The powder collects on sunglasses, around lips, and in the moist corners of the eyes. Barreling into a dust-stormed gully, we enter a section of exposed rocks too fast, and we're both slammed against the ceiling.

Garry grapples with the bucking Kenworth, plowing the rig through a sand berm at the bottom of the creek bed and into a motocrosser's nightmare of boulders and hip-deep ruts. As the gully bottoms out, there's a nauseating crunch behind us, the sound of metal being torn apart. Fighting to maintain momentum, Garry stomps the throttle, downshifting twice a second as we bore into the soft sand. With each lower gear the engine roars an agonizing note, and the tires burrow deeper. Overcome by grit and gravity, the big truck bogs to a stop.

As the dust rises around us, Garry grabs his window crank to seal off the cab. The crank falls off in his hand. He lets out a bellow. "Bloody mongrel roads," he says at last.

Over breakfast at Archer River, I had asked Garry if he enjoys his job.

At the time, with his buddies around him and a hot meal in front of him, his response had been balanced: "I suppose when the roads are good it's all right. But sometimes — these roads are mad."

Since then, Garry's mood has darkened. After we dig out of the gully, the top leaf spring on the tractor's left front wheel — a two-inch-thick, eight-hundred-dollar piece of hardened steel — shears. The next day, the bolts holding the intercooler to the frame snap apart. At the Aurukun aboriginal settlement, an impatient road crew worker tries to squeeze past the truck with his pickup, smashing two taillights. The road surface has gone from sand to hard red soil with deep corrugations that deliver a kidney punch each time one of the fourty-four wheels slams into one. The vibration is hellish; for the past three hours we haven't been able to get higher than second gear — that's second gear out of eighteen.

Garry pops a couple of Panadols for his back and squints at the clouds coming down from New Guinea. Then he looks over at me.

"You'd have to be mad to enjoy this."

Over the jackhammer sound of the stutter-bumps beating the youth out of his Kenworth, I ask Garry why he keeps making the run.

"To tell you the truth, I've been thinking about chucking it in. This may be my last run up here. They'll all be on their own then, as far as getting fuel up here."

I ask him if he's ever considered hiring a helper, an apprentice mechanic to ride shotgun and provide an extra pair of hands.

"I'd never be able to find anyone who wouldn't make a dog's breakfast out of everything he touches."

By the time we've finished unloading at the aboriginal settlement at Mapoon, a fuel discharge valve has stripped bare, and a fitting has torn from the air-system expansion tank. The fuel tanks are literally coming apart at the seams — some of the welds have cracked and fuel is trickling out.

Garry refuses any assistance with the repairs, and the farther north we go, the crabbier he gets.

There's smoke and charred earth everywhere, and lots of small blazes still kindling in the bush. When a scrap of smoldering debris blows across our path, I look back at the fuel leaking from the cracked tanker.

"Don't splatter your bladder, mate."

Diesel isn't nearly as volatile as gasoline, Garry tells me. I'm not completely reassured, but at this point the thought of exploding in a spectacular fireball seems preferable to a slow death by corrugations. In a few minutes I see Garry nervously eyeing his rearview mirror. Suddenly, he yells "Fuel!" and hits the kill switch. Chaos erupts. The crossover line connecting the tractor's tanks has torn loose, and fuel is gushing out by the barrel. We both fly into action, crawling under the prime mover into the diesel juice and dust that's quickly turning to mud, twisting valves shut under each of the four drive tanks.

When the flow is stanched, we climb out from under opposite sides of the truck. I see Garry looking at his watch with a stunned expression. Diesel fuel and dirt cover him like brown batter on a piece of fish. I let out an involuntary chortle, and when Garry looks up from his watch, he's wearing a dazed smile.

"Bugger me dead," he says. "It's my birthday."

We limp into Weipa and head to the fuel depot to reload. The depot manager, Vince, comes out of the office. One of Garry's best friends up here, Vince listens sympathetically as Garry details the last three days, listing the repairs he'll need to make before we can continue to The Top. Vince offers to help work on the truck, but Garry waves him off.

I mention to Vince that it's Garry's birthday.

"Fair dinkum?"

That's Aussie for "No lie?" Vince immediately gets on the phone to round up some people for a celebration. He tells Garry that he'll chain the gates if he tries to leave before we have a night out.

Vince's wife, Leann, will be joining us, and I ask Vince if she'll be bringing along any single girlfriends. He looks dumbfounded.

"Uh, Sheilas are a bit of a problem up here, mate. They're strictly B.Y.O."

I decide to tell Vince about my conversation with Garry — about how he told me he's thinking about calling it quits.

Vince laughs out loud. "He's been saying that for years, he has! He whinges [complains] nonstop, but the thing is, he loves this stuff. The reason nobody else brings fuel up to The Top is because he won't let anyone else have the run."

I'm beginning to see how Garry's world works. The pain is part of the package — just as it was for the heroes of the American "outlaw trucker" movies of the seventies. In those fabulously clumsy epics, the trucker-hero, like Jesus, must suffer. In *Convoy*, Kris Kristofferson gets his eye poked out. In *High Ballin'*, Peter Fonda gets his ass kicked with tire irons. In *The Great Smokey Roadblock*, Henry Fonda keels over after a heroic battle with the cops.

But if you're a Hollywood trucker, at least you have good roads. And you can share the burden with your buddies. You get on the CB, call up a convoy, and crash the roadblock, sayin', "Let them truckers roll, ten-four!" But if you're Garry White, swaggin' across the torture tracks of Cape York, you're on your own. You can't have a helper — of course you can't — because *you're the one who helps*. You handle everything the world throws at you. You deliver the blood to your flock. You light up their tropical nights. You cool their beer.

And if you happen to love it, you sure as hell don't let them know.

The Jardine is the largest river on the peninsula, the only one that can't be forded by a vehicle during The Dry. A small cable ferry shuttles vehicles back and forth, but when we drive up, the ferry is on the other side of the river, and the last four-wheel drive is rolling up the bank, joining a couple of other vehicles making tracks into the rain forest.

"That's Ben's truck," Garry says, hitting the horn. But Ben, the ferry operator, doesn't look back as he turns the corner and heads out of sight. So we're stuck here. For ten hours.

A Toyota Land Cruiser pulls up, filled with Torres Strait Islanders, people of Melanesian descent who inhabit the islands and part of the mainland at The Top. We strike up a conversation with one of the guys.

Garry says he knows where Ben hides the key to the ferry, and he knows how to get the boat across the river. "But the only way to get over there is to swim."

He looks at me. I look at the Islander. He looks at Garry. They both look at me. I take a step back.

"Y'know," the Islander says, "I used to swim across here every now and again. But not since that bloke got taken."

The "bloke" was in our situation a few months ago, and he decided to go for it. Apparently, he made it about a third of the way across before his companions saw an eighteen-foot log drifting toward him. It was drifting . . . upstream. The shore-side screams caught his attention, but fate was already in gear.

So we fire up some steak and onions and gaze over at the opposite bank, where our ride will sit for the next ten hours guarded by a prehistoric underwater antitheft device.

That night, thick clouds blot out the stars, and the monsoon rains come in hard just before dawn. There's no doubt that The Wet is on its way, and that we're running out of time.

In the morning, after Ben arrives and brings the ferry over, Garry noses the truck down the riverbank. But when the Kenworth's front wheels transfer their weight to the boat, the shorebound end sinks under the load, sending the other end rearing out of the water spectacularly, nearly throwing Ben's helper overboard. Upended, the ferry seems poised to shoot out of the water. When the drive wheels connect with the ferry, they claw it back down under the truck. Garry balances the truck on top of the teetering deck and jumps out. Ben runs over, wild-eyed.

"Garry, what's vehicle weight on this bastard?"

"About forty tons."

"Y'know, the capacity's only twenty-eight." Garry looks away like a guilty schoolboy, and does a little whistle through his missing front teeth.

"Well, I guess she's on now," Ben says, and yells at his helper to fire up the cable motor. In no time, the truck's on the opposite bank, and we roar off into the jungle.

Safely away, Garry looks over at me. "I rounded down," he says.

North of the river, the road narrows and snakes into a series of tight turns. The soil changes from hard red dirt to white boggy sand. The bumps stretch out and yield into soft, forgiving moguls. Garry works up through the gears, wrestling the beast through the hairpins, finessing torque and momentum into distance.

The track narrows further as jungle encroaches on both sides. We stop to remove the antennae before they're torn off, and Garry eases the big truck into the trees. Branches elbow out, grabbing at the mirrors. Vines reach down, clawing at the windshield.

Finally, we pull into Pajinka's gates and roll up to the generator tank. We decide to go up front before we unload the fuel, to say hello and see who's around, maybe rustle up some tucker. Peter, the cook, brings over a round of stubbies and tells us to help ourselves to whatever's in the fridge.

Three guests come in from fishing and join us in the shade. They're sweaty and sunburnt. When they get their beers, each of them drains half a bottle in a long, appreciative guzzle.

In a few minutes, Garry and I will venture back into the sun to unload the fuel. Then I guess we'll have to start thinking about heading back down the peninsula before The Wet catches us and bogs us in.

But for the moment, we're in the shade kicking back and savoring cold beer and conversation — Garry White's great gifts to The Top.

DAVE EGGERS

Hitchhiker's Cuba

FROM *Time*

ON THE ROAD outside Havana, where weeds grow through the
train tracks, and the crumbling buildings, colors fading into a dec-
orator's dream, alternate with wild trees and shrubs in the most
gorgeous, postapocalyptic way, is where it first happened, when we
first got an idea of how it all worked.

We had missed a turn (we suspected) and so had stopped to
ask directions. We pulled over next to a median strip, on which
stood eight or ten people, half with shopping bags, presumably
waiting for a bus. We rolled down the window, smiled sheepishly,
and directed our confusion to one of the men (tall, black, in a
shiny Adidas jersey). With a swift sort of purpose, he nodded and
stepped forward from the island and toward us, in a gesture we
took as exceptionally friendly and helpful, getting so close to better
relate the coordinates . . .

Then he was in the car. It happened before we knew it had happened. He just opened the door, and then suddenly he was giving
us directions from within the car. The smallish backseat was empty,
then full, full with this large man, his knees cramped up near his
chin. He was so nonchalant, and had not uttered any commands or
taken out a gun or any of the other ostensible signs of carjacking,
and so it dawned on us that this was what happened in Rome. In
Cuba, that is. Here hitchhiking is custom. Hitchhiking is essential.
Hitchhiking is what makes Cuba move. All those other people on
the median strip? All waiting for rides. Perhaps a bus, yes, if they
have a few hours to lose. But until then there are cars, and occasionally the back of a bicycle, and the hope that someone will stop.

So the man in our car tells us where we're going, and then we're off, eastbound, through the outer parts of Havana, along the train tracks, more and more green, past the heartbreaking roadside propaganda, ten miles, fifteen miles out of the city's center.

His name is Juan Carlos. And while he speaks a little English, thankfully in the passenger seat is a translator/navigator (T/N), and she duly interprets.

What does Juan Carlos do for a living?

He's a basketball player-coach.

Where are we taking him?

Home. Is that okay?

Of course, sure. Is he married?

Yes. Actually, he says, his wife is the starting center for the Cuban women's national basketball team. Do we want to meet her?

Hell, of course we want to meet her.

His building is a concrete complex overgrown with weeds and drying laundry. Neighbors stare from above, their arms draped over balconies. Through the door and inside Juan Carlos's apartment suddenly there is Judith, easily seven feet tall. Eight? She's huge. She leans down to offer her cheek for kisses. The walls are crowded with images of Michael Jordan. We say we're from Chicago. They nod politely. Juan Carlos thinks the Suns will take it this year. The Suns? We nod politely.

Judith is practicing for the Sydney Games, with her team playing against three other teams in the Cuban women's intramural league. From the four teams, the squad for the national team is chosen. Does she think she'll have any trouble making the team? She chuckles. Dumb question. No, she'll be starting.

They ask when we'll be back in Havana. We don't know. When you come back, they say, this is your home. Their in-laws live down the street, so they'll stay with them and we can have their bed. We say fine, but for now we have to move, must get back on the road (but not before getting a quick snapshot, for which Judith changes into her uniform), because we're heading up the coast, and we have more people to pick up and move, from here to there.

That becomes the point — it had not been the plan at the outset but now is the mission, one thrust upon us — the picking up of people, because, as we learn soon enough, the most common roadside scenery in Cuba, besides the horse-drawn wagons and broken-down classic American cars, is its hitchhikers. The roads are littered with people everywhere, along the huge highways and two-laners, all strewn with mothers and their daughters, grandmothers, working men, soldiers, teenagers, schoolchildren in their white, white shirts and mustard-colored pants or skirts, day and night, in the rain or otherwise. All waiting.

They wait for hours for the occasional bus or a spot on the back of a truck, waiting on the median strips, at the intersections, sitting with their possessions or on them, along the gravelly highway shoulders, patience their essence because gasoline is scarce and expensive, cars are owned by few and function for fewer, and the buses are terrible and slow and always so full. And so we are driving in our Subaru, a tiny thing but big enough for five, and we're Americans come to move the Cubans from place to place. Feel our luxury! Hear our engine's roar!

Up the coast, and in ten minutes we stop for Jorge, who gets in at a stoplight and is going toward Varadero, a beach town on the north coast. Jorge is about eighteen, in khakis and a pink shirt, with a very hip-seeming haircut, freshly gelled, a kind of haircut that makes him look half monk, half member of a dancing, harmonizing teen quintet. Jorge's father, he says, left for the U.S. years ago. He was one of the so-called *balseros,* the rafters who left from the Bay of Mariel in 1994 during one of Castro's periodic spurts of permitted emigration. Now he's in Miami.

T/N: What does he do there?

Jorge: I don't know. I haven't talked to him since he left.

T/N: Oh, that's too bad.

Jorge: No, no. It's okay.

We drop the subject of dad of Jorge. We pass miles and miles of oil pumps along the ocean, some pumping, their bird heads rhythmically dipping their beaks, others inanimate, the surf spraying over. We ask Jorge what he does for a living. He says he's a student of astronomy.

"Oh, so what does that entail?" I ask the rearview mirror. T/N translates.

"Oh, you know," he says. "Cervezas, sodas, comida . . ."

Oh. Ha. Not astronomy. Gastronomy. Big laughs all around. The sky is watercolor gray, and the clouds hold rain. We all go over the mix-up three more times. Not astronomy. Gastronomy. Yes. The beach comes into view, palm trees bent by a wicked ocean-borne wind. Jorge wants to know if we need someplace to stay. Jorge, like every last man in Cuba, knows of just the place, the perfect *casa particular* — the Cuban version of a bed and breakfast — and he, like most, is very difficult to convince of one's lack of *casa particular–based need.*

No thanks, we say.

I know just the place, he says.

No thanks, we say.

Very nice place.

No thanks but —

Clean, very cheap.

Thanks, no.

Have your own kitchen, very private.

No, no.

Only eighteen dollars.

You are too kind but —

You want me to show you?

We drop Jorge at the beach at Santa Maria del Mar and get back to moving down the coast. Minutes later we pull over for two girls, each carrying a cake, each about twenty, giggling to themselves in the backseat. Sisters? No, just friends. They're on their way home, to the next town, Guanabo. We pass a photo shoot, by the water: a skeletal blond woman, a photographer, a band of Cuban men, grinning in matching shirts, all standing in front of a mid-fifties Chevy, powder blue. We all wonder who the model is. Anyone we know? The girls giggle more. We're suddenly pals, they and all hitchers instantly familiar, completely at ease — as if we've picked up classmates on the way to the minimart. Safety here is assumed, trust a given. Where is there danger in Cuba? This is unclear.

Sand covers the road. We almost get blindsided by a mural-burdened van from Pastors for Peace. Bumper stickers thereon: END THE EMBARGO! ¡VAMOS A CUBA! Terrible drivers, these guys.

We drop the cake-bearing girls on the corner just past Guanabo's main drag and pick up a much older woman, sixty or so, who's been visiting her mother and needs to go just a little ways out of town. Ten minutes later — *¡Aqui, aqui!* — she gets out. She smiles thank you, and we smile good-bye — and again we're empty. We don't like to be empty. Through the Cuban countryside we feel ashamed to have the backseat unpeopled — all this room we have, all this fuel. It's getting dark, and as the roads go black, what was a steady supply of hitchhikers, punctuating the roads like mile markers, quickly disappears. Where they go is unclear. What happens when night comes but a ride hasn't? It's a problem of basic math we cannot fathom: always there are more riders than rides, a ten-to-one ratio at best, so what are the odds that all riders will be transported before sunset?

At Varadero, there is money. Resorts and busloads of European tourists waiting impatiently in lobbies for their bags to be ported to their private beachside cabanas. There are buffets and games of water polo organized in the main pool — a ridiculous sort of comfort level for about one hundred dollars a night. (Best yet, the help is obsequious and a fifty-cent tip would do just fine!) After being turned away at the daunting gates of the massive Club Med, we drop our luggage next door and set out to the area's most fiery hot spot, the Café Havana, a huge disco/Hard Rock–style fun provider. The place is overflowing with tourists from around the world, come to see how the Cubans entertain.

We sit at a table by the stage, and after some fantastic salsa-dancing action — women wearing little beyond sequins and feathers — there is a magician, ponytailed, with two ponytailed assistants. And this magician's specialty is doves. Everywhere he is making doves appear. From his sleeve, a dove. From a newspaper, a dove. A balloon is popped, and a dove appears and flaps wildly. The crowd loves it. The doves appear, each one flailing its wings for a few seconds of chaos and quasi-freedom. Then the magician, with fluid nonchalance, grabs the dove from the air, two-handed, making from the explosion of feathery white a smooth inanimate sculpture of a bird. Then in one swift motion he shoves the dove into a small cage, with little steel bars, on a stand by his waist. Once inside, the doves sit docilely, staring ahead through the tiny silver bars. Though there is a hole just behind them, they sit, cooing — one dove, then two, three, four, five, six, all in a row. When he is done, the magician is applauded. We all love him. The birds in their cage, content and so pretty. How does he do it? He is fantastic. Then the band comes on, and everyone dances.

The next day we're off, Varadero to Cienfuegos. First passengers, from a roadside crowd of fifteen or twenty: a mother-and-child duo, the mother skinny and snaggle-toothed, the baby perfect and in pink, eleven months old, little black shoes, shiny; they're headed home. We roll with them past horse-drawn wagons and slow, lanky cows. Egrets skim over the road, perpendicular. Air warm, sky overcast. The car screams.

They get out near Jovellanos, and we never get their names. In Jovellanos, a medium-size adobe town of narrow streets, we get lost, quickly and irrevocably. At a street corner, there appears beside us a man on a bicycle. He knows where to go, he says — just follow him. We rumble behind him and his bike at fifteen miles per hour, the streets full of onlookers watching our parade — left turn, right, left, left, right, left, ten minutes and there we are, back on the main road. He points ahead, toward the on-ramp. Aha.

We pull up next to him. He is sweating profusely and grinning. We slip him five dollars — for many, we're told, that's almost a month's salary — because we are wealthy and glamorous Americans and we appreciate his help. So easy to change the quality, the very direction, of Cubans' lives! It seems possible that, between our ride sharing and tip giving, we can single-handedly redress whatever harm has been done. Oh, if only!

Just outside Jovellanos there's Estelle, chatty, about thirty-five, and her ten-year-old Javier, who jump in at a dusty corner. Estelle sighs and laughs as she gets in and says hello. Had they been waiting long? Yes, yes, she says, they'd been waiting an hour and a half. They're going to a town called Australia, twenty minutes away. "Why is there a town in Cuba called Australia?" we ask. Estelle doesn't know. She turns to Javier. Javier has no idea. She shrugs and smiles.

We dodge more wagons, their drivers frequently asleep, the donkeys as sad as donkeys insist on appearing. There are men in uniform waiting for rides. There are women with groceries and babies waiting for rides. Some of the hitchers raise their hands to a passing car, but most don't. Some express frustration when they feel that a passing car could fit more people (i.e., them), but most don't. Most just watch you pass, squinting beyond you, for the next slowing car or truck. But when a car stops, never is there competition for the ride. Never is there shoving or even the most mild sort of disagreement. Each time we pull over, whoever's closest simply walks to the car and gets in. There is no system in place for the rewarding of longest wait, or oldest, or most pregnant. It's both perfectly fair and completely random.

We drop Estelle and Javier in Australia and pick up a family just outside of town. Grandfather, mother, daughter. They had been visiting a friend at the hospital and are going where we're going, to Playa Giron, home of the Cuban monument to the heroes of the Bay of Pigs. Our merengue tape, bought at a gas station, tinkles quietly from the speakers. We offer them — we offer everyone — water, cookies, crackers. They decline, and like most riders, this family says nothing unless we speak first; they don't even talk to one another. They watch the countryside pass, content. We are surprised, with them and most riders, that they do not want to know where we're from. Why are they not curious about us, the Americans here to save them? At their house, a bent-over salmon-colored ranch on a brown-dirt street, they ask us if we'd like to come in for a cold drink. We decline, must move. They scoot out. In the process, the daughter's shoe catches on the seat and loses its heel. She looks up, embarrassed, horrified. "New shoes too," says Mom. We all chuckle and then sigh. Kids.

After Giron, we're headed to Cienfuegos, through more fields of tobacco, then bananas. When night comes again, there are no streetlights, no lights anywhere, and on the winding two-lane roads, the avoidance of donkey carts and tractors and people requires tremendous, arcadelike hand-eye coordination. All is dark, and then things will suddenly be in front of us, lit as if by a camera's flash; swerving is an essential skill. Up ahead a car is parked, hazards blinking. There is a group of people around the car. Obviously an ambush. We should not stop. In the U.S., we would not stop.

We stop. Four people are standing around a white, early-seventies Volvo. They're out of gas; can we help? Yes, yes, we say, of course. They want to siphon from our tank. They have an actual siphon right there. We don't have enough, we say, noticing that we're almost out ourselves. We'll take them to the next town. Another man, Esteban, about nineteen, gets in the backseat, as does Marisa, twenty-four, petite, in silk blouse and black jeans. They hold the gas container on their laps. It's fifteen minutes to tinytown Roda and its one-pump gas station.

As we wait, we talk to Marisa, who we learn is studying English; she wants to get into tourism. She is married to an American, a photographer from Los Angeles. She was just coming back from Havana, as a matter of fact, where she was seeing him off at the airport.

So who are the others in the car?

She doesn't know. It's a taxi.

A taxi? A taxi running out of gas?

Big laughs all around.

The taxi was taking three passengers the three hours from Havana to Cienfuegos; the driver had grossly miscalculated how much fuel that would require. They had left at three that afternoon. It was now at least nine. We fill up their container and are ready to go.

But the Subaru won't start. It won't even turn over. In a flash, Esteban is out of the car and pushing. I'm driving, and he's barking orders, which need to be translated instantaneously by T/N. I have no idea what we're doing. We stop. Esteban, sighing loudly, takes my place, and then I'm pushing. Down the road, and before long we're out of the town and into the dark fields. The road is red from the taillights and slippery and I can't get a grip, but then boom, Esteban pops the clutch and the Subaru whinnies and I get in while it's moving and we're off, Esteban at the wheel. Like a getaway car! In a minute Esteban's doing eighty miles per hour. He's veering on and off the road. *"¡Flojo! ¡Flojo!"* Marisa is saying, urging him to slow down, but young Esteban has something to prove to her and to T/N, so eighty it is, the engine hitting high notes with full vibrato.

We get to the taxi. They fill up the Volvo while we wait. We meet the third passenger, Dale, an English-speaking med student from St. Kitts, who decides he's sick of speaking Spanish, so he'll ride to Cienfuegos with us. He's studying Spanish there, the first year of seven he'll spend in Cuba on his way to a medical degree. We follow the taxi into Cienfuegos, drop off Dale at his barbed wire–surrounded dormitory, check into a hotel with red light bulbs and a lounge singer plowing through the high points of the Billy Joel songbook, and we're done for the night.

In the morning, on the way to the town of Trinidad, it's all rolling hills and farms, and the people have been waiting for us. At an intersection ten miles out of Cienfuegos we stop at a gathering of twenty or so, mostly young men, some in uniform. One gets in, followed by a woman, running — she's just jumped out of another car and into ours. Her name is Maela and, like the vast majority of Cuban women, Maela is a devout spandex enthusiast. She's in a black-and-white bodysuit, bisected with belt, and she's laughing like mad at her car-to-car coup, the soldiers tossing her a wide variety of obscene gestures as we drive away. The soldier we've got is named Jordan; he's doing the mandatory military service — two years — and is heading home for the weekend. Maela was in Cienfuegos with friends and is going home too. He's quiet, but she's bubbly, and through the countryside we roll.

Ten miles and Jordan gets out at a tiny town called Pepito, where Condela gets in. Condela is about forty-five and has crumbs all over his mouth and hands — he has been eating a pastry while waiting for a ride, standing just outside a bakery. He's a butcher in Trinidad, so he'll be with us the rest of the ride, about an hour more. Condela has been visiting friends and is on his way back home. He asks where we're from. *Los Estados Unidos,* we say. Ah, he says. He has family in Miami. (Everyone has family in Miami.)

We drop off Maela; she giggles thanks, and in comes Belgis, about forty, pregnant, in a white frilly blouse and floral spandex leggings. She was waiting for three hours. She was visiting her family, and is on her way to Playa Yaguardabo to see her in-laws, ten minutes up the road. We get there, and she's out. Condela stays put and seems perturbed — the backseat is not so big — when we welcome a young couple, Alexander and Yaineris, who bustle in, exhaling with relief. They have a chicken with them. A live chicken. Condela laughs at our surprise. The chicken is small and in a plastic bag — its red, confused little head poking out. Alexander and Yaineris are married, and have been visiting her parents; they're headed back home to Trinidad. The ocean is a few hills to our right. Tour buses whip past us doing seventy-five miles per hour. The tour buses are always empty, always doing seventy-five, and they don't stop for anyone.

Halfway to Trinidad, while we are passing La Guira, something recklessly symbolic happens. At the bottom of a small valley, there is a split second when a huge, bulbous green army truck passes us, heading in the other direction. At the same instant, we are passing on our right a straw-hatted farmer on horseback and, to our left, a woman on a bicycle. Symbolism contained: each of our vehicles represents a different element of what makes Cuba Cuba. The bicycle (1) is the Cubans' resourcefulness and symbiosis with their Communist brethren (about a million bikes were donated by the Chinese, decades ago). The army truck (2) is the constant (though relatively sedate and casual, we'd say) military presence. We are the tourists (3), perhaps the future, our dollars feeding into Cuba's increasingly dominant second economy, largely inaccessible to Cuba's proletariat; and the horseback farmer (4) represents, of course, the country's rural backbone. All caught, for one split second, on a single linear plane.

At Trinidad, a colonial town four hundred years old, sun-bleached and ravishing, we drop off Condela. He shows us his shop, right on the main cobblestone drag. "If you need anything," he says, pointing to a storefront, "I'm right here." Trinidad is much too perfectly aged and brilliantly colored to be free of tourists: Germans, Spanish, Italians, even a few Americans drawling Indiana *r*'s.

On to Sancti Spiritus. Carlos, about thirty, and Armena, twenty-five, get in just outside Trinidad, where three dozen others are waiting with them. Carlos works in construction now, after a five-year stint as a policeman in Havana. Armena has been in Trinidad looking for work.

"What kind of work?"

"Anything at all," she says.

"Is it hard to find work?"

Eyes are rolled. Yes, yes. These days, yes. We drop off Armena at a little yellow house, clothes hanging in the windows. Carlos gets out soon after. At Banao, a tiny town, there is a crowd of forty waiting; a dozen or so people wave us down. We can't stop right in the middle — too confusing. (Oh, to have a bus!) We drive to the end, where the throng thins. We nod to a woman, and she jogs forward and gets in. Dayami is about thirty, lipsticked, in tight black jeans with a black mesh shirt over a sports bra. She's a doctor, on her way to pick up her daughter at school. We ask if it's hard to get medicine. After all, on the way from Havana, a billboard had read, YANKEE EMBARGO: GENOCIDE AGAINST CUBA. She says no, not really.

We pass a barefoot, shirtless boy on the back of a donkey. A mile later, a man on horseback, galloping, beams as we go by, takes his hat off, and waves it to us in mid-gallop, even as we're passing him going sixty-five miles per hour. Is Cuba cinematic? It is.

At a corner outside the city, we grab a tallish, redhaired woman in a white medical jacket. When she gets in, she and Dayami laugh. They used to work together, and begin chatting. She's a dentist, and had loaned her bike to a friend. We drop Dayami off at her daughter's school and park in Sancti Spiritus' central square. A school band practices in an auditorium above us. Mopeds buzz to and fro, soldiers talk to schoolchildren, and within minutes we see the dentist. She rides by on her bicycle and rings her bell. "I got my bike back!" she sings to us. Cuba has become one huge Richard Scarry neighborhood.

Then we're off to Santa Clara, too dark to pick up anyone, but the next day it's Santa Clara to Havana, and en route there is Wendy. Wendy is talkative and insists on tapping T/N on the shoulder and saying "*¡Mira!*" ("Look here!") every time she has a question or statement. She's married, has a three-year-old, and works at a peso food market. "Oh, I knew you weren't Cuban," she says. Why? we ask.

"Cuban couples won't pick people up," she says. "People in groups or driving alone but never couples."

(Shoulder poke) "*¡Mira!*": She has family in New York, New Jersey.

(Shoulder poke) "*¡Mira!*": She also cleans houses, to make ends meet.

(Shoulder poke) "*¡Mira!*": "You know how the situation in Cuba is, right?"

She's on her way home. Her husband's in prison, she says — she has just been visiting him. He was convicted, with nine others, of stealing gasoline. He was originally sentenced to four years, but with a lawyer — he is innocent, was set up, she insists — he was able to get the sentence reduced to twenty months. She gets out and is replaced by a cheerful trio — a large blond woman, her sister and her sister's daughter. Havana? they ask. Yes, yes. Oh, they cannot believe their luck. They cannot believe they're getting a ride all the way to Havana. Waiting long? Hours. Are things always like this? Getting worse every year. Castro, they say, is getting too old, senile maybe. Things are not good. Are we aware of the situation here? Things are getting worse. The past ten years, they say, much worse. Fidel is obsessed with the U.S., they say, which is fine, but he must start taking care of things here at home. When we drop them off, at about noon, they're astounded that they're home before nightfall. They are beside themselves. When we're in Cuba again, they tell us, we have a home, we have a family. We take pictures.

And finally, there is Yuricema. About twenty, dark-brown skin, wide white smile. She gets in on the Malecon, just shy of the Hemingway Marina. She's coming home from school; she's a business and law student. We're in the suburbs of Havana, and the sky is purplish and getting darker as we approach the city's center. Yuricema claims that her English is bad, but then she speaks it, and it's kind of perfect, at least in terms of the words she does know. The accent sounds more California than Havana. We ask her where she learned English.

"My professor was Michael Bolton," she says.

I almost veer off the road.

"Michael Bolton?" T/N says.

"Yes, yes, he is very good. I love him."

Is it possible? Was Michael Bolton ever a teacher of English in Cuba? We hit the main drag of the Malecon. The ocean is bursting against the wall, spraying the waves up and over the road, thirty feet high. It's almost dark. T/N wants one more shot at it.

"So, wait, Michael Bolton was your English teacher?"

Yuricema bursts out laughing. We laugh too. She asks T/N the English word for *"¡Ojala!"* T/N translates, "I wish!"

She had been trying to say "My preference is Michael Bolton" but said instead "My professor is . . ." She had one of his albums, but she loaned it to a friend, and then he claimed never to have seen it. Yuricema rolls her eyes to underline how stupid her friend is. We offer to send her a new Michael Bolton tape. I throw in that we'll send her whatever Michael Bolton stuff we can find. Posters, books, everything. "Very easy," I say. So easy to send wonderful things from America! She is beside herself. She gives T/N a pre-emptive gift — a wallet-size plastic calendar featuring an advertisement for a new kind of Vaseline. We thank her. I picture the sending of the Bolton care package. She will be so happy. She will never forget us. No one will ever forget us. Cuba will not forget us. We will come back, with not only the Michael Bolton stuff but a bigger car. No, a fleet of cars — and buses. We will sneak into the country from America, this time with legions of drivers — there are more of us coming all the time; it's getting so easy, embargo or no — and with enough buses and cars to get everyone everywhere they need to go. With our dollars and new tires, we will empty the roadsides and move the people place to place. The cars and buses will be huge and shiny, and we will flood the roads with them, get this place going — faster and faster, no more waiting for anything. Cars for everyone! We'll bring in some trains maybe. Hovercrafts, mono-rails. It'll be great. And all we'll ask in return is some hearty thanks and a nice beach to enjoy when we're in the neighborhood.

We wind our way through the dark streets of Old Havana, as Yuricema directs us to her home. When we get there we realize she lives a block from our hotel, the Hambos Mundos, a bargain at $120 a night. She gets out of the car and asks if we'd like to come in. We decline. She smiles.

"Don't forget me," Yuricema says, getting out and backing into her doorway. "Because I will never forget you."

Oh, just you wait, Yuricema. You haven't seen the last of us.

DAVID HALBERSTAM

Nantucket on My Mind

FROM *Town & Country*

THERE IT WAS last summer, one of the many real estate advertisements in our weekly newspaper, this particular one not even particularly large. It mentioned four houses for sale, all of them said to have great views. I did not doubt that, for one house was listed at $5 million, another at $4 million, a third at $3.5 million, and the fourth, clearly a bargain, at a mere $3 million. One would hope they had great views. It was one more sign of the times, of the increased value of property on this strange, semiquaint, once-remote, old-time Quaker island that has now become a target for the young, stunningly wealthy winners of Wall Street. In the past we were more middle class than many of the chicer East Coast watering holes, but now we have become a trophy island where the masters of the universe, as Tom Wolfe called them, can build their magnificent houses for their wives and families — twenty-room houses for four or five people.

I do not remember exactly when it was that the real estate market crossed the magical seven-figure barrier — in Nantucket real estate terms, surely the equivalent of that marvelous moment when aeronautical engineers were able to design jet planes that could break the sound barrier. I think it was two or three years ago, somewhere in that heady period when the Dow was shooting up some three thousand points in under three years. Like many people who have come to Nantucket for years and were drawn here by its simplicity rather than its chicness, I do not think it is a cause for celebration, though clearly in financial terms at least I am a beneficiary, and my wonderful and venerable old house — half-simple and half-gentrified, surely a house with a divided soul (and most assuredly unbeatable) — is certainly worth more now than ever. If, of course, I can continue to afford to live in it.

Because the new wealth is so great, we have lost the one thing that protected us in the past — our inaccessibility. We were thirty miles out to sea, distinctly farther than the Vineyard and much harder to reach. The constant threat of fog made getting here a nightmare: I have several lasting friendships that were fashioned during the long hours of waiting in Logan Airport while the island remained socked in, then finally taking a death-defying late-hour shot at Nantucket — *Well, folks, they say the fog out there's still pretty thick, but what say we give it one little old last try* — followed by a hair-raising approach, the pilot sometimes pulling up at the last second and going back to Boston, where the airline dispensed with us at a less-than-imposing hotel for a few hours, until early morning, when we got on a bus to Hyannis in order to make the approach by sea. It was the kind of experience that cemented friendships forever. It was also the kind of experience that warned young ambitious Wall Street winners that the island, no matter what its joys, was not worth their time and suffering.

But the newcomers have not let ancient, time-honored barriers of geography and low airport ceilings stand in their way. *They come equipped with their own air force.* Private jets — fog-proof, it would seem — have now appeared and are mandatory equipment for these recent arrivals, as fishing rods, tennis rackets, Labrador retrievers, and old jeeps were mandatory to those who came before. Indeed, I have a friend who notes that some of the new people do not even own land on our island but fly in only to play at its new golf course (which initially cost $250,000 to join and filled up in a matter of weeks), and suggests that they are doing it not for the sport, but just to show off their jets. After all, what is the point of having a showcase private plane if there is not some difficult, essentially inaccessible place to fly in to? Be that as it may, the commute, once so hard, is now a piece of cake. On one recent Fourth of July, our small airport was the busiest in all of Massachusetts, with, it was said, 1,200 takeoffs and landings in a single day, busier than even Logan.

The truth is, I am, almost without knowing it, in the midst of a lover's quarrel with Nantucket; I still love it, but these days I do not always like it. This is therefore something of a cranky piece, and I do not like to write as a crank: I am not in general nostalgic for the past. The Fourth of July, I believe, is not now and never was what it used to be. A few years ago I wrote a book about the fifties, a decade in which I came of age, and it convinced me that for all our myriad contemporary failings, life in America is infinitely better and richer, more diverse and more tolerant than it was at the midcentury mark. But nevertheless I am also uneasy about what happens when so much wealth — wealth to many of us of an incomprehensible nature — strikes an island so small and fragile.

Long Island, befitting its name, is very big. Nantucket is not. Essentially, the island is a triangle of which the two barrier sides are roughly eight miles and fourteen miles long, depending on how you measure them. Despite the thousands and thousands of vehicles that crowd onto the island during the summer, when the population swells from roughly 7,000 year-round residents to some 40,000 part-time owner residents, we still do not have a single traffic light. Our size therefore is finite; the texture of our daily life oddly delicate because we are so small that when something goes wrong socially, we feel it immediately.

This is my thirtieth year as an owner here. I bought my house in 1969, the year I began working on *The Best and the Brightest*, the moment when I went over to writing books full time. Over the years I have come to love the island — it has given me sanctuary in a demanding and difficult and often volatile professional life, allowing me to work diligently each summer while putting myself back together among people who I know love and care about me. It is a place to work and to heal. I leave the island in the early fall rested, but with a great deal of work done. I stumbled on it at first — my friend Russell Baker brought me here in 1968 and I thought it was the most beautiful place I had ever seen. It seemed to have more of the good things of life and fewer of the bad than any vacation spot I had ever seen before; it offered an almost-perfect balance between the possibilities for friendship and the right, when I needed to work, to my privacy. Because the happiest part of my peripatetic childhood was spent in a small town in northwest Connecticut, Nantucket — with its strikingly handsome library, the sense of community manifest at high school football games — reminded me of the best part of my youth. People knew one another and treated one another with respect. The people who did have money (and it would be considered small money these days), those old Yankee families said to be very wealthy, very consciously did not manifest it. In the great houses along Hulburt Avenue, our show-case street that runs along the harbor, the houses were, as they always had been, a little worn down, with bathroom sinks stained green by the relentless drip of the water — a reminder of plumbers never summoned.

It was still very much a middle-class island in those days. Unlike other East Coast watering holes, we did not have much in the way of a writer's community, and that too appealed to me, because I had spent one summer in the Hamptons and the pace of the social life had been far too intense. My own social circle was eclectic, filled largely with people I would not have been friends with in New York — people I fished with, or, in time, those my wife and I enjoyed cooking with. Not surprisingly, as our daughter grew up, our friends were people who had children who were her friends.

We formed, I think, the squarest of summer communities. Our friends were, it seemed to me, people brought to Nantucket not because it was chic but because it was beautiful and family-oriented, and because they liked the pleasures of the island — the fishing, the sailing, the tennis, and the birding, things that, as they did for me, recalled the happier parts of their own childhoods, even if they now lived in tough, demanding urban environments.

Soon it was the texture of friendships as much as the beauty of the island that held us, friendships that were not work-connected and that near the end of spring we always looked forward to renewing. Those friendships were based on simple things: fishing with my friend David Fine; going to the beaches with Pam and Foley Vaughan and their children; dinner with Bill Euler and Andy Oates, who ran our best store, Nantucket Looms, a friendship tentative at first because they were so private; rowing in a double scull with Marc Garnick; and finally, after I sold my fishing boat, fishing with Tom Mleczko, who doubled as a schoolteacher in New Canaan the rest of the year. These were the touchstones of our summer, the friendships sweetened by the many years in grade from the past.

There was over the years, starting in the eighties, a dramatic change in the cast of characters who came here — the rising prices on the tickets of the houses automatically narrowed down the possibilities of who could afford the island. (One summer I called a friend of mine who was a journalist and asked if he was going to rent again. No, he answered, the rent had just tripled, and so he was going to Tuscany for a month — it was cheaper.) In addition, in a number of cases I thought I sensed a change in what people sought from this island — an increase in the importance of status. That has been particularly noticeable in the last few years with the coming of such stupendous wealth, wealth that seems with is vast annual rewards disconnected from the reality of daily life. I realize there is some degree of generalization to what I am going to say, and I am sure that some of the new people are as nice as or nicer than the old, and that some of the older people, given half a chance, would be greedier than the new. But I am not sure that the new people are brought to the island by the old and abiding pleasures that drew us.

The new people seem not only very rich, but very young to be that rich; and all too often they seem quite imperious. I suppose that is not too surprising; they have been raised in a modern pressure cooker: starting out in demanding day schools, and then demanding boarding schools, and then making the cut at demanding elite colleges, and then again making the next level, at demanding law or business schools, and then becoming winners in the brutal competition in the world of finance. There, if you are a winner, an annual reward of $10 million is thought to be small; it is where people now talk of making a unit as a mark of success — a unit being earnings of $25 million in a year. I think something like that begins to affect a person's sense of proportion.

On our island we are, I think, the worse for it. There is a sharp, indeed an alarming, decline in the requisite courtesy and manners that are so critical to the texture of life in a small town, and that are, comparably, so unimportant in a city like New York. When these people want things — houses to be built, gardens to be made green, rugs to be woven and delivered — they want them right now, with a special immediacy, as if they were back in the city ordering out from a neighborhood Chinese restaurant. If they buy a piece of property for $2.5 million and plan to tear it down and build a new house for $3 million, the money is no longer an object — but the speed of completion is. *By July 1, if you please — otherwise we'll have to go elsewhere.* That has a ripple effect throughout the island — the cost of everything goes up accordingly, and other work orders, small assignments, the repair of a house here, an addition to a house there, tend to be shunted aside. Two summers ago, our gardener fired us because all we wanted was upkeep on our garden, and it was impossible for us to compete with the gargantuan projects offered her by newer arrivals.

The houses being built are different now. The old Nantucket had houses of modest size, and in keeping with the traditional respect for the sheer beauty of the island, they were often nestled in the landscape itself. By contrast, many of the new houses are huge flagships to show that yes, there is a great deal of wealth in the family, and they seem to violate the natural contours of the land as violently as possible. The cars on our island are bigger and fancier, too — they used to be deliberately downscale, and exceptionally well rusted, but these days everyone seems to be driving sport-utility vehicles (SUVs, to use the vernacular) that seem to be like jeeps on steroids.

Worse, the manners of the drivers seem to have declined in inverse proportion to the size of their cars and wealth. Many of our rural roads are paths more than roads, and it was common courtesy, when you were driving down a rural road wide enough for only one car and you spotted a car coming at you, to pull over if at all possible in a niche alongside the road and let the other car go by. Part of that same courtesy was for the driver of the other car to wave as he or she went by signaling some respect for your manners — as if to say, you did it for me this time, I'll do it for you the next. Now you pull over — you had better, because the other car is sure to be twice as big and powerful as yours — and more often than not, there is not the slightest wave of a hand or the beep of a hor They are telling you that you pulled over because it is your pro place in the universe to pull over for them — and you'd bette prepared to pull over the next time as well.

Somewhere in here is no small amount of irony. The is more crowded than ever, more gentrified than ever, and more building going on than ever before, more huge tr ing down on our narrow streets and roads. Yet if the isla crowded, I suspect it manages to remain aloof from most ardent new suitors. I have this theory — that ma pleasures of Nantucket are not easily gained and c chased on demand, that they have to be, like everything else in life, earned, and you have to take time and serve something of an apprenticeship in order to get the full measure of the pleasures available.

For all of the crowding downtown, many of the beaches remain secluded; the nature walks are pleasant and accessible, and there is no line for them. If you want to picnic, and have a boat, there are places in Polpis, the large inner harbor, where, if you know the tides, you can miraculously enough go and picnic in a beautiful spot — more of an idyll than one can imagine on the East Coast — and never see another soul. I am a fairly serious fisherman, and our light-tackle saltwater fishing is arguably the best along the East Coast, perhaps because we are so far into the Gulf Stream, But it takes time and skill to learn how to fish here, and money will not do it all for you — you have to learn to handle a boat in what are daunting waters, going out on days when the weather changes, when the shoals are murderous and when the fog rolls in so suddenly that unless you know what you are doing, it can all be quite terrifying. I know, because I had a boat for ten years, and it was a difficult and exacting apprenticeship, not so much learning where the fish are — that part was easy — but how dangerous the Atlantic Ocean can be. So perhaps it is not surprising that, for all the money being spent on boats, many of them with GPS/Loran guides that should make dealing with fog and shoals virtually idiot-proof, on the July Fourth and Labor Day weekends, the most crowded days of the year, you can be at choice spots for fishing for blues or stripers only thirty minutes from Madaket Harbor and not see another boat.

I realize that what I'm writing reflects not just the change in the economy but the change in the writer himself, the changes in the eye of the beholder: that the adventurousness of a young man come to a new place in his thirties is very different from a man in his sixties, wanting things always to be as they once were, bemoaning, almost unconsciously, the loss of his own youth. And I am aware that one of the critical things that I liked about the island remains as true as ever: that it can, in a country as dynamic and volatile as ours, offer you a sense of the seasons of your own life, as life in a city rarely can, the kind of texture and feeling that Thornton Wilder captured in *Our Town* — a sense of the rhythm of your life as it touches those around you. If over the years we have had friends who for various reasons have moved away, and if our list of friends is not exactly what it was two decades ago, there is nonetheless a sense of being rooted here as we are not rooted in New York, and an ability to monitor the seasons of our lives from the changes in the lives of those around us.

In New York our friendships tend to be with peers, more often than not professionally driven, and while we tend to know the children of our friends, by and large, with few exceptions, the friendships bloom in the evening and the children tend to remain in the background, seen but not really known. That is not true of Nantucket: over the past thirty years I have watched the children of my friends grow up, go off to college, and come back and have children of their own. I have fished with my friend David Fine for twenty-eight years now, and our routines aboard the boat — who will catch the first or the biggest fish — have the quality of old vaudeville routines, the sweetness of conversations so oft repeated that they have by now become second nature. Paul and Joan Crowley became our friends because they were friends of David and Sue Fine's, and in time we watched Melissa Crowley grow from a young girl and a superb athlete to a confident, extremely successful magazine editor in New York. Both David Fine and I in time gave up running our own boats, and we have fished for the last few years with Tom Mleczko, who is our best fisherman, and we have had the pleasure of seeing his and Bambi's children, who worked as strikers on his boat, grow up to become strikingly handsome young people, one daughter in Boston, a son about to start college, and another daughter, whom I wrote about, become a star of the championship U.S. Olympic hockey team, an article that gave me as much pleasure as anything I've ever written. Their cousins, the Gifford kids — how many letters written to directors of admission at different boarding schools and colleges? — have morphed into tall, handsome, confident young men and women. John Burnham Schwartz, who appeared with his parents at my house when he was nine, beautiful and beguiling, and whom I used to take fishing every summer, has remained a friend and a light of my life. We gave his engagement party and the book party for his second novel; he is now a successful novelist, and a peer, someone I count on not merely for friendship but for advice.

The friendship with Bill Euler and Andy Oates, a bit hesitant at first, grew stronger every year, and dinners with them became the evenings we looked forward to with singular pleasure, in time raucous evenings of more wine than normal and world-class gossip. Five years ago I dedicated a book to them (it was a baseball book, and someone, not knowing of our friendship, saw their names and asked, "Euler and Oates — which team did they play for?"). This year, Bill, who was my age, died of leukemia, and it was like nothing so much as a death in the family, for he was a shy man who had quietly enhanced many other people's lives, and seemed not to know how much he was cherished and how much he would be missed. We've watched our own child, and those of our friends the Vaughans and the Clapps and the Durkes, grow up together and go off to college. Our daughter on occasion reminds us that she thinks of Nantucket, not New York, as her real home and thinks about living in our old house some day with her own children. And when she talks like that, we are reminded that we have become in some way *of* the island, that it binds us and forms our lives in ways that we do not entirely understand, and yet are unconsciously dependent upon.

The places you love will do that to you.

MARK HERTSGAARD

The Nile at Mile One

FROM *Outside*

WHERE THE NILE enters Lake Albert, in the northwestern corner of Uganda, lies a tiny fishing village named Wanseko. It is the end of the line, the last stop on the public bus route from Kampala, the run-down capital nestled among the hills above Lake Victoria, 160 miles to the south. The trip took nine hours the day I made it, crammed inside a 1960s-vintage American-made school bus that for some reason had been painted chocolate brown. Bench seats originally meant to accommodate two schoolkids each were now packed with four and five Ugandans of all ages, the small sitting on elders' laps amid high-pitched chatter and good-natured jockeying for space.

Apart from the close quarters, the drive was pleasant and cool for the first two hours. The farther north we traveled, the drier the land became, yet it remained beautiful and apparently fertile. On either side of the road stretched plains of golden grass, dotted by cone-roofed huts and oblong structures whose white crosses identified them as the schools and churches bequeathed by European missionaries a century ago.

By the time we reached Wanseko, it was late afternoon and I was one of only three passengers still on the bus. Wanseko was little more than a few low-slung shacks grouped around a dusty clearing the size of a football field. To the west, across Lake Albert, I could dimly make out the mountains of Zaire through a bluish haze. There was nothing like a hotel in town, so I paid the equivalent of a single U.S. dollar to spend the night inside a barren concrete room behind the general store.

I had come to Wanseko while retracing a trip that Winston Churchill made through Africa in 1907. At the time, the future British prime minister had just begun his first significant government appointment, as parliamentary undersecretary of state for the colonies, a post that naturally included Africa among its concerns. Churchill's expedition took him by ship across the Mediterranean, through the Suez Canal, and around the Horn of Africa to the old Arab port city of Mombasa, located on the Indian Ocean in what is now Kenya. The newly constructed Uganda Railway carried him west to Nairobi and on to Lake Victoria, the presumed source of the Nile. He crossed the great lake and followed the Nile through Uganda, Sudan, and Egypt to Cairo. The expedition was a combination of business and pleasure for the thirty-three-year-old Churchill, undertaken during Parliament's autumn recess and paid for in part by a book he would write about the experience, *My African Journey*.

Part travelogue, part policy paper, *My African Journey* is a short, impassioned book of dazzling prose and keen observation. It articulates virtually all facets of the ideology that shaped industrial man's impact on Africa in the twentieth century — the values, fears, goals, and justifications that animated European efforts to recast the human and physical environment of Africa. Churchill saw the continent through the eyes of an inveterate colonizer, an unashamed imperialist who believed that colonialism benefited colonizer and colonized alike. Even more than his white skin, what set Churchill apart from the Africans he encountered was the technology at his disposal — guns, steamships, railways, the telegraph, and other emblems of the industrial era. Technology had brought wealth and progress to the people of Britain, argued Churchill, and it would do the same for the population still mired in the "primary squalor" of Africa.

When I pulled a copy of *My African Journey* down from a friend's bookshelf in Nairobi, I was in the midst of traveling around the world, researching a book about the many environmental pressures crowding in on the human race at the end of the twentieth century. Churchill's unqualified enthusiasm for technology had helped convince me to retrace his African journey, for technology, of course, lies at the heart of humanity's relationship with the environment. Yet to many contemporary environmentalists, technology is almost a dirty word. The root of the problem, as they see it, is the arrogant belief that modern man can, by virtue of his technology, live separate from, even superior to, nature — "to tame the jungle," as Churchill put it.

It is easy for a late-twentieth-century observer to condemn Churchill's boorish insistence on conquering nature. But there is no denying that technology has been inseparable from human progress since time immemorial. From the moment our first human ancestor picked up the first stone tool more than two million years ago — an event that, according to the fossil record, may have occurred less than three hundred miles northeast of Wanseko, in the Great Rift Valley — the fate of our species has been inextricably linked to the creation of technologies that gave us more efficient means of extracting food, water, shelter, and other essentials from the physical environment. Churchill's generation had particularly good reason to regard technology as a liberating force. For millennia, the vast majority of humans had lived on the edge of starvation, struggling against natural forces beyond their control. But the industrial ascent of the nineteenth century — notwithstanding the often abominable working conditions imposed on the laboring classes — had shown how the application of technology could raise living standards for nearly everyone.

Like other champions of the industrial order then and now, Churchill had big ideas about what technology, properly applied, could achieve. I was following in his footsteps partly because *My African Journey* had made such a trip sound like irresistible fun, with enough risk thrown in to keep it interesting. But I also wanted to see how Churchill's ideas compared to African reality nearly a century later, and what that implied about our contemporary environmental dilemma.

That night in Wanseko, I wondered whether Churchill had managed to arrange better accommodations than I had. I slept poorly in my concrete hovel, awakened repeatedly by the chickens — or was it rats? — that, inches from my head, rustled and scratched against the wall outside.

The next morning, determined to remain as faithful to Churchill's itinerary as I could, I rented a bike in Wanseko for the trip to Murchison Falls, praised by Churchill as the most spectacular waterfall to be found on the Nile's 4,037-mile journey from Lake Victoria to the Mediterranean. Churchill wrote that a bicycle was "the best of all methods of progression in Central Africa," for it offered both speed and mobility. In the process, he came up with what may be the first literary paean to the glories of single-track riding: "Even when the track is only two feet wide, and when the densest jungle rises on either side and almost meets above the head, the bicycle skims along, swishing through the grass and brushing the encroaching bushes, at a fine pace."

Actually, I had little choice but a bike if I hoped to reach Kabalega Falls, as Murchison Falls is also known. I had been told back in Kampala that I could catch a bus to the falls from Wanseko, but that turned out to be false. Walking was not advisable; the distance was twenty-seven miles, and the area was frequented by rhinos and other dangerous wildlife. There were also bandits; indeed, soldiers hunting them had boarded the chocolate bus the day before and aggressively questioned each of the male passengers (except me, the only white). Begging a ride from a passing vehicle was a possibility, but it could be anywhere from five minutes to five days before a vehicle passed. On the other hand, there were lots of bicycles around: the Ugandans seemed as fond of them as Churchill had been, and they almost never traveled without passengers or large quantities of goods perched over their back wheels.

How I managed, amidst such plenty, to select the singularly pitiful specimen of bicycle I ended up with is something I cannot easily explain. Some people just have a sixth sense about these things. After my test ride, I did tell the owner — a teenage boy with a round, eager face — that something was wrong with the left pedal; it was cocked at a funny angle, and my foot kept slipping off it. Besides that, the back tire was treadless, the front wheel had no brakes, and the rusted metal seat offered a standard of discomfort unknown since the Middle Ages. But the owner assured me that the pedal was no problem. And since it was already midmorning, I was in such a hurry — always a mistake in Africa — that I didn't doubt him.

The first six miles of hard dirt road passed quickly enough, and in half an hour I reached the turnoff to the falls. I pedaled east, twenty-one miles to go. The road became a dusty track through clusters of thatch huts where children played in the shade beneath mothers' watchful eyes. A teenager in a torn white T-shirt who introduced himself as Robert began riding his bike alongside me and appointed himself my new best friend for life. The track soon began to climb through sparse, dry bush — and climb, and climb some more. After three or four miles on my one-speed stallion with a thirty-pound rucksack on my back, I was feeling the strain. Robert was, too, I think, but the smile never left his face as he casually asked whether I had an extra T-shirt or notebook I could spare.

Suddenly, as if to mock my exertions, a white jeep barreled past us in a blizzard of dust. It was a chance in a thousand, but if I had waited at the turnoff with my thumb out, I could have been in that jeep. Instead, I faced another sixteen miles of hard labor beneath a sun that, in Churchill's words, "even in the early morning, sits hard and heavy on the shoulders. At ten o'clock its power is tremendous." It was now after eleven; the sun was a huge, hazy white mass.

I had gone only another two hundred yards or so when my bicycle's left pedal abruptly collapsed beneath my foot like a cliff after too much rain. The bike keeled over sideways, and my pack and I went sprawling. As I lay in the dust trying to collect my wits, Robert looked down and helpfully observed, "Your bike is faulty, I think."

I reassembled the pedal and banged it back into place, but I had no tools, so there was no means of securing it firmly. I climbed back on anyway and got about five feet before the pedal gave way again and I toppled over a second time. I banged it back into place again, climbed on, and toppled over again. After a couple more rounds of this sport, I devised a crabbed method of pedaling that took me another five hundred yards or so before the pedal fell off and had to be reset. When the path turned from navigable clay to wheel swallowing sand I was flung to the ground once more. By now, Robert had seen enough of my antics; he murmured good-bye and disappeared down the hill.

It was at this point that I began to suspect Churchill of grossly overstating the attraction of Murchison Falls, not to mention the virtues of bicycle travel in Africa. I covered the next five miles on foot, pushing my bike before me through the sand like a bedouin trudging along behind a reluctant camel. Finally I saw the gate to Kabalega Falls National Park, manned by a park ranger wearing ragged cutoffs and no shirt. He examined my bike, ducked inside his hut, and returned with one of the most beautiful pieces of technology I had ever seen: a pair of battered pliers. He took my park entrance fee — ten U.S. dollars — and for no extra charge restored my bike to semiworking order by binding the pedal together with a spare piece of wire.

When I finally arrived at the campsite an hour later, weak and light-headed, the first sight to greet me was the white jeep that had left me in the dust, now parked under a big tree next to a small party of lolling white tourists. I stumbled off the bike into the shade and collapsed on the ground, whereupon one of the jeep riders, who turned out to be an Englishman with uncommon powers of deduction and tact, gasped, "Was that you on the bike? We almost stopped to pick you up!"

Churchill felt no shame in observing that Africans were members of "an inferior race." Nevertheless, he argued, they could make the leap to modernity with the help of the British Empire. The "four millions of these dark folk" living in England's East Africa Protectorate could improve their standard of living if they would only accept the guidance of Europeans and embrace industrial development. Of course, Africans were not given much choice in the matter. This was the era of untrammeled European imperialism in Africa, and Britain was determined not to lose out in the carving up of the continent. Occupation of Kenya required the removal of such tribes as the Kikuyu and Masai from lands they had occupied for centuries, a task local British authorities pursued with relish. The author Peter Matthiessen has written that by 1939, "four-fifths of the best land in Kenya was the province of perhaps 4,000 whites; a million Kikuyo were to make do with the one-fifth set aside as the Kikuyo Reserves." Ugandans were more successful at resisting such expropriations. The country has suffered through terrible civil strife and an AIDS pandemic in recent decades, but partly because land ownership is far more evenly distributed than elsewhere in East Africa, hunger and poverty are noticeably less prevalent.

Churchill insisted that Britain's intervention in eastern Africa would benefit all parties, but in retracing his journey roughly nine decades after the fact, I found the economic disparity between Africa and the industrial world as vast as ever. The forces of progress that Churchill championed seemed to have changed everything and nothing here. The physical environment had certainly been altered, but the prosperity derived was limited and narrowly distributed.

The first leg of Churchill's sojourn was the magnificent train ride from Mombasa to Lake Victoria. When I took that same train ride, I was impressed, as we pulled out of Mombasa, to see numerous signs of a functioning industrial society: smokestacks, power lines, petroleum refinery tanks, and row after row of low concrete warehouses awaiting replenishment from the half-dozen container ships moored in Kilindini Harbor. Next to a chemical processing plant, clusters of silver piping thrust themselves skyward like industrial dandelions, while overhead a red-and-white jetliner screamed its approach to the international airport. But the lives of the people were another matter; I often felt as if an African version of *A Tale of Two Cities* was playing out before me. As the descending airliner disappeared below the jagged skyline, the train chugged slowly past a squalid shantytown whose tin-roofed shacks of rotted wood contained the shops and meager households of the urban masses. Sprawled on the ground not ten feet from our click-clacking wheels, a man in trousers and a short-sleeve shirt slept open-mouthed, as if poisoned or drunk. Past the city limits, small children scampered from their mud and grass huts to gather along the track, wave and cheer, and plead with outstretched palms, "Give me pen! Give me sweet!" or merely, "Something!"

Meanwhile, the gulf separating the races of eastern Africa remained as wide as when Churchill was writing condescendingly that it was impossible to "travel even for a little while among the Kikuyu tribes without acquiring a liking for these lighthearted, tractable, if brutish children, or without feeling that they are capable of being instructed and raised from their present degradation." Black-on-black tribal violence was still common, there was no love lost between black Africans and the Asian merchant class, and the dominant emotions between Africans and Europeans were distrust and fear. The closest interactions most whites had with blacks occurred within master-servant relationships. Spend an evening in the company of whites and one certain topic of conversation would be the relative honesty and competence of their maids, cooks, and gardeners. "You just never know what they'll fancy," one Nairobi matron, recalling alleged stealing, mused while being served Christmas dinner by a squad of middle-aged servants.

There was no more revealing symbol of the chasm between blacks and whites than the *matatu,* a vehicle in which most whites never set foot but that was the primary means of transport for blacks. To be sure, there were good reasons not to set foot in a *matatu* — unless terrible overcrowding and a high risk of death or dismemberment were your ideas of excitement. *Matatu* was a Swahili term for privately operated minibuses that were much faster than public buses, far more numerous, and only slightly more expensive. They also had lots more personality. Every *matatu* in Kenya had a nickname painted in bright colors across the front and back of the vehicle, with speed the usual theme. I rode one *matatu* called the Singaha Quick. Other names I saw included the Road Shark, the Gusii Express, and inexplicably, the '90s Explainer.

When I reached Lake Victoria, the only way to carry on to Uganda was by *matatu.* (The ferry Churchill took across the lake had long since gone out of service.) The bus stand in Kisumu, a bustling town on Lake Victoria's eastern shore, was a beehive of cheerful chaos when I arrived the next morning. While hawkers whistled, clapped, and shouted out their destinations, passengers milled about, occasionally hoisting their belongings up onto the roof before boarding their *matatu* of choice. I was assigned to an older *matatu* that already looked more than full. Twelve adults sat facing one another on metal benches that extended in a horseshoe down both sides of the van. Each person's hips and shoulders were wedged firmly against his or her neighbors'; I couldn't move my legs without kicking the person across the row. The last passenger on board, a broadly smiling young man wearing a dark wool suit (wool!) and carrying a large cardboard box, was directed to sit in a nonexistent space across the aisle from me. I watched him with my own eyes and still don't know how he managed to fit.

While we waited to depart, the skipping guitar riffs of African pop music filled the air and hopeful vendors approached the van. A hand would suddenly thrust its way inside the open back door, six inches from my face, and flash bottles of soda, or boiled eggs, pineapple slices, sweets, cheap wristwatches, plastic bowls and cups, cassette tapes, wrench and screwdriver sets, handkerchiefs, earrings, or, most bizarre of all, packet after packet of unlabeled pills.

When we finally departed, the crowding inside the *matatu* made it impossible for us passengers to see much outside, which was just as well. Daredevil speeds and passing maneuvers are matters of honor among many *matatu* drivers, and grisly accounts of highway deaths are a staple of the region's newspapers. One story featured photographs of a *matatu* that hit a petroleum tanker head-on while struggling to pass another *matatu;* the passengers had been charred into blackened lumps where they sat. Africans I talked to were aware of the dangers of riding these minibuses — how could they not be? — but they accepted them with placid nonchalance. On a continent where one infant in seven does not survive to age five and a woman of fifty is considered old, death is regarded not as a distant stranger, but as a familiar companion. Africans accept death and discomfort because they have no choice, just as they ride *matatus* because the only alternative is to cover the same distance on foot.

Wherever I traveled, urban Africans seemed caught in a kind of purgatory, somewhere between the seductions of modernity and the habits of tradition. They had access to some of the same trappings of city life found in Europe and the United States, but these trappings were always compromised. There was mass transit, but it was wildly dangerous; newspapers, but they were only four pages long; public schools, but without books. Of the feast of materialism that Churchill had promised them so long ago, the vast majority of Africans had tasted barely a bite.

At the Ugandan border, I had to switch to yet another *matatu* to make the trip to Jinja, a town on Lake Victoria's northern shore near the source of the Nile. Churchill had ridiculed Jinja as an "outlandish name" for a town that geography and geopolitics had plainly destined for greatness; he wanted to rename it Ripon Falls, "after the beautiful cascades which lie beneath it, and from whose force its future prosperity will be derived." What was needed, he added, was to build a dam and "let the Nile begin its long and beneficent journey to the sea by leaping through a turbine." Easy to say, but it was 1954 before this vision was actually accomplished.

On the ride to Jinja, my *matatu* passed the electric power station that now hummed beside the dam. But the other blessings forecast by Churchill — "the gorge of the Nile crowded with factories and warehouses" and "crowned with long rows of comfortable tropical villas and imposing offices" — had yet to materialize. And later that afternoon, when a few greedy *matatu* drivers suddenly raised the price of the trip to Kampala by the equivalent of ten cents, more than half of the passengers angrily disembarked and prepared to wait two more hours for a later *matatu* rather than pay the higher fare.

The source of the Nile, where the world's longest river emerges from Africa's largest lake, should rank as one of the great scenic spots on earth. But because of the dam two miles downriver, "the beautiful cascades" of Ripon Falls have disappeared beneath the waterline, so now no one spot stands out as the precise beginning of the Nile. Gazing down from the tidy park that overlooked the Nile, I watched a flock of long-necked, brilliantly white birds wheel lazily across the river before settling back among the branches of a half-submerged tree. On the far bank, swaying in the light breeze, were row upon row of rubbery-leafed *matoke* trees, which provide the banana-like staple of the local diet. Off to my left, Victoria Bay, calm and spacious, curled out of sight to meld seamlessly into the great lake. Without question, this remained a place of uncommon beauty and peacefulness. Yet a feeling of loss and incompleteness was inescapable. What this cosmic site on the earth's surface looked like before the coming of industrial man could now barely be imagined. Churchill provided an inkling: here the Nile was "a vast body of water nearly as wide as the Thames at Westminster Bridge, and this imposing river rushes down a stairway of rock . . . in smooth, swirling slopes of green water."

Leaving the park, I stopped to chat with the young man who had sold me my entrance ticket. Neatly dressed, wearing flimsy eyeglasses with black plastic frames, he lounged beneath a tree with a friend, taking refuge from the midday sun. Yes, he agreed, this was a very beautiful place to work, but day after day, week after week, it sometimes got boring. Spying his newspaper on the ground, I asked why he did not bring a book to read. It was a foolish question, but his answer was polite.

"It is very difficult to obtain books in Uganda," he explained. "Our shops are usually empty. And any book for sale costs a great deal of money."

When I marveled at how lovely this place must have been before the dam, he was again a step ahead of me, seeming to read my mind and discern my unspoken assumptions.

"Yes," he smiled, with the enchanting gentleness I found to be so common among East Africans. "But the dam has done much good for us, giving us electricity."

"You trade one for the other," I said.

He beamed with the pleasure of having communicated perfectly across our cultural divide. "Yes! You trade one for the other."

Compressed in that brief exchange is the essential dilemma facing the human species as it approaches the twenty-first century. Can the material strivings of the entire human family be reconciled with the need to protect the planet's already strained ecosystems? Of course that young Ugandan deserves books, and electric light to read them by. And if he must, he will accept a great many aesthetic and environmental woundings in return for such benefits of progress. But must he? Can prosperity be achieved only through the kind of ruthless "development" that has turned so much of the Third World — from the industrial hellholes of China to the clearcut forests of Brazil — into environmental wastelands? Can we not learn to choose technologies that help us work with, rather than against, nature, and thereby preserve as much of it as possible in its original, wild state?

Churchill was lucky enough to observe Murchison Falls, where my travels in his footsteps finally concluded, in the first light of dawn. "The river was a broad sheet of steel grey veined with paler streaks of foam," he wrote. "The rock portals of the Falls were jetty black, and between them, illumined by a single shaft of sunlight, gleamed the tremendous cataract — a thing of wonder and glory, well worth traveling all the way to see."

I was about to find out if my efforts to reach this remote point along the Nile, not to mention my taxing bike ride from Wanseko, had been worth it. The jeep riders had arranged for a park ranger to ferry them upriver later in the afternoon so they could see the "tremendous cataract" up close, and they invited me to join them.

We didn't see another human being the entire trip. Indeed, we saw no signs that humans had ever been here — just the pristine fecundity of a healthy ecology humming with activity. The River Nile, as the locals called it, was often hundreds of yards wide and surrounded on both sides by steep hillsides covered with thick greenery. The river looked amazingly blue and clean, its rippling surface sparkling in the afternoon sun. The park's wildlife population was said to have been all but eliminated by rampaging soldiers during the Obote and Amin dictatorships of the 1970s and 1980s, but if so, the subsequent recovery had been remarkable. I saw more wild animals along this thirteen-mile stretch of the Nile than I had seen in many weeks of wide-ranging travel in neighboring Kenya. There were literally hundreds of hippopotamuses — some plodding up the riverbanks, others squatting in the shallows with only their bulging eyes visible, still others disappearing underwater only to reappear half a minute later on the other side of the boat. Sharing sandbars with the hippos were dozens of plump brown crocodiles. Nearly all of them were stretched out on their bellies with their jaws open wide, revealing long rows of nasty-looking yellowish teeth. This open-mouthed posture was actually a cooling reflex, like a dog's panting, but it lent the reptiles a peculiar aspect, at once menacing and lazy.

The animals rarely shied away from us. Often the boat came close enough to the hippos and crocodiles that I could have reached over the railing and touched them. Along the shore were numerous graceful giraffes and self-possessed elephants, as well as a few shaggy, skittish waterbucks. And all around was an extraordinary array of waterfowl: goliath herons; fish eagles; saddle-billed storks with yellow, orange, and black beaks that resembled miniature Ugandan flags; and most entertaining of all, pied kingfishers, which hovered forty feet above the water like hummingbirds for minutes at a time before diving straight down to snag their unsuspecting prey.

After two hours of steady chugging, our boat passed a long calm stretch of water and rounded a bend, and suddenly the waterfall swung into view. Even from half a mile downriver, it was fearsome to behold — a glistening cascade of white fury that carried such force our boat could not advance against the current. This extraordinary power stemmed from the fact that, as Churchill explained, above the falls the banks of the Nile "contract suddenly till they are not six yards apart, and through this strangling portal, as from the nozzle of a hose, the whole tremendous river is shot in one single jet down an abyss of a hundred and sixty feet." Transfixed, we admired this sight for I don't know how long before the captain finally turned the boat around and, with the surging current at our back, returned us to camp in half the time it had taken to get there.

The next morning, the jeep riders invited me to accompany them overland to the top of the falls. Churchill may have been lubricating his tale somewhat when he claimed that the falls could be heard from ten miles away, but they were certainly audible from five. When we finally clambered down to the shoreline the roar was fantastic, like the fiercest windstorm imaginable. In the last few hundred yards of its approach to the falls, the Nile seems to sprint so impatiently forward that the foamy green water gets ahead of itself and leaps exuberantly upward, as if ascending an invisible escalator. Just before the fall line, the river separates into separate flows. The one feeding the cataract is over the edge in an instant, crashing down into the bubbling pool below. The others loop around a massive stone outcropping and supply a second waterfall, shorter but far wider than its famous brother. The spray, the din, the water's irresistible force and volume are as overwhelming to the senses as the knowledge of its distant destination in Egypt is to the mind.

Murchison Falls remains a glorious natural spectacle, but only because Churchill did not get his way. Churchill, that incorrigible champion of industry, wanted to build a dam at Murchison Falls. Its "terrible waters" itched at his restless nature. They had to be put to some productive purpose: "I cannot believe that modern science will be content to leave these mighty forces untamed, unused, or that regions of inexhaustible and unequalled fertility, capable of supplying all sorts of things that civilized industry needs in greater quantity every year, will not be brought — in spite of their insects and their climate — into cultivated subjection." Of course, the dam whose construction Churchill was advocating here would have covered up forever the very falls he had praised as one of the great wonders in all Africa. Prudently, he ignored this contradiction. He did seem to sense there was something unholy about his proposal, however. His reflections on damming the Nile were interrupted, he later wrote, by "an ugly and perhaps indignant swish of water" that nearly drenched him.

ISABEL HILTON

Spies in the House of Faith

FROM *The New Yorker*

CHOEKYI GYALTSEN DIED, unexpectedly, on a freezing night in the Tibetan monastery of Tashilhunpo in January 1989. Better known as the tenth incarnation of the Panchen Lama, he was the reigning religious authority in Tibet — the second most important figure after the Dalai Lama, who was living in exile. The Panchen Lama had been assumed dead once before — during long years of imprisonment in China — but that time he had returned; this second death, at the age of fifty, seemed all the more cruel to his followers, because it dashed the hopes he had revived.

The event did not go entirely unnoticed in the West. In London, I watched a ninety-second report on the TV news. And there were judiciously critical obituaries, which recalled how the Panchen Lama had remained in Tibet when the Dalai Lama fled to India, thirty years earlier. The obituaries told of the Panchen's early collaboration with the Chinese occupiers of Tibet, and then of his official disgrace, in 1964, his thirteen years of detention spanning the Cultural Revolution, and his return, in the final decade of his life, as a public figure and occasional critic of the regime.

For me, at the time, it was just another landmark in the passing of old Tibet. Most Westerners had never heard of the Panchen Lama, and I knew only the sketchy details of his life that I had heard during my student days in China in the early seventies. I had no idea that his death was to become an issue that would convulse the Tibetan and the Chinese worlds, or that I would be drawn so deeply into the drama of it. The process began, for me, five years later, the first time I met the Dalai Lama.

*

In February of 1994, I made the first of what were to be many journeys to Dharamsala, in northern India, to interview the Dalai Lama for the BBC. I was making a film about Petra Kelly — the radical co-founder of the German Green Party, who had been killed by her lover a couple of years before, and who had known the Dalai Lama. The film's director, Jonathan Lewis, and I arrived in Delhi on a chilly Wednesday morning, then waited for the night train to the small city of Pathankot. From there, we took a taxi for four and a half hours, winding north along deep river valleys into the foothills of the Himalayas.

It was my first encounter with Tibet-in-exile. As the taxi climbed the vertiginous, twisting roads, India seemed to fall away. The Indian men, women, and children who had thronged the streets for most of the journey gave way to flocks of young Tibetan monks in maroon robes, old men in *chubas,* and old women in long skirts and striped aprons, walking slowly and counting their rosaries. On a rock at a bend in the road, FREE TIBET had been painted in English and in Tibetan. The muddy streets of McLeod Ganj, the mountain village that is the commercial heart of the exiled Tibetan community, were lined with shops selling Tibetan trinkets, books, and religious paintings. Among the crowds on the streets were groups of drifting foreigners: backpackers, tourists, and the occasional shaven-headed Western Buddhist monks and nuns. From the balcony of my hotel I could see the brilliant winter sunshine reflected from the golden roofs of the compound that housed the main temple. Farther up the hill lay the Dalai Lama's residence, a modest building set in a luxuriant garden.

The Dalai Lama's life in exile, I discovered, is a curious mélange of archaic court ritual, modern security, and impoverished informality. His predecessors — the theocratic kings and incarnations of the Buddha of Compassion who had governed Tibet since the seventeenth century — commanded the respect of most of Central Asia. But this Dalai Lama has been forced into a new kind of international celebrity. Banished from his country, he uses his personal charisma and his moral authority to keep Tibet's cause alive. In India, he and his followers have re-created what they could of their former culture. There are monasteries, an elected government, a library, and schools that offer education in English and in Tibetan. It appears at first glance to be a success, a tribute to human resilience. But it is a fragile success that depends, to a degree that worries many, on the Dalai Lama himself.

Two days after our arrival, Jonathan and I waited in the long, low bungalow that houses his audience room. The Dalai Lama appeared, walking briskly.

"You must be the BBC," he said.

"And you must be the Dalai Lama," Jonathan replied.

The Dalai Lama laughed as though it were the funniest thing he had ever heard. "Yes," he said. "Yes, I am the Dalai Lama," and launched into another storm of chuckles.

There are those in his community who believe that the Dalai Lama's famous laugh is his best weapon. "Be careful," I had been warned by one Tibetan intellectual. "He uses that laugh when he doesn't want to say anything." It is certainly an unanswerable laugh. His shoulders heave, his head goes back, and he rocks in his chair until it passes. It is a great full stop of a laugh, putting an end to any further pursuit of a line of inquiry and deflecting impertinence or hostility. But there is one matter about which he rarely laughs: the Chinese occupation of Tibet.

After the interview, we said good-bye, neither of us expecting to see the Dalai Lama again. That evening, we dined with an expatriate Englishwoman at the Hotel Tibet. At a neighboring table, three Tibetans listened politely as an American lectured them on the finer points of Buddhism. In the bar, a less spiritual group could be heard warming up on the hotel's brightly colored cocktails. Our own conversation turned to the Tibetan religious system, and I asked our companion about the fate of the tenth Panchen Lama.

"He died," she reminded me, "in 1989."

"And his reincarnation?" I asked. Buddhists believe that death is a passage to another life. For Tibetan Buddhists, the Panchen Lamas are incarnations of the Buddha of Boundless Light, an enlightened being who returns to human life to help others. The Panchen Lama's absence was only a temporary affair, and it was the duty of his followers to find the next incarnation — the child who would be recognized as the eleventh Panchen Lama.

"He hasn't been found yet," she said. I was immediately filled with curiosity. Who was looking for the reincarnation? Were the Chinese interested? She answered as best she could: yes, it was an important issue and, yes, by now, under normal circumstances, the child should have been found. Everyone was concerned, but whatever was happening was happening in secret. It was one of the key problems facing the Dalai Lama's government-in-exile. I stayed on for a few days and asked everyone I met about the Panchen Lama. I had little knowledge of the structures and beliefs of Tibetan Buddhism, or even what precisely was meant by reincarnation. I spoke no Tibetan and found the names so hard to grasp that I had to write them down, laboriously, before they slipped away. I was anxious to speak with the Dalai Lama about the search for the new incarnation, but didn't know whether he'd agree to discuss the issue with an outsider. I mentioned the idea to Tsering Tashi, an assistant in the Dalai Lama's private office. Tashi was encouraging. It was an important story, he said, and should be told. On the last day of my visit, I left a letter for the Dalai Lama, asking whether he would be willing to cooperate with a documentary about the search. Then I took the winding road back down from Dharamsala to the dust and noise of India.

On January 27, 1989, the night before the tenth Panchen Lama died, he had been on a visit from Beijing to his former home, Tashilhunpo Monastery, in Shigatse, in central Tibet. Thirty-nine years had passed since China invaded and occupied Tibet. Nine years after that, in 1959, the Tibetans had risen up in protest, but the rebellion was brutally crushed by the Chinese in a matter of days. That was when the Dalai Lama, Tibet's secular ruler as well as its highest spiritual incarnation, had fled to India. Over the next few months, a hundred thousand Tibetans had followed him. The Panchen Lama stayed behind and was briefly considered a puppet of the Chinese regime. In the early sixties, however, when he asked the government to moderate its policies in Tibet, he lost official favor and was bound and paraded through the streets to be jeered at and spat upon, and then thrown into prison. Since his release, in 1977, the Chinese government had not allowed him to live in Tibet, and his visits there were rare.

Toward midnight on the evening of the twenty-seventh, after a day of festivities, the Panchen Lama grew tired and retired to his room. He asked an attendant to bring him an extra blanket against the cold. When the attendant returned, however, he found his way blocked by an unusual number of Chinese security personnel.

They snatched the blanket from him and told him to leave. To his alarm, he recognized none of them. Accounts of what happened next are murky and contradictory. According to Xinhua, the official government press agency, at about 4 A.M. on the twenty-eighth, the Panchen Lama felt a chest pain and called a doctor; he was given some medication, after which he slept again. He woke again at eight-thirty, and the medical staff checked his heart. Five minutes later, he collapsed and died.

The suspicion that he had been murdered spread like a blaze in a dry pine forest. A case could be made, of course, for natural causes. The Panchen Lama was a huge man, who gloried in his bulk. There had been a biting wind that day and the ceremonies had been long. But those who sought a motive for murder pointed to the outspoken views that the Panchen Lama had begun to express. They recalled a speech he had given five days before, at a high-level meeting between government and religious leaders, during which he had revealed his real feelings about the Chinese occupation of Tibet. "Since liberation," he had said, "there has certainly been development, but the price paid for this development has been greater than the gains."

Whatever the cause, the death of the religious leader devastated the monks of Tashilhunpo. Sonam Gyelpo, a monk now in exile in India, remembers it as the beginning of the end of his life in Tibet. "People just couldn't believe it at first," he told me. "The monks were beating their heads against the walls so hard that the walls were stained with blood. They were crying that there was no point in staying in the monastery any longer."

Posters went up, demanding that the Chinese authorities prove that they had not murdered the Panchen Lama. The Tibetan New Year, which had become a time of tension and protest, was approaching. On March 5, members of the People's Armed Police opened fire on a crowd in Lhasa, sparking a full-scale riot. At least twelve Tibetans were killed. Two days later, martial law was declared.

In this tense atmosphere, the significance of the death of the Panchen Lama — a man who, in his last ten years, had tried to mediate between his restive compatriots and the Beijing authorities — was inescapable. But more important was a question that his death had raised: Who would control the search for his reincarnation? The Chinese? The Tibetans? Or their exiled leader, the Dalai Lama?

This was the story I wanted to follow. The Dalai Lama did not respond to the letter I'd left with his office in February 1994, so I telephoned. I wrote another letter. I e-mailed his office. Finally, in July, I heard back. The Dalai Lama would speak with me about the search for the eleventh Panchen Lama and would allow me special access to follow its progress, but, whatever happened during the search, my discretion was required until it was concluded. (I have changed certain details in this article to protect those involved who are still living in Tibet or China.)

In October I returned to Dharamsala. As I waited in the Dalai Lama's audience room, I had many questions. Somewhere in the world a boy had been born, and for the Tibetans only that boy would do. How did they know how to find him? How did they know who he was? The process was a mystery to me. There were certain things the Tibetans looked for, but the authenticity of the child depended ultimately, I thought, on the power of their belief. I was not looking for a religion, but I wanted to understand that power.

And I wanted to understand how that belief would express itself, given the repressive restrictions the Chinese had placed on it. Tradition ruled that the Dalai Lamas and the Panchen Lamas would play the decisive role in the recognition of each other's incarnations. But this was the new Tibet, a Tibet under the rule of the Chinese Communist Party. For two decades after the 1959 rebellion, the Chinese had tried to eradicate religion in Tibet. Thousands of believers had been imprisoned, and 99 percent of the country's religious buildings destroyed. But the campaign, in the end, had done little to help the Chinese cause; it had simply strengthened Tibetan nationalism. Since 1979, the Chinese had been trying, instead, to co-opt Buddhism, to make it work for them by controlling it. Would they allow the Dalai Lama to participate in this important religious event?

The Dalai Lama appeared, moving quickly and energetically, and settled into an armchair opposite me. His face assumed that air of expectancy — just short of impatience — which signaled that a moment of high seriousness had arrived. "This," he said, leaning forward to emphasize his words, "is a spiritual matter."

In old Tibet, he told me, the search for the Panchen Lama's reincarnations was initially conducted by the lamas of his monastery, Tashilhunpo. Only in the final stages did it involve such a senior figure as the Dalai Lama. Back in August 1989, Beijing had overseen the formation of an official search committee at Tashilhunpo (which some of the monks suspected was infiltrated by Chinese spies), but so far had allowed only one contact, an indirect one, between the Dalai Lama and the monastery's administrator, Chadrel Rinpoche. In 1993, Chadrel had sent a letter through the Dalai Lama's brother, and the Dalai Lama had replied immediately, inviting Chadrel to come to India to discuss the search. But after that there had been nothing. All formal requests from the Dalai Lama to send representatives to Tibet to take part in the search had been ignored by Beijing.

In the meantime, the Dalai Lama had initiated investigations of his own. From all over the Tibetan world, he told me, names had come, some sent by hopeful parents, others by lamas who had been alerted to look out for unusual children born at the right time.

What was it, I asked him, that qualified these boys to be considered candidates?

The Dalai Lama smiled and began to enumerate the signs. "There is a boy from Gyalthang," he said. "Whilst this child was still in the mother's womb, he recited a mantra. The mother heard it. Then, on the day the child was going to be born, he spoke from inside the womb, and said, 'I am going to be born today' — exactly as it happened." He laughed. "Talking before birth — and immediately afterward. Curious," he said, shaking his head.

Moments before, we had been analyzing politics. Now we were discussing a talking fetus. I looked at the Dalai Lama, hoping for some clue to how I was meant to take this. He was a sophisticated man and very aware of the power of the media. But I could find no trace of irony in his expression. I was reminded of a conversation I'd had a few days earlier with a young Tibetan monk in southern India. When I'd asked whether any of his fellow monks had known the late Panchen Lama, he told me that he himself had.

"I was with him in prison," he said. "I told them to beat me."

"What happened then?" I asked.

"I died," he replied.

"I see," I said, my mind reeling. "Do you remember that?"

He grinned. "No. It was in 1962. Maybe 1963. That was in my previous incarnation. Have you heard of Tina Turner?"

"Then, there is another child, in Amdo," the Dalai Lama continued, "who also seems to be very bright. In both cases, the previous Panchen Lama had a special connection with the families. That is generally taken as a clear indication. Then, there's a child that local ladies say has declared himself to be the Panchen Lama's reincarnation. You see, there is competition," he said, laughing, "particularly among the local ladies. And there is another one, in Dharamsala. The father is a lama inside Tibet, who had some close connection with the Panchen Lama. The mother escaped while she was pregnant. I saw her with the baby. That baby was very small, but he looked at me and smiled" — the Dalai Lama beamed at the memory — "very beautifully." He added, "Frankly speaking, at the moment my mind is in a state of confusion and indecision. You see, in my case Lhamo Latso Lake gave a clear indication: it showed the house where I was born."

Lhamo Latso is a holy lake, in central Tibet, and is one of the first ports of call for any search party looking for a reincarnation. On the surface of its waters visions appear to those who can see them. Tashilhunpo had sent a party to the lake in 1989, at the start of the search for the Panchen Lama, and there had been, the Dalai Lama told me, several visions, among them a vision of a house guarded by what might have been a Sikh policeman; it was thought to be a sign that the new Panchen Lama had been born in India. But since then the claims of the boys from Tibet had been put forward, and the evidence in their favor seemed equally plausible.

Cut off from the search, the Dalai Lama knew that his picture was incomplete. Dharamsala had telephones and fax machines, even e-mail, but the telephone lines were often down for days at a time. The Tibetan phones were assumed to be tapped, and any communication into China was likely to be monitored by both the Chinese and the Indians. The Indian government had been generally hospitable to its population of exiled Tibetans, but their presence posed a complicated political problem, and India had no desire to annoy its powerful neighbor.

Still, it was clear that in this world of religious allegiances the Himalayas were at least partly porous. Messages were carried across the Tibetan-Indian border by hand. Secrets were exchanged, clandestine arrangements attempted. The Dalai Lama had recently sent a covert message to Tashilhunpo Monastery, for example, asking the search committee to return to the lake to confirm its visions.

Had the Chinese communicated with him about the search? I asked.

In the beginning, he explained, Beijing had declared that the Panchen Lama's reincarnation would be found within China and had indicated that the Dalai Lama could not be involved. But he had recently received a different message from the Chinese authorities. "It said that they will announce the new Panchen Lama very soon," the Dalai Lama told me. "They were inquiring as to my response. This is a little illogical, a little delicate. They want me to say yes." He chuckled. "I don't think I will say yes. What do you think? Yes or no? I think no, don't you?" His voice trailed off into a gale of laughter.

I left, with the sound of the Dalai Lama's merriment still in my ears. It was clear that the search had reached a critical stage. The Dalai Lama was anxious to be involved, and Beijing was determined to exclude him. The Chinese wanted the process concluded, and the Tibetans were trying to delay. Over the next year and a half, it would become an intricate battle between the power of the Chinese state and the resilience of Tibetan religious faith.

The following January, the Dalai Lama would give a *Kalachakra* initiation — one of the most important teachings in Buddhism — in the south of India. Thousands of people would attend, and among them, he hoped, would be one of the senior lamas involved in the search. Once he had had the opportunity to consult with that lama, he planned to send his own search parties into Tibet to test the candidates. If the Chinese cooperated, the search parties could travel openly. If not, they would proceed clandestinely. That, the Dalai Lama observed mildly, would be more complicated. But it had been done before: a monk the Dalai Lama had sent to search for a lower incarnation had succeeded in finding the child and had smuggled him to India in 1993. The Dalai Lama had said that it might be possible for me to accompany the search party, and I returned to London to wait for word.

It came nearly three months later, one night in January. My telephone rang at 2 A.M. On a terrible line I made out the familiar voice of Tsering Tashi, from the Dalai Lama's office in Dharamsala. "You have to come to India immediately," he said. Why? I asked. He didn't know. "His Holiness is in the south and has sent a message asking us to tell you to come right away."

Part of the difficulty of following this story was that, given the secrecy of the affair, I could never just call the Dalai Lama for something I'd forgotten to ask in person. To get an answer to a simple question, I had to travel three thousand miles. So it occurred to me that the latest development might be something quite minor. But there was no doubt in my mind that I would go.

Four days later, with visa and tickets arranged in record time, I flew to Delhi, then headed north to Jammu and took a taxi across Kashmir. The journey to Dharamsala is so preposterously inconvenient that some have come to suspect that the Tibetan refugee community was put there by the Indian government under pressure from the Chinese — in the hope that Dharamsala's inaccessibility would slow down the flow of visitors attracted by the Dalai Lama. But the truth is that one of the Dalai Lama's advisers had chosen it for the beauty of the scenery and the purity of the water.

There was the usual parade on the road: slow-moving water buffalo, gaunt cattle, an occasional moth-eaten camel, a troop of monkeys. As the car crawled up the final ascent to McLeod Ganj, it broke down. I got out and stretched. The late-afternoon sun was painting the valley a mellow gold. I picked up my bag and strolled along a path to a small hotel that lay in the woodland shadows.

The next morning, after the briefest of greetings, the Dalai Lama came directly to the point. He had just returned from southern India. There, during the *Kalachakra* teachings, a monk had approached his assistant and said that he had an important message.

"Actually, we told him to go away and stop making a nuisance of himself," the assistant told me later. "There were thousands of people who wanted to see His Holiness. I told him at least to tell me what it was about. But he wouldn't."

Finally, the assistant relented. The monk, it turned out, had an extraordinary story to tell. He was an exile, he said, living in India, and he had just returned from a visit to Tibet. While he was there, the Tashilhunpo monks had asked him to carry a set of scriptures back to present to the Dalai Lama. It was imperative for the monk to return to India at once, he was told, and he must return via Nepal, where he would meet a messenger who had another package for the Dalai Lama. In a state of agitation, the monk traveled to the border crossing at Nepal. There he was joined by the messenger, who accompanied him all the way to Delhi and then gave him a package. It was this package that the monk had brought south. The messenger stayed in Delhi. He could not be seen anywhere near the Dalai Lama, he insisted.

The Dalai Lama opened the package and discovered that it contained a complete list of the boys whom the Tashilhunpo search committee had under consideration. There were more than twenty photographs, and a long letter from the head of the committee, Chadrel Rinpoche, explaining the evidence in each case. There was, the Dalai Lama read, a candidate whom Chadrel favored. A highly respected Tashilhunpo lama, who had taken part in the visit to Lhamo Latso, had interviewed the boy and was convinced that he was the one. But the final choice, Chadrel wrote, was to be the Dalai Lama's.

Chadrel Rinpoche was a reincarnate lama himself, of a minor lineage. He had no great reputation as a scholar, but he was a good manager, and his monks respected him for his honesty and fair-mindedness. He understood, however, that any religious freedom he had depended on the continuing favor of the Chinese, and so far he had played along with them. He had been rewarded with a house and a large salary. But he was now faced with a difficult decision: He and the search committee had delayed the conclusion of the search for the Panchen Lama for almost six years, hoping that there would be some way to include the Dalai Lama, but they could not keep it going much longer. The Chinese were insisting that the final authority over the search lay with them. If Chadrel conceded to Beijing's demands, his career would continue on its upward path. But without the Dalai Lama's recognition, the child — and Chadrel — would earn the contempt of Tibet's monks. And there was also, of course, his religious conscience.

Chadrel began what was to be the most dangerous game of his life. He proposed a subterfuge: The Dalai Lama would recognize the child now, but the child's name and the fact that the Dalai Lama had identified the boy would remain a secret. Once Chadrel had the name, he would take the search through its closing stages, ensuring that the Dalai Lama's candidate emerged as the choice of the committee. The child would be presented to the Chinese, approved, proclaimed, and installed in Tashilhunpo Monastery, all without a sign from Dharamsala. Only when Chinese approval had been given would the Dalai Lama make it public that the boy had been his choice all along. If it worked, Chadrel argued, everybody would gain, and, however angry the Chinese might be over the deception, it would be too late for them to do anything. But if any hint of the plan were to leak out prematurely, Chadrel warned, they would be sure to reject the Dalai Lama's candidate and impose their own.

Not without reservations, the Dalai Lama told me, he had consented. Chadrel, he assumed, was a better judge of the internal politics than he was, and the Dalai Lama felt that he had little choice but to try to make the plan work.

I was beginning to understand why my telephone had rung in the middle of the night. The Dalai Lama needed an outside witness: it was important to him that there should be no confusion among Tibetans about who had made the real choice, and when. It would be better still, he explained, if the witness were a Western journalist who could film the process.

I was astonished by the speed of events and the proposition that was unfolding. I had hoped at some point to join a search party. Now the child was about to be chosen, and I would be recording the result. Suddenly, I was intimately involved in an extraordinary story that I could reveal to no one.

The Dalai Lama had, he said, conducted a divination. It had told him that it was time to decide. In two days, the monk would reach Dharamsala. The Dalai Lama would then perform further divinations and complete the process of recognition. A reenactment of the monk's arrival (the Dalai Lama called it "playacting"), the written proclamation of the recognition, the dispatch of the letter back to Tibet — all was to be filmed and dated, so that when the moment came there would be no question of the authenticity of the choice.

We talked on, discussing the risks involved. The biggest risk — and the one that preoccupied the Dalai Lama the most — was to Chadrel Rinpoche.

"I am very worried," he said, "about the Chinese reaction when they discover that there has been — shall we say? — a subterfuge. They are bound to be angry. Chadrel Rinpoche says that he is prepared to risk his life. But this is a matter of great concern."

I had a more mundane concern. Since I had known nothing of these dramatic developments when I left London, I had neither a film crew nor a camera. I was halfway up a mountain in northern India, and the monk was due in Dharamsala in two days. I ran through the options with Tashi. There were film crews in Delhi, but there was no means of guaranteeing their discretion. Then Tashi remembered two visitors who had preceded me that morning into the audience chamber — a Finnish film crew.

Over lunch at the Hotel Tibet, I asked the Finnish filmmakers why they were in India. They were making a religious film, they said. Both were Buddhists, and the highlight of their trip had been their audience with the Dalai Lama. They were planning to leave Dharamsala the next day.

I could not explain why, I told them, but if they could stay another couple of days and were prepared to promise not to reveal what they saw they would have several opportunities to meet the Dalai Lama again. I was aware of how strange it must have sounded, but they took it solemnly, asking only for my assurance that nothing dishonorable would be expected of them.

Two days later, on January 26, we met in the gatehouse of the palace. The Dalai Lama was cheerful as the morning's work got under way. We filmed the reenactment of the arrival of the monk — a thin middle-aged man with prominent ears — and his prostration before the Dalai Lama. From the depth of his maroon robes, the monk drew the package. The Dalai Lama opened it, and a litter of photographs of young boys spilled onto a low table in front of him. Suddenly, the process, which had been somewhat abstract, became very real. Life was about to change radically for one of these children. The Dalai Lama picked up a photograph and looked at it for several minutes.

It was my first sight of an image that was to become known around the world. In it, a child stared at the camera, his head slightly tilted back, his lips parted. He was sitting in what seemed to be one of those large brown leather armchairs that used to be the universal official furniture in China. He wore a dark-blue shirt with an orange tunic over it. His eyes, widely spaced, betrayed nothing of the emotions he might have felt as the photograph was taken. He was Gedhun Choekyi Nyima, the eleventh Panchen Lama.

The Dalai Lama spoke of the burden of trust that had lain upon him since the death of the tenth Panchen Lama. He had regularly consulted the oracles and had learned that the child had been born, he said, but until the beginning of 1994 the oracles had not told him that the moment to identify the child had come. Then Chadrel's list of names had arrived.

"I made a divination, immediately," the Dalai Lama said. "It pointed to one boy, a boy of six. When I looked at that boy's picture, I felt a warm feeling, which developed the more I looked at it. Then, yesterday, I made another divination, and the name of the boy came." The Dalai Lama had used a traditional method of divination, in which slips of paper bearing the names of the candidates were introduced into identical balls of kneaded *tsampa* — roasted barley meal. The balls were then placed in a bowl, and the bowl was rotated as the Dalai Lama prayed, until one of them jumped out. The process was repeated to confirm the result. "Now," the Dalai Lama said, beaming, "I feel relieved of a huge responsibility — one stage of the responsibility. But, because of today's situation, the next question is: How should this true reincarnation be installed and have a proper education, proper care? The problem is how to resolve this" — he laughed — "with our new masters. It's all very sensitive. So one worry is over, but another begins."

The boy came from Nagchu, a remote district in central Tibet. He had been born on April 25, 1989, in the Year of the Earth-Snake. According to Chadrel's letter, he had not figured high on the original list, but when the search parties went to visit the candidates he made a deep impression.

"This boy showed no excitement or fear," the Dalai Lama said. "He greeted the lama as though he were an old friend. And when the lama asked him where he came from, the child replied, 'I come from Tashilhunpo.' When the monk had to leave, the boy asked to go with him." There was more, he explained. The monks had found special signs on the child's body.

"What happens next?" I asked. Traditionally, Gedhun Choekyi Nyima would now have been educated for a life of prayer and devotion in Tashilhunpo Monastery, and his family raised to positions of wealth and respect. But that Tibet no longer existed. What did the future have in store for this child? Would he grow up to be a puppet of the Chinese or a patriotic Tibetan leader? Would he ever meet the Dalai Lama, his spiritual brother, who had just taken a step that would change his life forever?

"Now," the Dalai Lama said, "I wait. I have to wait for a signal from those who have taken this great risk. I am responsible for their lives."

The next day, I said good-bye to my Finnish film crew. I wasn't sure whether they had understood what they had witnessed. In any case, they were sworn to secrecy. Then I packed the tapes and traveled to Delhi with the monk and Tsering Tashi to meet the original messenger, who was waiting to carry the Dalai Lama's answer back to Tibet. The four of us spent an emotional day together in Delhi, taking photographs and discussing the future. At the restaurant where we ate lunch, a group of people who appeared to be Tibetans sat down next to us, and a frisson ran around our table as we wondered whether they had been sent to spy on us.

At the end of the day, we said our good-byes. I planned to follow the story into Tibet, but India was not the place to ask for a visa. It was the middle of winter, not the tourist season, and the Chinese embassy in Delhi would have been suspicious. So I was returning to London to arrange the trip from there. Tashi and the monk were going back to Dharamsala. The messenger had the hardest journey ahead of him; he was nervous, but proud of the trust that had been placed in him. We wished each other luck. Despite their anxiety, my three companions were bright with expectation. I shared neither their nation's history nor their religion, but it was impossible not to be moved by the faith that impelled them to take such risks.

The messenger left the next day. It must have been a lonely trip. He took a bus to Kathmandu, but when he got there the weather worsened. A heavy snowfall closed the road across the mountain pass to the border. A snowfall like that could lie for weeks. The messenger knew that he could not wait. His letters were urgently needed. If he could not travel by car, then he would walk through the snow-covered mountains. It took him the best part of five days.

In London, I got a visa and found a cameraman to film what I thought would be the closing stages of the search: Chadrel would ensure that Gedhun Choekyi Nyima was chosen by the search committee, and a party of Tashilhunpo monks would be sent to bring him to the monastery. I wanted to be there — or, at the very least, to arrange for someone less conspicuous to film it for me. Things did not, however, go as planned.

I made it to Lhasa, the capital of Tibet, two weeks later. I had flown to Chengdu, in western China — a city in the grip of the redevelopment fever that had consumed the country since Deng Xiaoping decided that getting rich lay within the new rules of Communism. My hotel, a vast and elderly building, was being ripped apart and refurbished. Half transformed, it seemed to embody the distracted condition of China itself, scrambling to discard the past in a desperate rush to modernity. In a cavernous, dusty ballroom, young prostitutes, in miniskirts and bright makeup, whiled away the afternoons, waiting for customers. Raucous groups of young men in baggy suits — the new money-making elite — occupied other tables, talking loudly into mobile phones and steadily filling ashtrays and spittoons. In the dark recesses of the hotel was the bureau of the state-run China International Travel Service, which held the key to travel to Tibet.

The manager in the C.I.T.S. office was in his thirties. He sat smoking behind a dark-brown counter that was bare except for a large Nescafé jar, now half full of wet tea leaves, which he topped up with water from a battered thermos.

"Lhasa?" he said. "No problem." He recommended a weeklong tour with limousine and two obligatory guides, to be paid for in advance. He named a price that made me think I had inquired about buying Tibet. If I agreed, I knew, a ticket would miraculously appear the next day. Otherwise, the flights might remain "full" for weeks. I declined but refused to leave. The manager rapidly lost interest. He ignored me for an hour, then, as his lunch break approached, he sighed theatrically and reached for the telephone.

"No limousine and no guides! She says she can't afford it," he shouted into the phone.

I waited for what I thought would be the inevitable refusal. But on the other end, in Lhasa, it was decided, apparently, that for that low-season week at least even an uncooperative tourist was better than none at all. Permission was granted, and there was a flight the next day.

The next morning, and the day after, however, the airport was fogbound. Its corridors were thronged with stranded travelers, who sat staring at gray murk outside the smeared windows. As I waited, I noticed a young Chinese man with a large camera. Carefully, he slipped into a squatting position and pointed his camera at me. I raised my own camera and pointed it at him. He lowered his lens and grinned sheepishly. He was smartly dressed and had no luggage. "I work for the South West Airlines in-flight magazine," he said. "Are you going to Lhasa? What is your name?"

In twenty years of traveling in China, I had never seen an in-flight magazine. I stared at him. "I don't understand," I replied. He shrugged and retreated. Ten minutes later, out of the corner of my eye, I noticed him again, still taking my picture.

At last, on the third day, the airport reopened. An hour after the plane had taken off, the billowing banks of cloud below us were pierced by jagged snow-covered peaks — the mountains of Tibet. We disembarked into a freezing baggage hall. I walked slowly, conscious of the effort of every step in the thin air. My luggage was covered with a thick layer of what were unmistakably — and inexplicably — chicken droppings. The rickety bus I caught outside the airport took three hours to get to Lhasa, and my spirits began to sink as we reached the outskirts of the city, bowling along a wide street lined with dreary compounds of small apartment blocks and single-story karaoke bars. Was this the legendary capital of Tibet?

But then the Potala, the former palace of the Dalai Lamas, came into view. It was a heart-stopping sight. It seemed to grow from living rock, its huge bulk floating above the city, its façade alive with the fluttering of the curtains that decorate its hundreds of windows. This was architecture as theater, an assertion of spiritual and temporal power, which still managed to impose its authority on a city it had once dominated. As I approached the Potala the next day, I saw that the little district of Shol, which had lain at its feet, was gone. In its place was a vast building site where Tibetans were working, I learned, on what was to be a huge plaza, part of a modernization plan that is clearly intended to erase the old city. When it's complete, the Potala will be marooned in a Chinese metropolis.

In Lhasa, I asked a friend whether a meeting with Chadrel was possible. Things were difficult right now, he said. Chadrel was under extreme pressure from the Chinese government, and a meeting with a foreigner would be ill-advised. While I was waiting, though, there was no reason that I shouldn't visit the monastery, which was promoted by the government as a stop for Western tourists. So I found a four-wheel-drive jeep and set out for Tashilhunpo.

As I sat in the monastery courtyard in the afternoon sunshine, a group of monks called to me to join them. They poured some hot butter tea into a bowl and gave it to me. We chatted, at first about neutral subjects. Then one monk began to talk about the late Panchen Lama. He was worried, he said, about how long it was taking to find the reincarnation, but the exact procedures were secret. Chadrel, he said, had just left for Beijing.

"Who should decide which child is the right incarnation?" I asked him.

"The Dalai Lama," he said firmly.

Chadrel's departure was a surprise. But there was a limit to how long I could wait for him to return without its becoming obvious that I was not a tourist. I had no choice but to go back to London, with the understanding that another friend, a schoolteacher in China, would call me when something happened.

Months passed with no word. I called the teacher from time to time and we exchanged coded messages. "When is the new teacher expected?" I'd ask. "I don't know. The principal is still away, and I don't know when he's coming back," he'd reply. I also kept in touch with the Dalai Lama, and we arranged to meet at the beginning of May, when he was in Dortmund, Germany.

The Chinese government had been waging a particularly virulent campaign against the Dalai Lama for the previous nine months, and he was staying, with his small entourage of bodyguards and personal attendants, at the Römischer Kaiser Hotel, secure behind the doors of the presidential suite. He had discarded his usual Doc Martens for a pair of flip-flops and seemed in a decided frame of mind. The elation of our last meeting in Dharamsala had been replaced by great uneasiness. The waiting, he announced, could go on no longer. Messages he had been expecting for months had not come. He knew that Chadrel was still in Beijing, but he had been unable to contact him, and, frankly, he was worried.

He had begun to doubt the wisdom of Chadrel's plan, he continued. He had not lost the fear that, even if it worked, it might put Chadrel's life at risk. His advisers and fellow exiles had also raised strong objections. It would not go down well in the exile community if the Chinese proclaimed a candidate before the Dalai Lama had pronounced, they said. Could he really afford to let it be thought that he was following the Chinese lead in this critical religious moment?

"I have thought of an alternative to Chadrel's plan," he told me. He would announce his recognition of Gedhun Choekyi Nyima on the next auspicious date and then appeal directly and publicly to the Chinese government to accept the choice. Encouraged by his advisers, he had begun to see this as a gesture of conciliation: after all, the boy was in Tibet, under the control of the Chinese government, and the Dalai Lama would make no attempt to remove him. The boy's relatives had never been in contact with Dharamsala, so they could not fall under suspicion of collaboration. And the choice was the same as the preferred candidate of the search committee in Tibet. What happier resolution than that both sides agree?

I was skeptical. This was a naïve view of the Chinese regime, I suggested. In the bankrupt ideology of Beijing, there was little firm ground to stand on, but patriotism and the supremacy of the Han race were still certain bets. Over the past year, there had been a renewed crackdown on religious practice in Tibet. New restrictions had been placed on the numbers of people entering monasteries, and they were told that, while Buddhism would be tolerated, allegiance to the Dalai Lama would not.

There were other problems, which neither of us knew about at the time. Two days before we'd made our film in Dharamsala, the Tashilhunpo search committee had drawn up a short list of seven names from Chadrel's original twenty-eight. According to a later Chinese account, there was an argument. Chadrel, waiting for the messenger to arrive with the Dalai Lama's choice, had fought to keep his candidate, Gedhun Choekyi Nyima, on the list. But he had failed to win decisive backing, and others on the committee had argued that the time had come to use the lottery of the Golden Urn.

The Golden Urn had been a present to Tibet from the Emperor Qianlong, a pious Buddhist, in 1792. He had suggested that, in the event of a disputed search for an important reincarnation, the candidates' names be placed in the urn and whichever was drawn be recognized. It had been used only occasionally, but now Beijing had seized on it as an essential symbol of China's power over Tibet. Chadrel, of course, had argued strongly against using the urn. In mid-February, while I was in Lhasa, he had set out for Beijing to argue his case in person, accompanied, as usual, by his loyal assistant, Champa Chung-la. Since Chadrel had arrived in China, however, his movements had been restricted and his telephone calls closely monitored.

The Dalai Lama felt that he had no choice but to make the announcement independently. The rumor that a lottery was being prepared had reached him in Dharamsala. It would be held very soon, the rumor went, and the results announced immediately. If the report was well founded, then the game had changed again. Beijing would announce first — and it might be the wrong child. The Dalai Lama and his advisers had scanned the calendar, guessing at a likely date for a Chinese announcement, and they feared that May 23, the anniversary of the treaty that had followed the Chinese invasion of Tibet, would be chosen, in order to stamp the choice with Beijing's political authority. The only auspicious date for the Dalai Lama to make an announcement before then was the anniversary of the day when the Buddha first gave the *Kalachakra* teaching, which fell on the fifteenth, he told me, ten days away. There was only one obstacle.

"I want to know Chadrel Rinpoche's opinion," the Dalai Lama said. He had not managed to reach him. Was there any way that I could get in touch with someone? he asked.

I felt myself being drawn more deeply into this process than I had ever envisaged. But it seemed absurd to refuse to make a telephone call, particularly when there was so much at stake. I promised to try to reach someone who might be able to help.

I went back to London and tried to call the schoolteacher. For several days, I had no luck: either nobody answered or a stranger would pick up the phone and I would have to hang up. Then, finally, I got through.

"They'll be announcing the new teacher's arrival on the fifteenth of May," I said. "But we need to know what the principal thinks."

That would be difficult, he said. The principal was traveling, but he would try to get the message through.

I heard nothing more. In Dharamsala, the Dalai Lama waited all week. The phones went down. A junior official was sent to Delhi to try to call Tibet, without success. Late in the morning of Saturday,

May 13, the Dalai Lama turned to his final resource, the method he had used repeatedly when faced with an impossible decision: he cast a divination. Was it the moment, he asked, to announce the choice of the eleventh Panchen Lama? The answer came back. It was.

The Dalai Lama had told me that he would make the announcement on the fifteenth, a date I took to be the fifteenth of May. As it turned out, he had been speaking of the Tibetan calendar, and the date he meant was May 14 in the Western calendar. I had, I discovered later, sent a message with the wrong date.

On the night of the thirteenth, a huge full moon hung over London. As I looked at it, I thought of what was about to happen. I had had to choose whether to be in Dharamsala for the announcement or to try to get to Tibet for the aftermath. I had chosen Tibet.

On the morning of the fourteenth, the Dalai Lama got up early, as usual, and spent his first hours in prayer. He was suffering the effects of a cold and was feeling feverish and short-tempered. Waiting for him in the hall of ceremonies at his hilltop compound was a hastily assembled collection of dignitaries. It was not a large crowd, but it included most of those whose opinion the Dalai Lama respected in the secular and religious balancing act that is his government-in-exile. At eight-thirty, seated cross-legged on his throne, he read a simple prayer that he had written for the occasion. He asked that Tibetans everywhere learn and recite it. It was a prayer for the long life of a six-year-old boy whose photograph was displayed to the Dalai Lama's right.

This was how the Tibetan community-in-exile, the Chinese government, and the boy himself came, finally, to hear the news that Gedhun Choekyi Nyima had been chosen as the eleventh incarnation of the Panchen Lama.

The Dalai Lama retired to nurse his cold, and the select group who had witnessed the ceremony fanned out to spread the news. Only a tiny circle had been privy to the long and complicated process that led up to the announcement. Those outside that circle assumed that the child's future was assured. Within a few hours, word of the announcement was running on all the major news wires, and the Voice of America was preparing to broadcast an audiotape of the Dalai Lama's special prayer into Tibet itself.

The following day, the announcement was reported in newspapers around the world. The Dalai Lama's office in Delhi was besieged with calls from news organizations that were picking up the story and trying to make sense of it. Beijing seemed equally nonplussed, and it took three days for a spokesman from the Bureau of Religious Affairs to respond officially: the Dalai Lama's announcement, he said, was illegal and invalid. But the story was far from over. What would happen to the child now? And to Chadrel?

I left London the day after the announcement. It was summer and the route from Nepal into Tibet was open. I reached Lhasa five days later. Everyone I spoke with sounded nervous. "This is a very bad time," I was told.

I met with a friend the next day. He was tense and anxious. As we drove along a main street, a motorcycle came up to the driver's side of the car, keeping pace with us. The motorcyclist, who was wearing dark glasses, stared inside, holding his position for nearly half a minute before dropping behind.

In the back room of one of the many bad Chinese restaurants in Lhasa, we ordered food that neither of us touched. He told me that by early May it had become clear to Chadrel that he had lost the argument against the Golden Urn and he had prepared to return to Tibet. He had one last hope: if there had to be a lottery, he would somehow see that the right name was drawn. He had been in Chengdu, waiting for a plane to Lhasa, when the news had broken.

"They moved too soon," my friend complained. "We thought it was going to be the fifteenth. When the message got to Chadrel, he said that they absolutely must not make the announcement. I was about to telephone to get them to stop, but then I heard that the announcement had been made. We thought it was going to be the fifteenth, but it was the fourteenth."

"It was the Tibetan calendar," I said. "But I thought that Chadrel Rinpoche must have agreed."

"He did not agree," he said. His face was a mixture of bewilderment and pain. I thought of all that these people had done and the danger they were now in. Chadrel and his assistant had been detained. "They suspect him of collusion. They want to know how the Dalai Lama got the name. He has refused to denounce the Dalai Lama or to reject the choice."

The proprietor of the restaurant pushed aside the curtain and started to refill our tea glasses. Behind us, a window gave onto a small courtyard. We talked in whispers.

I had brought a copy of the Dalai Lama's statement and the prayer, but now I wondered whether it was safe to hand them over. I imagined the car being stopped after I left him, the incriminating documents found.

"If you don't want to take them now," I said, "I can keep them."

"No, I'll take them," he insisted, and they disappeared into his pocket. "Chadrel Rinpoche hasn't been tortured yet," he continued. "But I am worried about his assistant. He isn't well known. They might torture him."

Lhasa was full of rumors. Among them were some fragments of news. It was said that Gedhun Choekyi Nyima had been taken away with his father and mother and older brother. The family had been seen in the custody of the security forces, in Nagchu, then in Golmud. In Golmud, they had been put on a plane, and all traces of them had vanished. I was told that the area around Choekyi Nyima's birthplace, which risked becoming a site of pilgrimage, was now heavily patrolled.

We sat in front of the cold food. My friend shook his head. "Chadrel Rinpoche said that, whatever happens to him, he will never renounce this child," he repeated. "He wants the Dalai Lama to know that."

The situation did not look good at the Tashilhunpo Monastery. A fifty-person "work team" — one of China's most effective tools of repression — had taken up residence there. Its mission was to force the monks to repudiate the chosen child and to demand a lottery to select another candidate.

The monks resisted. By mid-June, the confrontation had hardened, and extra troops were drafted into town to keep the peace. On July 10, the monks were told that the government had proof of contact between Chadrel and the Dalai Lama. Chadrel's assistant, Champa Chung-la, had been brought to the monastery in handcuffs and interrogated. How, his interrogators wanted to know, had Chadrel collaborated with the Dalai Lama? How had he sent his letters, and had he sent any other documents? Champa Chung-la began to speak. He wanted to confess, he said. There had been contact, he admitted, but, with touching devotion, he insisted that he alone had been responsible. "I just wanted to ensure that we found the right child," he said.

The authorities, confident now of their case, called a meeting in the monastery. The monks arrived in a truculent mood. They whistled and booed the senior Party leaders who had come to address them, and interrupted the local Party secretary's long denunciation of Chadrel with catcalls. The meeting was abruptly abandoned, and the official cars drove off in a shower of stones thrown by angry monks.

At nine-thirty the next morning, three trucks, filled with police in riot gear, pulled into the gates. The crowd of Tibetans who had come to take part in one of the monastery's festivals became witnesses to the monks' final resistance. From behind the gates, they could hear the monks shouting, demanding that the Panchen Lama be brought to Tashilhunpo, and calling on the townspeople to enter the compound. After midnight, police raided the living quarters. Thirty-three monks were beaten and handcuffed, then driven in trucks to a prison nearby.

"They were in a terrible state," said a monk who had seen them arrive from the window of his own prison cell. "They were handcuffed, their clothes were torn, and they were covered in blood." The group included many senior religious figures and several who had been personally close to the Panchen Lama. In prison, the cries continued as the monks were beaten into "confession."

The next day, the town was under the control of security forces. Chadrel was formally dismissed, and a man whom the monks had long regarded as a Chinese puppet was given his job. Of Chadrel there was no news. He was "ill," Chinese authorities said, and was undergoing medical treatment.

Beijing named its own Panchen Lama a full four months later, on November 29, 1995. Just after midnight, in the chilly first moments of the day, several hundred monks and a smaller group of high-ranking government officials assembled in the dim interior of the Jokhang Temple, in Lhasa. Three young boys, who had also appeared on Chadrel's list of candidates, took their seats. Among the monks were the new leaders of Tashilhunpo and a respected lama, Bomi Rinpoche, who had been chosen to perform the ritual.

At 2 A.M., three ivory tallies, each inscribed with a name, were solemnly shown to the officials and to the parents of the three boys. The tallies were then wrapped in yellow silk and placed in the urn, which was waved around like an oversized cocktail shaker. Then Bomi Rinpoche drew out a tally and handed it to the chairman of the Tibet Autonomous Region, who read out a name. The officials burst into loud, if rather artificial, cheers. The monks sat expressionless, eyes downcast.

The boy whose "lucky number" had come up, as the official report put it, was named Gyaltsen Norbu. His parents, unlike Gedhun Choekyi Nyima's, according to the Dalai Lama, were both members of the Communist Party. Given the strictures against Party members' observing any religious belief, the recognition of their son as a reincarnate lama in any other circumstances would have landed the couple in hot water. To date, however, their deviation has gone unpunished. In another departure from orthodoxy, the official press publicized accounts of miraculous, authenticating evidence of a kind that had rarely graced the pages of any official newspaper. The boy's birth, it seemed, had been accompanied by a series of remarkable events. People had "beamed with happiness" and commented that he "might be the incarnation of a god." A bird with the beautiful wings of a peacock had turned up a few months later (perhaps delayed by the fierce prevailing winds) and had circled the family house for several days before nesting on the roof. A teacher had observed the sacred letter *Ah* on the boy's tongue, and his mother had dreamed that one of Tibet's most honored guardian deities was cradling him in her arms.

In Dharamsala, the Dalai Lama issued a statement describing the Chinese action as "unfortunate" and appealed to all governments and religious and human rights organizations to intervene to ensure the safety of the real Panchen Lama. Beijing's response was a long attack on the Dalai Lama's nominee. The boy, it said, had "once drowned a dog." His parents were "notorious among their neighbors for speculation, deceit and scrambling for fame and profit." In case ordinary pious Tibetans took a different view, possession of a photograph of the boy was banned.

Nine days after the Golden Urn lottery, Gyaltsen Norbu was enthroned in a heavily guarded ceremony in Tashilhunpo Monastery, then flown to Beijing. There he was filmed exchanging *khatas* —

ceremonial scarves — with a beaming President Jiang Zemin. But the limits of the government's success became apparent when the boy was not returned to Tashilhunpo Monastery. Instead, he was installed in a heavily guarded villa that lies in the hills on the outskirts of Beijing. It is a comfortable prison, but it was an odd choice for a child whose destiny was to be a religious leader in Tibet. Were the authorities afraid for the safety of the child, or was his confinement intended to remove him from the influence of the Tashilhunpo monks?

In the outside world, there were protests. The European and Australian parliaments passed resolutions of condemnation, as did the United States Senate. Such protests were unacceptable, the Chinese government said: the selection of the Panchen Lama was an "internal affair."

In May 1996, the Chinese government finally acknowledged that it had detained Gedhun Choekyi Nyima. Summoned to answer for his whereabouts before the United Nations Committee on the Rights of the Child, China's ambassador to the United Nations in Geneva admitted that the boy had been put "under the protection of the government." His parents, he said, had requested the detention, fearful that he might be kidnapped by "Tibetan separatists." Last year, the Chinese Foreign Ministry announced that he was "living with family members and everything is good."

News of Chadrel's fate did not come out until the spring of 1997. He had been found guilty, an official announcement said, of "leaking state secrets" and "splitting the country." He had been sentenced to six years in prison. His assistant, Champa Chung-la, was convicted on the same charges and sentenced to four years. The trial was held in secret, according to the official explanation, because the charges against the defendants involved "state secrets." The messenger who carried word of the Dalai Lama's choice through the mountains was sentenced to a prison term of two years.

I saw the Dalai Lama again several times, and we discussed the sad end of a story that had begun with such high hopes. The Dalai Lama was grieved by the outcome, and worried about the Panchen. I asked whether he regretted making the announcement that had precipitated the final crisis.

"No," he replied. "I conducted my own religious investigation as to whether I should make the announcement and it was positive. So I have no regrets."

But earlier this year, when I broached the subject with him again, he revealed how much personal anguish the whole affair had cost him. "I feel that I committed the crime here, and they took the punishment there," he said.

The consequences reached far beyond Tashilhunpo. Traditionally, the Panchen Lama must recognize the new incarnation of the Dalai Lama. This Dalai Lama is now sixty-four, and at some point he, too, will take temporary leave of this world and seek a rebirth. Who will now have the authority to recognize his reincarnation? Gedhun Choekyi Nyima may never emerge from the shadows of his confinement, and a reincarnation identified by Gyaltsen Norbu would carry little authority. The present Dalai Lama has often said that he may be the last of the line. I asked him why.

"It's up to the Tibetan people," he replied. "If in twenty years' time they feel it is irrelevant, then there will be no more Dalai Lamas." He continued, "Sometimes I think this present stupid Dalai Lama may not be the best, but he's not the worst, either. I think it might be better to make a dignified farewell, in case some other Dalai Lama comes along and disgraces himself." He burst out laughing, then resumed, "But if there is another Dalai Lama I have made it clear that the next reincarnation will certainly appear outside Chinese control."

As he looked at the photograph of Gedhun Choekyi Nyima, I asked him what he imagined the child was feeling.

He sighed. "I don't know. As a human being, he will feel frustration and fear, and I think he will have a lot of questions. When I look at his photograph, I feel very sorry that he should have become a political prisoner through no fault of his own."

But, while supporters around the world were preparing petitions and letter-writing campaigns on behalf of "the world's youngest political prisoner," the Dalai Lama was, on one level, serene. If the child was the correct choice, as he believed him to be, then he would remain the Panchen Lama, whatever happened.

His followers in Tibet seem to agree. Copies of Gedhun Choekyi Nyima's photograph have appeared in homes across Tibet. The more the Chinese denounce him, a refugee monk told me a few weeks ago, the more the Tibetans will believe in him. To that extent, if there is a moral to this strange contest, it is the old lesson that force rarely triumphs over faith.

Faith, however, had not proved able to save the child from his life of confinement. I asked a well-informed Tibetan in Beijing what he thought the Chinese would do with Gedhun Choekyi Nyima. "If I were them," he replied, "I would bring him up stupid."

There were no winners in the search for the Panchen Lama. Tibet now has two Panchen Lamas and no Panchen Lama. The child in whom Tibetans believe is deprived of the religious education he needs to fulfill his role. The other, the government boasts, can now "recite sutras for three successive days." Gyaltsen Norbu, according to the Xinhua news agency, "is now the esteemed and beloved religious leader of Tibetan people," something the Chinese have long hoped to achieve.

But in June of this year it was clear how far the official claim is from the reality. Four years after the government crushed the Tashilhunpo revolt, Gyaltsen Norbu was briefly returned to the monastery to attend the most important annual religious festival. The boy arrived in a twenty-one-vehicle police motorcade that swept past the waiting foreign press and the congregation. He stayed only an hour before he was spirited away again, his visit to Tashilhunpo just another instance of the empty ritual that Beijing calls religious freedom in Tibet. Played another way, the search for the eleventh Panchen Lama might have brought a measure of reconciliation between Tibet and China. The Chinese have their Panchen Lama now, but they have damaged — perhaps fatally — the institution itself.

CLIVE   IRVING

The First Drink of the Day

FROM *Condé Nast Traveler*

THERE SEEMS TO BE an unwritten code that the earlier the hour, the more iniquitous the idea of a drink. (And, conversely, that the longer you wait, the more respectable you will be.) The only exception is the champagne breakfast. Few would regard this as a guilty pleasure. For some reason, it has been elevated above delinquency. Alas, for me the champagne breakfast does not work. My aversion dates from a morning in January 1961 at the Hotel Metropole in Moscow. I was part of a group of journalists waiting for a promised interview with Nikita Khrushchev. We knew that everything in the hotel was wired to the KGB — phones, bedside lamps, clocks — even though, as was the tradition, the bathtub came without a plug. Our hosts thought they might loosen our tongues with a champagne breakfast. In fact, the champagne, in black bottles, was excellent, from Georgia. The breakfast, however, was abysmal: underboiled eggs and bread like a blotter. The combination was lethal, and I've never since been able to face champagne before noon (I'll return to the virtues of that).

But in spite of this experience, I have long realized that there is a seriously neglected connection between the first drink of the day and the ultimate satisfaction of travel and place. It's my contention that, when traveling, the first taste of the right drink at the right moment in the right place (and ideally with the right partner) is the highest form of serendipity. In my case, most of the formative experiences seem to have been in France.

For example, the French brasserie (sadly, a fast-diminishing species) is founded on the principle of communal comfort, a place where every little need of the day is catered to without a second thought, and hospitality is dispensed to a regular clientele as well as to any stray visitor. When I lived in Paris in the 1950s, I quickly adopted one particular daily habit that prevailed on the avenue de Wagram: a glass of marc at about ten in the morning, backed up by a cup of black coffee. Marc is a drink that ranges from firewater to something of magnificently rounded body. Most of the great wine areas of France produce a marc, otherwise known as an eau-de-vie. The word *marc* actually means "residue": the distilled spirit begins as the liquid pressed from the pulp, or cake, of grape skins left after the wine is drawn off — a process called maceration. Good marc comes with the wine region's name attached — Marc de Bourgogne is my favorite because it is infused with the inimitable plumminess of Burgundy, and should at its best taste like it has seeped from warm saddle leather.

The brasserie on the avenue de Wagram was close to the Place de l'Etoile. It had zinc-topped tables, wicker chairs, and waiters who knew every nuance of their regular clients' moods. The place was popular with taxi drivers, and it was they who seemed most in need of the early marc, since they were the ones who had just navigated the frenzied morning rush of the Place de l'Etoile, the unpoliced confluence of eleven boulevards, and a strident ballet of unyielding metal.

What I had discovered in Paris was a kinship between my metabolism and a shot of Marc de Bourgogne. Taken midmorning, it powerfully clarifies the mind, in addition to usefully beginning the murmurings of the gastric juices (the coffee provided the double whammy). As it happens, an early marc is also a favorite tipple of that great philosopher-sleuth Inspector Maigret, the invention of Georges Simenon, a Belgian who knew his way around all the French appetites. It only works, however, in a brasserie. Any real brasserie, anywhere in France. This affirms three key truths about first drinks of the day: their efficacy rests on personal chemistry, ambience, and — this is the last, indispensable truth — the ability to inspire reminiscence.

These conditions apply whatever the time of day. There will be days, even in the best-regulated life, when the first drink will arrive rather late. If this happens to be about five in the afternoon and I happen to be in Italy, there is only one solution: a glass of Punt e Mes. This bitter vermouth with a color of poppylike red, served

with a splash of soda and a slice of orange, embodies the Italians'
gift for rendering into liquid the kinetic rush of their cities' cafés.
Punt e Mes began its life, allegedly, in the Carpano bar in Turin,
a bustling, mercantile, not particularly pretty town. It is near the
part of Piedmont where several families jealously guard old, secret
recipes for vermouths made partly from the neutral-tasting bulk
white wines of Piedmont and elsewhere, flavored with a mysterious
mulch of mountain herbs. The Carpano bar happened to be near
the city's stock market, and — so the tale goes — one afternoon in
1870 a harassed broker was so wound up from dealing that as he
called for a mix of bitter and sweet vermouths, he used broker-
speak: *punt e mes* ("point and a half"). It was taken to mean the ratio
of bitter to sweet and, if you believe the story, the name and the for-
mula stuck. The taste has a lingering, slightly medicinal cleansing
effect that requires (and enhances) rapid resort to a serious meal.
It is low in alcohol — only 15 percent.

The French and Italians make many vermouths, in many shades,
and sweet, dry, or bitter. "Vermouth" derives from *Wermut,* German
for "wormwood," used to flavor absinthe but, oddly, never used
in vermouth. And, of course, the most ubiquitous vermouth is the
French Martini — the brand, not the cocktail, dry white or sweet-
ish red. The brand name was somewhere transmuted into the
defining American cocktail, which for excellence requires only a
glancing acquaintance with vermouth and mostly a potion of superior gin.

I have to confess that the American martini is excluded from my
pantheon of first drinks of the day. Remember the criteria: personal chemistry, ambience, reminiscence. On a cold Thanksgiving
morning in 1963, my first American publisher served me three
martinis before lunch. These obliterated any chance of reminiscence, canceled ambience, and paralyzed chemistry.

Those three martinis (or even one) were and are the antithesis
of my thesis. A martini doesn't stir the taste buds; it shuts them
down. A vermouth is supposed to be an aperitif. An aperitif is part
of the foreplay of gastronomy. The beauty of a great aperitif is that
it will prefigure the flavor of pleasures to come, and in that sense it
is the quintessence of what a first drink of the day should be.

For me, nothing puts the subtlety of vermouth more firmly into
the context of a place than a glass of Chambéry. It's an obscure,
decorous aperitif, possibly because it originated in a part of France

dedicated to nursing arthritic bodies. Chambéry is white and delicately dry — its herbal quality softens the sharpness of the grape.
Although Chambéry is now made in Piedmont (and sold in the
United States under the brand name Boissière), the eponymous
town is in Savoy, the mountainous eastern French province where
the lakes are still unpolluted and where, on Lake Annecy, they
serve a superb local fish, *omble-chevalier.* If you order this for lunch
(preferably at the two-star Auberge du Père Bise in Talloire, a place
that had faltered in quality but is now back on form), begin the experience with a glass or two of chilled Chambéry, which sets you up
nicely for a bottle of Roussette de Seyssel, a local white wine that
should absolutely go with the fish.

France also delivers another little-known aperitif called Pineau
des Charentes. Charente is the home of cognac. It's a flat, unevent-
ful part of western France, where the white grapes are too poor to
make decent wine but hold the root essence of great cognac. The
juice is distilled into spirit and aged in cellars, where, evaporating
slowly from the barrels, it leaves a dark mold on the walls that in
turn seems to feed age back into the cognac.

Pineau des Charentes is made as a wine from cognac grapes and
is limited to the low alcohol level of 10 percent. It is then fortified
with cognac to an alcohol strength of between 17 and 22 percent,
in a process called mutage. Pineau comes in rosé or white, each a
blend of several grape varieties. I greatly prefer the white. When it's
a *vieux* Pineau, aged between ten and twenty years, it makes a perfect eye-opener at around noon, served chilled with a splash of
soda, as a kind of supercharged spritzer.

Charente is not far from Périgord, where the best goose pâté is
made. By happy chance, while in the cognac capital of Jamac, I began my day's gastronomy with a glass of Pineau and a plate of
Périgord foie gras, sharpened with a few *cornichons,* those tart little
cucumbers that counter the liver's richness. This instantly fulfilled
all three of my essential criteria, and the reminiscence part means
that I cannot ever again pass through Charente or Périgord without the first drink of the day being a chilled Pineau with foie gras.

Try it. It alone is worth the trip.

Farther south, moving with careful intervals of research, I found
that since 1989 the Gascony region has been serving an aperitif to
compete with its rivals in Cognac called Floc de Gascogne. Like

Pineau it is made from the grapes otherwise rendered into the region's wonderful *digestif,* Armagnac. (A warning: The Armagnac sold direct from "farms" is often little more than moonshine, unlike the real thing sold in wine stores.) Floc comes in a pale yellow or a rather sickly red that reminds me of that ancient and rather coarse aperitif called Dubonnet; the lighter Floc is perfect with the livers of the fine fat ducks served in the region.

And so to the neighboring Pyrenees. Things are wilder here. You sense the temperaments of border people — Basques in the west and Catalans in the east — who have both Spanish and French allegiance. The distilled spirits are infused (a suitably chemical term) with the mountain herbs and blended into liqueurs with an indelible whiff of place.

If the mountain air alone doesn't jump-start your day, try a glass of Izarra, either green- or lemon-colored. This concoction comes from a Basque recipe, originating in the town of Bayonne in 1835, proud that it is a blend *"aux plantes des Pyrénées."* Taken neat, it can be too unctuous; it's a sticky liqueur, and I learned the trick of lessening its viscosity by, again, adding a blast of soda and a slice of lemon. I tell you, sitting by the old harbor in St.-Jean-de-Luz at about nine in the morning, as the tuna boats unload, with a breakfast plate of thickly cut smoky *jambon de Bayonne* and a green Izarra (the same tint as Chartreuse), gets the chemistry bubbling wonderfully.

The idea of anticipating food with the first drink of the day should not, however, become a rule. It might make the habit seem a tad more respectable, but if you're looking for respect this isn't the place. There are those days on any journey when knowing the quickest route to an appropriate libation is vital. I'm not speaking of a medical emergency but an emotional one.

It could be that the bags lost by the airline have not turned up. It could be that the rented car has blown a tire. It could simply be that last night's dinner — and probably the last drink of the day — were too much. Whatever. For me the cure is, when available, Pernod, the sanitized descendant of that ruinous lubricant absinthe (or, if Pernod is not available, the Ricard equivalent). It's of the anise family, with a pronounced undertow of licorice and fennel. The yellowish spirit turns magically milky white with the addition of water, and in this form, as a long drink, it has amazing restorative powers (don't take ice with the water — it seems to mask the flavor). My great Pernod moment was on the small Mediterranean atoll of Gozo. This satellite of Malta is eccentric. I had rented a car that even Rent-A-Wreck would have rejected. It was better downhill than up — until, one hill too far, the brakes failed on descent. Instead of using the gears to brake, I stupidly froze in neutral and hurtled toward a small town square. Luckily nobody got in the way, and I circled the square until I found first gear and rolled to a stop — right outside a bar. Two Pernods later, I was able to call the rental agency with some composure. The manager treated me as an effete wimp and sent a minion to demonstrate how to drive the car back without brakes, clearly a local custom. In any event, ever since, Pernod has been my hot-button drink of choice.

Of course, some cultures are more tolerant than others about drinking before noon. I wouldn't, for example, try asking for a cognac with breakfast in Toronto. (In Montreal, maybe.) It's in those cities built to deal with heat — when the streets have been watered, the sun is still below the rooflines, and yet the bar on the corner of a square is open — where they understand the place of the first drink as a prelude to the day's urbanity. Barcelona is such a place. A glass of Manzanilla, the only sherry that is unfortified with brandy, served very cold with a dish of olives and salted almonds, exactly catches the moment — say, at around 9 A.M.

Sherry has never really been a success in America, and yet it is one of the great wines — possibly the most stylish first drink of the day you can imagine, since it comes in a variety of strengths and styles, enough for any mood. The finest Manzanillas are the finos, with a bone-dry, nutty quality. The best of these come not from Jerez, the sherry capital of Spain, but Sanlúcar de Barrameda, near Cadiz, and seem to capture the aristocratic restraint of Moorish Spain. Nobody could possibly find a breach of manners in a glass or two of fino taken early, least of all the Brit-loving Andalusian snobs who make it.

Finally, I come back to champagne. Rare among wine, this is one drink for which you almost always get what you pay for: the more expensive it is, the better it should be. I fear that few champagnes are great wine, and they are not cheap. When they are of superior quality, they are just too good to be taken on the run. For me, a great champagne has the tiniest bubbles, which release the flavor of bursting fruit, a foaming, yeasty, and ineffable balance of ripeness and impending rot. Champagne at this level exists sublimely and briefly between its life in the bottle and its death in the air. Ideally, if you want champagne as the first drink of the day, wait until you are comfortably settled in a ravishing place and have an appreciative partner. Then, on the dot of noon, break open the bottle and make it last at least an hour. Don't complicate things with a meal, or even thoughts of a meal. Other ideas will occur.

Lard Is Good for You

FROM *Coffee Journal*

IN COSTA RICA, I lived on lard and coffee. There was lard in the bread, in the rice, and in the beans. There was lard in the cookies, in the imitation Doritos I ate at the school where I taught; it was coating the potatoes and being used to fry bananas in the cafeteria. Damaris, the woman I lived with, normally bought only three food items when she went to the supermarket in the city: a sack of rice, a sack of beans, and several sticks of *manteca vegetal* — vegetable shortening. Everything else we ate came off the farm.

The lard came in a fat plastic tube and, unopened, looked like slice-and-bake cookie dough. For some reason, there were drawings of clover leaves on the packaging. I watched Damaris fold back the lard's plastic skin and insert a large metal spoon as she prepared a pot of rice. She scooped out a generous dollop of the viscous, bone-white mush and plopped it into the pot.

"Why do you put lard in the rice?" I asked Damaris as she stirred.

Damaris furrowed her brow slightly as she turned to look at me.

"Lard is good for you," she said.

Out on the farm, Rafael was cutting broccoli. "Wait until you see this broccoli," he had promised. "It's beautiful, perfect." Everything Rafael planted grew into something beautiful and perfect. I helped him work seeds into the soil sometimes. He was demanding; he threw work boots at me when he needed my help, then instructed me on how to bury the seeds, and when the seeds grew into shoots, how to replant them. For broccoli it was three shoots to a hole. He dug the holes by twisting his machete into the ground, and I planted. Dirt pressed under my nails, fast against the quick. This was, unofficially, how I earned my keep. My labor supplemented the checks that Rafael and Damaris received from the government in exchange for my room and board. I did it with pleasure.

Rafael's farm was dominated by coffee bushes, the arabica variety, produced for mass consumption. Banana trees between the coffee bushes were there to provide shade; the bananas that grew on them were a bonus. The other things Rafael grew — broccoli, chayote, blackberries, sweet lemons — were not intended to be sold, as the coffee was, but rather were for him and his family to eat.

"Look at this, *doña*," Rafael said, as he entered the kitchen with a full satchel. He opened the satchel on the cable and flawless stalks of broccoli spilled out onto the waxy checkered table cloth.

"Nice," Damaris murmured approvingly. "Berta!" she called. In a moment her five-year-old daughter scampered into the living room. Berta was precious and wiry and wild, a real gift of a child. Her stick-straight hair hung down over her face. Her feet were bare; she refused to wear socks in the house, and Damaris had given up pushing worn, white socks over her heels just to have Berta peel them off when she wasn't looking. Anyway, most of the children in La Victoria, especially in our neighborhood, ran around barefoot. "Gee me four eggs," Damaris told Berta.

I looked at the broccoli on the table, longing to eat it just like that, still dirt-encrusted, hard, and cold. To feel something crunch between my teeth. Before I knew it, Damaris had cleaned and cut the broccoli, thrown it into the frying pan, broken the eggs over it, and dumped the remaining lard — maybe three large spoonfuls — into the pan.

I ate the soggy, eggy broccoli already planning how I would sneak out in the morning with my Swiss Army knife, saw off a fresh stalk, and relish it raw as I ate it hidden among the coffee bushes. I would have to do it in secret to keep people from thinking I was crazy. Nobody in La Victoria ate vegetables raw; it just wasn't done. You might as well eat dirt or tree bark.

Lard was a component of everything edible, like butter where I grew up, only butter made things taste good, and lard just made things heavy and greasy, as far as I could tell.

But I learned. I ate so much lard that my body began to require it. It was one of two substances that had that effect on me.

*

The other one was coffee. As for the coffee, my addiction had been intact for some time before my arrival. It had little to do with my being in Costa Rica, though it was one of the things that drew me to Costa Rica in the first place, along with the rain forest, the beaches, and the chance to see a three-toed sloth. As it turned out, my job placement found me spending most of my year in the highlands, hours away from the beaches and rain forests I had once associated with Costa Rica. I did see a sloth once, clinging to a tree on the side of the highway. Moss grew in its fur and when it turned to look at me, it moved as if its batteries were running down.

But coffee — coffee was everywhere I looked. I lived in a town where coffee bushes lined the road, where half of the men over the age of thirteen picked coffee for a living. I loved being surrounded by this drug of mine, seeing it in all of its stages of growth, the red and yellow berries littering the dirt road during coffee-picking season.

Sometimes, during that wet, ripe season, I picked the ready coffee cherries off the bushes and sucked on them like candy, unleashing their juices with the pressures of my teeth. They tasted fresh, the texture fruity but the flavor distinctly caffeinated.

The best berries would be roasted in a nearby city, then exported to countries like the United States. If you've ever read the menu at Starbucks you'll have seen a Costa Rican blend called Trés Rios. If you've ordered this blend, you may have tasted the beans of which I speak — perhaps the very beans that I watched grow outside my door, on Rafael's farm, bursting into festive reds and yellows during the rainy season.

Within Costa Rica, you can find choice coffee — Café Americo, Café Britt — in hotels and restaurants that cater to tourists. Off the tourist path, you're more likely to find "inferior" blends, some of them cut with sugar, like Café Maravilla.

But I had trouble telling the difference between those grades of coffee, as well as the flavor of the beans from which they were made. On Rafael's farm, I picked the harder, younger green berries before they turned their warm hues and sucked on them as gleefully as I sucked on the red and yellow ones. Those berries were as delightful as what would become of them.

The lard, however, I could have done without.

I heard voices in my head. There were two of them. Some people have the devil on one shoulder, nudging their id, and the angel on the other, appealing to their superego. I had the Tourist and the Traveler, two entities that were, in my mind, just as polarized. On my left shoulder sat the Tourist. When it spoke to me, it encouraged me to ditch this dinky town and make a beeline for the beach, where I could stay in a nice hotel and sleep in a bed with fresh sheets free of that mildew smell. The Tourist sometimes wished I could speak English instead of struggling with Spanish all the time, and maybe hang out with a few more *gringos*. On Thursday nights around ten o'clock, the Tourist whispered in my ear, "You know, Alden, if you were in the States right now, you could be curled up on the couch watching *E.R.*"

The Traveler sat on my right shoulder, embarrassed that it should have to share a body with someone as crude and culturally insensitive as the Tourist. When I was coming home from the city, even when I had enough money to take a cab, the Traveler encouraged me to take the bus like everyone else in La Victoria. "You're not a spoiled *gringa*," the Traveler tried to convince me. The Traveler reveled in the fact that I lived many kilometers — only the Tourist still thought in miles — from any American hotels or restaurants, and it would object to the term "American," since Costa Rica was as much a part of America as the United States.

When the Tourist watched me being served food fraught with that tasteless, pointless lard, its little voice sounded in my left ear: "No, Alden. Don't eat that. It's just not worth it. It will make you fat, and besides, it sits like cement in your stomach. You would never eat that at home."

Then came the voice of the Traveler, the one who wanted me to fit in. "Shut up," it told the Tourist. To me it said, "Just do whatever you have to. You're not here to challenge anything, you're here to learn. You want to be Costa Rican. So eat the lard, *gringa*! EAT THE LARD!"

Lard I ate. I had no choice; it was lard, or starve.

At home there was no coffee. I found this strange, like living on a farm in Idaho and not having potatoes in the cupboard. In the mornings I was served *agua dulce,* a sweet hot drink made from sugar cane. Damaris used a knife to scrape off bits from what looked like a big block of brown sugar and stirred it into hot water. It looked and tasted like watered-down maple syrup.

"Coffee is bad for the stomach," Damaris explained. "Imagine the pain I had, Alden. The doctor told me coffee has cocaine in it."

I thought for a moment. "Do you mean caffeine?"

"Yes," Damaris corrected herself. "*Cafeína*. So the doctor told me to stop drinking it."

I yearned for coffee, and I lived in the one house in La Victoria — on a coffee farm, no less — where coffee was banned. I was a contemporary version of the Ancient Mariner: coffee, coffee, everywhere, and not a drop to drink! There were no restaurants in La Victoria, only a cantina, and Rafael had forbidden me from going there.

He had pointed out the cantina on my first day in town. It was a one-room building with a Coca-Cola sign painted on the wall, and it had swinging doors, like a saloon. "The only women who go there are prostitutes," Rafael had explained to me with a warning stare. He was often very stern with me, as if I were an unruly twelve-year-old, and not a schoolteacher of twenty-two. Then, after a second, Rafael softened and said, "Well, not prostitutes really, just bad women." I doubted they would serve anything other than beer and *guaro*, anyway. The men inside were bored-looking, always hunched over their drinks, and if they caught sight of me as I walked by, they hissed: "*Macha! Ay, gringa!*" They scared me. No, the cantina was not the place to go for coffee.

There was nowhere else to buy it either. La Victoria was a very, very small town. There was one road. Everyone swore it would be paved by the time I left; it never was. Along the road there was a church that doubled as a *pulpería* (they sold candy Coke, batteries, diapers), a nursery school, and an elementary school for grades one to six. A woman sold vegetables out of her house. That was it. The high school was in a town nearby called Juan Viñas. Some took the bus to go to school in Juan Viñas, but high school was optional and many teenagers chose to pick coffee, cut sugar cane, or have babies instead.

My life was at the school. My life was with the kids, teaching them English, and learning Spanish from them. We traded word for word. I liked the arrangement, though the time in between sometimes dragged. Especially without coffee.

Things changed when I met Ana. I was outside on the patio, munching on cookies between classes, and she walked up to me, just like that.

"You're *La Teacher*," she observed. I wasn't that hard to pick out. I was blond, and my clothes were different. La Victoria had never had a gringa teacher before, so I was something of a celebrity. "Yes," I said.

"My son Jason is in the first grade," she said. Jason . . . dark eyes, quiet in class. I met so many people during my first months in La Victoria, and it was always, somehow, a shock to connect relatives to each other. It was made more difficult by the fact that everyone seemed related. "Why don't you come over to my house after school?" Ana suggested. "Have a little coffee."

Coffee? "Okay," I said. She pointed across the street. "Just go over there and ask for Ana," she said.

Ana lived in the compound next to the church. Her son, Jason, was an excellent little soccer player with enormous brown eyes. He was shy, but get him in the school yard with a soccer ball, even a little plastic one, and watch the kid go. Ana had those same saucer eyes and black, feathered hair. Their house was one in a row of tiny boxlike houses that the government had built for low-income families. I walked through Ana's open door to find her sitting in front of the television, watching a *telenovela*.

"That Eduardo," she said, shaking her head at the television screen. "He's no good. He cheats on Maria Luisa and last week he slapped her. He's just like my husband."

"Where's your husband?" I asked, looking around suspiciously. The house was tiny and I already knew that there was no one else in it.

"He left me," said Ana, and her eyes started to tear. "He's been gone for a year." Just as I was beginning to wonder if I should comfort her, she pushed her tears away with a fist and stood up. "Would you like some coffee, Teacher?"

"If you wouldn't mind," I said casually.

Ana walked into the kitchen and plugged in the coffeemaker. In my house, a mesh bag that Damaris had once used to make coffee hung on the wall. Coffee grains were placed inside the bag, boiling water poured through it, and a coffee cup held underneath. Ana was more modern; she had a Mr. Coffee. Ana also had an electric stove, as opposed to the wood-burning stove that Damaris used.

Ana prepared a plate of crackers while the coffee was brewing, slapping margarine on one and then placing another cracker on top, like margarine sandwiches. "Not worth it," whispered the

Tourist, who had snuck into my left ear. I sighed. When the coffee was ready, Ana poured a big mugful and added three spoonfuls of sugar from the sugar jar on the table.

"My husband is going with another woman now," Ana said, handing me the mug. Like a Pavlovian dog, I felt my heart speed up as I brought the cup to my lips. The coffee was bitter without milk, but full, and delicious.

I sipped at my coffee as Ana showed me her photo album, pausing over pictures of her husband, a very young-looking man with a mustache. "He's not the best man," said Ana. "He hit me. He hit Jason. But Jason needs a father, you know."

"It seems like you're better off without him," I offered.

"I don't know," Ana said, shaking her head. It was clear to me that she would take him back in a second.

Suddenly, I had a friend. A friend who filled and refilled my coffee cup until my hands shook. I was happy.

I told Rafael and Damaris over dinner. "I went to Ana Solana Coto's house after school," I said. "She's very nice; we had a good chat."

I watched Rafael and Damaris exchange a look and I wondered why they didn't say anything. Finally Rafael said, "Ana is not a good woman." I brought my attention back to my rice and beans and left it at that.

Between classes, when I had nothing to do, I hung out in the cafeteria with Doña Ruth, the cook. Doña Ruth was an enormous woman who came to town on the bus. She served up rice and beans for lunch every day, plus *mortadela* — a mysterious kind of sausage — or other meat products when the school's budget allowed. Later in the year, I saw on the news that mortadela was made from horse meat. They showed footage of skinned horses strung up on meat hooks. The skinned horses were red and looked strange, as if they were wearing costumes.

"Eat the horse, *gringa*," Traveler whispered.

I was brave. I continued to eat mortadela, and whatever else was served to me. That was the point, after all — embracing a foreign way of life in its entirety, not just taking the good parts and shunning the less appealing ones. Still, when I saw Doña Ruth scoop such generous helpings of lard into the rice on the stove, the other voice rang in my head. "Make her stop!" it said. It was Tourist. "Tell her she doesn't need to put in that much!"

"She's kind of right about that," conceded Traveler in a moment of weakness, and I asked Doña Ruth why she put lard in the rice.

Doña Ruth looked at me sideways.

"That is how you make rice," she explained simply. After all, she was the professional.

"When I make rice," I said, "I don't add any lard at all. Only just the tiniest bit of oil."

"You can't make rice without lard," Doña Ruth said. "It would get all stuck together."

"That doesn't happen when I make rice," I said.

"You must have a different kind of rice in the United States," said Doña Ruth, and she scooped another spoonful out of the tub, adding it to the pot of beans.

We drank coffee during morning recess. The teachers made it in the school's electric coffeemaker. I helped carry out the tray of coffee cups and the metal sugar container with its lumpy, yellow sugar. I was getting used to drinking coffee with lots of sugar and no milk.

The teachers laughed at me as I drained the last of the coffee pot into my cup. "Ay, Teacher," said Elsita, the second-grade teacher. "What a *cafetera* you are."

I loved it that they had a word for someone who drinks a lot of coffee.

Miraculously, despite my eating habits, I did not gain weight. I lost weight. Maybe some chemical bond between the caffeine, lard, rice, and beans, and occasional chlorophyll molecules made energy burning more efficient, I considered. Or perhaps the fact that food was beginning to lose its appeal. I couldn't take all the lard-ridden food; digestively, it just didn't agree with me, so I ate less of it. And I was becoming downright skinny. I learned that in Costa Rica, one's appearance was an open topic for conversation. If you looked pale one day, several people might grimace and say, "Ay Teacher, you look really pale today." At the first signs of weight gain you would be called *gorda*, fat girl. If you were fat enough, Gorda might become your permanent name, as Teacher had become mine. Then, suddenly, for the first time in my life, I became *flaca*, skinny girl. Ana soon commented on my newer, bonier self.

"Teacher," Ana said. "You're wasting away! Is Damaris feeding you?"

"She's feeding me plenty," I told her.

What I didn't tell her was that Damaris and Rafael had finally given me a little talking-to about my visits to Ana's. They didn't like Ana — not one bit. She wore spandex shorts, for one thing. Also, Rafael was friends with Ana's husband, and thought the breakup had been Ana's fault.

"She drove him away," Rafael said. "She was a bad wife."

"But Ana said her husband used to hit her, and their son," I objected.

Rafael looked at me blankly. "You have to teach them somehow," he said.

I still snuck over to Ana's house after school, on the sly, like a teenager with an undesirable boyfriend. Ana was my best friend. She always gave me coffee and filled me in on the telenovela that was her life. In March, there was big news. "The woman!" Ana said, slamming her hand down on the fake leather of the couch. "Did you hear about the woman?"

"What woman?" I asked innocently. I had an idea of which woman she was talking about, but I didn't like to jump to conclusions.

"That harlot, that loose woman, the one my husband is seeing. She's having a baby! She's already big!" Ana started to cry, plump tears sliding onto her hot-pink T-shirt. The T-shirt was tight, and I thought to myself, Rafael would have something to say about that shirt. I put my arm around Ana and let her cry like that for a while.

"He's a jerk," I assured her. "You're better off without him."

My words never seemed to comfort Ana, though she did seem happy to have someone who would listen to her. Some people in town had lost patience with Ana's endless lamentations about a guy who wasn't worth missing.

"He's not a good fellow," the first-grade teacher told me when I inquired about him. "He left Ana — she's a handful anyway, always complaining — and now he's back in the house he grew up in, living with his mother. Twenty-nine years old and he's still being taken care of by his mama!"

I never met Ana's husband, but I saw "the woman" at school. She wasn't as pretty as Ana. She had buckteeth and hacked-off bangs.

Her first daughter — I didn't ask who the father was — came to kindergarten in a cute blue jumper. The woman picked her daughter up at the school every day at noon, and soon I noticed that her belly was growing round.

One day, Rafael entered the house after work with a huge smile on his face and requested coffee. "Please, doña," he begged Damaris. "Could you make some coffee? Just a little coffee?" He whined like a child and flirted with Damaris until she giggled, flattered by the attention, and headed towards the kitchen. I was shocked. I hadn't realized that Rafael still had an appetite for coffee, or that Damaris kept a stash of Café Maravilla on the top shelf of the cupboard. She put a pot of water on to boil and spooned the powdered coffee into the sack on the wall.

"Would you like some?" she asked me. "Oh yes, I love coffee," I hinted. Then she yelled into the bedroom, "Berta? *Café?*"

"*Sí,*" Berta called out from behind the curtain.

Damaris served me my coffee in a heavy glass mug, with several spoonfuls of sugar and powdered milk. The powdered milk was a gift from the government via the school; the kindergarten teacher thought Berta was too skinny and that the milk would help fatten her up. The coffee tasted like hot melted ice cream. Rafael received his mug and slapped Damaris on the thigh in thanks. Berta got her coffee in a bottle. She drank it with childish sucking sounds.

"Do you like coffee, Berta?" I asked her.

"Mmmpg," she said enthusiastically through the nipple.

A few days later, Dave, my American director, came to visit me in town. He observed my classes and offered feedback.

"Let's show my boss how smart we are, shall we?" I urged my second-graders. Dave sat in the back of the classroom as the kids and I went through the alphabet, shouting out the words we had learned. "What are some words that start with *s?*"

"Sun! Sit down! Stomp your feet!"

"'Stomp your feet'?" Dave said after class. "I'm impressed." We were sitting at the school, outside of the office. Dave stood out dramatically in the town, even more dramatically than I did because he stood over six feet tall. You could spot his blue eyes from sixty meters away. People — especially women — stared at him. Some even walked out of their houses to get a better view. "Are there any problems I should know about?" he asked. "I'm not having any at the moment," I said. I had already told him about the constant precautions against catching lice. So far my hair was still nit-free. "But my five-year-old host sister drinks coffee out of a bottle."

"Kids all over the country drink coffee," he said. "It's available, it always has been. No one worries about stunting their growth."

"And then there's the lard thing," I said. Dave smiled. He was, of course, used to gringas complaining about the lard content of the Costa Rican diet. There were over seventy volunteers in the country at the time, doing what I did, and I was not the only one with a Tourist on my shoulder.

"Ah, *manteca*," he said. "Years ago in Costa Rica, few people could afford to eat meat. Most lived on rice and beans. The thing is, you need a little fat in your diet, just like you need protein and carbohydrates, and there is no fat in rice and beans. So the government advised everyone to start using *manteca*."

"People eat meat now," I observed.

"Lard has become a staple in the Costa Rican diet. Just like coffee." Dave smiled. "So you see, Alden, lard is good for you." He squeezed my shoulder. "Anyway, you look like you're wasting away. You could use a little meat on your bones."

The pregnant woman — I still did not know her name — walked by the school yard. She was not shy; she craned her neck to stare at us as she passed. "Look," I said, nodding my head in her direction. "That's the woman who's pregnant with my friend Ana's husband's child. But Ana's husband doesn't live with either of them. He lives with his mother."

My director laughed at me. "Ay, Alden," he chuckled. "You're becoming quite the *chismosa*" — the girl who gossips. Finally, something I learned in high school that I could apply to real life.

The pregnant woman had her baby, another girl. "He didn't even go with her to the hospital," said Ana. She didn't seem to know how to feel about this. She smiled, as if gloating; then her brow wrinkled and her gaze fell, as if she felt the indignation of single mothers around the world.

I was teaching animals that week. In my first-grade class, I held
up a picture of a dog. "Dog," I said. The kids repeated the new
word.

I barked. The kids laughed at me, then barked. "Who wants to be
a dog?" I asked.

Soon hyperactive Rosa Elena was on all fours, barking and howling, crawling up to her classmates and nipping at their heels.
Twenty-five first-graders were laughing, screaming, and pretending
to be dogs. It always amazed me how such little people could make
such big noise.

Ricardo's shrill voice cut through the din. "Look!" he said, pointing outside the classroom door, "it's the Red Cross!"

A wave of gasps passed through the room. I looked out the door
and there it was, the Red Cross van, bouncing over the rocky road,
heading east. The Red Cross only came when something bad was
happening. This was the first time I'd even seen it; until now, I'd
only heard about it in the context of horror stories, like the time
Rafael told me, "Gemelo's brother got run over by a tractor and the
Red Cross had to come."

Ana's son Jason sat in the back row. He was so quiet, so obedient
and sweet. All the quiet kids got stuck in the back. Jason sat at his
desk, staring at me attentively, not knowing that down the road, his
twenty-nine-year-old father was having a heart attack.

"The doctor said it was the lard," Damaris explained later. "It
clogged up his heart."

Word spread like wildfire through the town: Ana's husband had
just dropped to the ground while he was picking tomatoes. The
closest phone was in the center of town, and by the time the Red
Cross got there, he was dead.

"He was so young," I said.

"So now we're supposed to stop putting so much lard in our
food." Damaris suddenly looked away. Her eyes turned pink. "Just
imagine — I didn't know it, but I was killing my husband! My food
could have killed him."

"Poor Ana," I said. It was the wrong thing to say. Damaris and
Rafael wouldn't talk about her. Any mention of her name and they
went silent.

"She's better off without him," the teachers in school whispered.

Ana cried after her husband died, but she said it was for Jason, and not for herself. "Jason needs a father," she said. She put a hand on her cheek in distress. "I'm working on getting him a new one," she said, a strangely out-of-place tone of mischief in her voice. "There's a guy in Juan Viñas who thinks I'm pretty."

That was how it was from then on, Ana telling me about the new men in her life. I listened attentively and sipped at the coffee she made me. The more I listened, the more coffee I drank. I walked home with shaking, sweating hands and a buzz in my head. I avoided telling Damaris and Rafael where I had been. *"Paseando,"* I told them — just passing around. And I sat down with them for a lard-reduced meal.

RYSZARD KAPUSCINSKI

The Truck

FROM *The New Yorker*

Translated by Klara Glowczewska

IN THE DARKNESS, I spotted two glaring lights. They were far away and moved about violently, as if they were the eyes of a wild animal thrashing in its cage. I was sitting on a stone at the edge of the Ouadane oasis, in the Sahara, northeast of Nouakchott, the Mauritanian capital. For an entire week now, I had been trying to leave this place — to no avail. It is difficult to get to Ouadane, but even more difficult to depart. No marked or paved road leads to it, and there is no scheduled transport. Every few days — or weeks — a truck will pass, and if the driver agrees to take you with him you go; if not, you simply stay, waiting who knows how long for the next opportunity.

The Mauritanians who were sitting beside me stirred. The night chill had set in, a chill that descends abruptly and, after the burning hell of the sun-filled days, can be almost piercingly painful. It is a cold from which no sheepskin or quilt can adequately protect you. These people had nothing but old, frayed blankets, in which they sat tightly wrapped, motionless, like statues.

A black pipe poked out of the ground nearby. This was the region's sole gas station, and passing vehicles always stopped here. There was no other attraction in the oasis. Ordinarily, the days went by uneventfully and unchangeably, resembling in this the monotony of the desert climate: the same sun always shone, hot and solitary, in the same empty, cloudless sky.

At the sight of the still distant headlights, the Mauritanians began talking among themselves. I didn't understand a word of their language. It's quite possible that they were saying, "At last! It's finally coming! We have lived to see it!"

It was recompense for the long days spent waiting, gazing patiently at the inert horizon, on which no moving object, no living thing that might rouse you from the numbness of hopeless anticipation, had appeared for a long time. The arrival of a truck — cars are too fragile for this terrain — didn't fundamentally alter the lives of the people. The vehicle usually stopped for a moment and then quickly drove on. Yet even this brief sojourn was vital to them: it injected variety into their lives, provided a subject for later conversation, and, above all, was both material proof of the existence of another world and a bracing confirmation that that world, since it had sent them a mechanical envoy, must know that they existed.

Perhaps they were also engaged in a routine debate: Will it — or won't it — get here? Traveling in these corners of the Sahara is a risky, unending lottery, perpetual uncertainty. Along these roadless expanses full of crevices, sinkholes, protruding boulders, sand dunes and rocky mounds, loose stones and fields of slippery gravel, a vehicle advances at a snail's pace — several kilometers an hour. Each wheel has its own drive, and each one, meter by meter, turning here, stopping there, going up, down, or around, searches for something to grip. Most of the time, the sum of these persistent efforts and exertions, which are accompanied by the roar of the straining and overheated engine and by the bone-bruising lunges of the swaying platform, finally results in the truck's moving forward.

But the Mauritanians also knew that a truck could get hopelessly stuck — sometimes just a step away from the oasis, on its very threshold. This can happen when a storm moves mountains of sand onto the track. Either the truck's occupants manage to dig out the road or the driver finds a detour — or he simply turns around and goes back where he came from. Another storm will eventually move the dunes farther, and clear the way once more.

This time, however, the electric lights were drawing nearer and nearer. At a certain moment, their glow started to pick out the crowns of date palms that had been hidden in darkness, and the shabby walls of mud huts, and the goats and cows asleep by the side of the road, until, finally, trailing clouds of dust behind it, an enormous Berliet truck drew to a stop in front of us, with a clang and a thud of metal. Berliets are French-made trucks adapted for road-less desert terrain. They have large wheels with wide tires, and air filters mounted high atop their hoods. Because of their great size and the prominent shape of the air filter, from a distance they resemble the fronts of old steam engines.

The driver climbed down from the cab using a ladder — a dark-skinned, barefoot Mauritanian in an ankle-length indigo djellabah. He was, like the majority of his countrymen, tall and powerfully built. People and animals with substantial body weight endure tropical heat better.

The Mauritanians from the oasis surrounded the driver. A cacophony of greetings, questions, and well-wishings erupted. This went on and on. Everybody was shouting and gesticulating, as if haggling in a noisy marketplace. After a while, they began to point at me. I was a pitiful sight — dirty, unshaved, and, above all, wasted by the nightmarish heat of the Saharan summer. An experienced Frenchman had warned me earlier: It will feel as if someone were sticking a knife into you. Into your back. Into your head. At noon, the rays of the sun beat down with the force of a knife.

The driver looked at me and at first said nothing. Then he motioned toward the truck with his hand and called out to me — *"Yallah!"* ("Let's go! We're off!") I climbed into the cab and slammed the door shut. We set off immediately.

I had no sense of where we were going. Sand flashed by in the glow of the headlights, shimmering with different shades, laced with strips of gravel and shards of rock. The wheels reared up on granite ledges or sank down into hollows and stony fissures. In the deep, black night, one could see only two spots of light — two bright, clearly outlined orbs, sliding over the surface of the desert. Nothing else was visible.

Before long, I began to suspect that we were driving blindly, on a shortcut to somewhere, because there were no demarcation points, no signs, posts, or any other traces of a roadway. I tried to question the driver. I gestured at the darkness around us and asked, "Nouakchott?"

He looked at me and laughed. "Nouakchott?" He repeated this dreamily, as if it were the Hanging Gardens of Semiramis that I was asking him about — so beautiful, but for us lowly ones too high to reach. I concluded from this that we were not headed in the direction I desired, but I did not know how to ask him where, in that case, we were going. I desperately wanted to establish some contact with him, to get to know him even a little. "Ryszard," I said, pointing at myself. Then I pointed at him. He understood. "Salim," he said, and laughed again. Silence fell. We must have come upon a smooth stretch of desert, for the Berliet began to roll along more gently and quickly (exactly how fast I don't know, since all the instruments were broken). We drove on for a time without speaking, until finally I fell asleep.

A sudden silence awoke me. The engine had stopped. The truck stood still. Salim was pressing on the gas pedal and turning the key in the ignition. The battery was working — the starter, too — but the engine emitted no sound. It was morning, and already light outside. He began searching around the cab for the lever that opens the hood. This struck me at once as odd and suspicious: a driver who doesn't know how to open the hood? Eventually, he figured out that the latches that needed to be released were on the outside. He then stood on a fender and began to inspect the engine, but he peered at its intricate construction as if he were seeing it for the first time. He would touch something, try to move it, but his gestures were those of an amateur. Every now and then, he would climb into the cab and turn the key in the ignition, but the engine remained dead silent. He located the toolbox, but there wasn't much in it. He pulled out a hammer, several wrenches, screwdrivers. Then he started to take the engine apart.

I stepped down from the cab. All around us was desert. Sand, with dark stones scattered about. Nearby, a large black oval rock. (In the hours following noon, after it had been warmed by the sun, it would radiate heat like a steel-mill oven.) A moonscape, delineated by a level horizon — the earth ends, and then there's nothing but sky and more sky. No hills. No dunes. Not a single leaf. And, of course, no water. Water! It's what instantly comes to mind in such circumstances. In the desert, the first thing a man sees when he opens his eyes in the morning is the face of his enemy — the flaming visage of the sun. The sight elicits in him a reflexive gesture of self-preservation: he reaches for water. Drink! Drink! Only by doing so can he ever so slightly improve his odds in the desert's eternal struggle — the desperate duel with the sun.

I resolved to look around for water, for I had none with me. I found nothing in the cab. But I did discover some: attached with ropes to the bed of the truck, near the rear, underneath, were four goatskins, two on the left side and two on the right. The hides had been rather poorly cured, then sewed together in such a way that they retained the animal's shape. A goat's leg served as a drinking spout.

I sighed with relief, but only momentarily. I began to calculate. Without water, you can survive in the desert for twenty-four hours; with great difficulty, for forty-eight or so. The math is simple. Under these conditions, you secrete in one day approximately ten liters of sweat, and to survive you must drink a similar amount of water. Deprived of it, you will immediately start to feel thirsty. Genuine, prolonged thirst in a hot and dry climate is an exhausting, ravaging sensation, harder to control than hunger. After a few hours, you become lethargic and limp, weak and disoriented. Instead of speaking, you babble, ever less cogently. That same evening, or the next day, you get a high fever and quickly die.

If Salim doesn't share his water, I thought, I will die today. Even if he does, we will have only enough left for one more day — which means we will both die tomorrow, or the day after, at the latest.

Trying to stop these thoughts, I began to observe him closely. Covered with grease and sweating, Salim was still taking the engine apart, unscrewing screws and removing cables, but with no rhyme or reason, like a child furiously destroying a toy that won't work. On the fenders, on the bumper, lay countless springs, valves, compression rings, and wires; some had already fallen to the ground. I left him and went around to the other side of the truck, where there was still some shade. I sat down on the ground and leaned my back against the wheel.

Salim.

I knew nothing about the man who held my life in his hands. Or, at least, who held it for this one day. I thought, If Salim chases me away from the truck and the water — after all, he has a hammer in his hand and probably a knife in his pocket, and, on top of that, enjoys a significant physical advantage — if he orders me to leave and march off into the desert, I won't last even until nightfall. And it seemed to me that that was precisely what he might choose to do. He would thereby extend his life, after all — or, if help arrived in time, he might even save it.

Clearly Salim was not a professional driver, or, at any rate, not a driver of a Berliet truck. He also didn't know the area well. (On the other hand, can one really know the desert, where successive storms and tempests constantly alter the landscape, moving mountains of sand to ever-different sites and transposing the natural features?) It was common practice in these parts for someone — perhaps after a small financial windfall — to hire another person with less money to carry out his tasks for him. Maybe the rightful driver of this truck had hired Salim to take it in his stead. And in Mauritania no one will ever admit to not knowing or not being capable of something. If you approach a taxi driver in the city, show him an address, and ask him if he knows where it is, he will say yes without a second's hesitation. And only later, when you are driving all over the city, round and round, do you fully realize that he has no idea where to go.

The sun was climbing higher. The desert, that motionless, petrified ocean, absorbed its rays, grew hotter, and began to burn. The Yoruba are said to believe that if a man's shadow abandons him he will die. All the shadows were beginning to shrink, dwindle, fade. The dread afternoon hours were almost upon us — the time of day when people and objects have no shade, exist and yet do not exist, reduced to a glowing, incandescent whiteness.

I thought that this moment had arrived, but suddenly I noticed before me an utterly different sight. The lifeless, still horizon — so crushed by the heat that it seemed nothing could ever issue forth from it — all at once sprang to life and became green. As far as the eye could see stood tall, magnificent palm trees, entire groves of them along the horizon, growing thickly, without interruption. I also saw lakes — yes, enormous blue lakes, with animated, undulating surfaces. Gorgeous shrubs grew there, with wide-spreading branches of a fresh, intense, succulent deep green. All this shimmered continuously, sparkled, pulsated — as if it were wreathed in a light mist, soft-edged and elusive.

"Salim!" I called. "Salim!"

A head emerged from under the hood. He looked at me.

"Salim!" I repeated once more, and pointed.

Salim glanced where I had shown him, unimpressed. In my dirty, sweaty face he must have read wonder, bewilderment, and rapture

— and something else besides, which clearly alarmed him, for he walked up to the side of the truck, untied one of the goatskins, took a few sips, and wordlessly handed me the rest. I grabbed the rough leather sack and began to drink. Suddenly dizzy, I leaned my shoulder against the truck bed so as not to fall. I drank and drank, sucking fiercely on the goat's leg and still staring at the horizon. But as I felt my thirst subsiding, and the madness within me dying down, the green vista began to vanish. Its colors paled, its contours blurred. By the time I had emptied the goatskin, the horizon was once again flat, empty, and lifeless. The water, disgusting Saharan water — warm, dirty, thick with sand and sludge — extended my life but took away my vision of paradise. The crucial thing, though, was the fact that Salim himself had given me the water to drink. I stopped being afraid of him. I felt that I was safe — if only until we were down to our last sip.

We spent the second half of the day lying underneath the truck, in its faint, bleached shade. In this world circled all about with flaming horizons, Salim and I were the only life. I inspected the ground within my arm's reach, the nearest stones, searching for some living thing, anything that might twitch, move, slither. I remembered that somewhere in the Sahara there lives a small beetle that the Tuareg call Ngubi. When it is very hot, according to legend, Ngubi is tormented by thirst, desperate to drink. Unfortunately, there is no water anywhere, and only burning sand all around. So the small beetle chooses an incline — this can be a sloping fold of sand — and with determination begins to climb to its summit. It is an enormous effort, a Sisyphean task, because the hot and loose sand constantly gives way, carrying the beetle down with it, right back to where he began his toils. Which is why, before long, the beetle starts to sweat. A drop of moisture collects at the end of his abdomen, and swells. Then Ngubi stops climbing, curls up, and plunges his mouth into that very bead.

He drinks.

Salim has several biscuits in a paper bag. We drink the second goatskin of water. Two remain. I consider writing something. (It occurs to me that this is often done at such moments.) But I don't have the strength. I'm not really in pain. It's just that everything is becoming empty. And within this emptiness another one is growing.

Then, in the darkness, two glaring lights. They are far away and move about violently. Soon the sound of a motor draws near, and I see the truck, hear voices in a language I do not understand. "Salim!" I say. Several dark faces, resembling his, lean over me.

Confessions of a Cheese Smuggler

FROM *National Geographic Traveler*

ELAINE HAS DONE ME a favor. A huge favor. As the public relations account executive for a major European hotel chain, she's managed to arrange several nights' accommodation for my wife and me at a very swanky establishment in Paris, the Hôtel Lutétia. During the high season, mind you. "Darling" — that's Elaine talking, not my wife; Elaine is very Continental and always calls me darling — "Darling, you're a very lucky man. The Lutétia is très chic." Elaine is from Los Angeles but she can get away with nonsense like this because she's married to a Parisian, though I doubt if her husband has ever said *"très chic"* in his life.

Anyway, I'm indebted. "Sweetheart," I say to her (these silly endearments are a game we play), "what can I bring you back from the City of Light? Foie gras from Fauchon? A lacquered tray from Palladio? Tell me, *mon petit écureuil,* what do you desire?"

Elaine does a little trilling laugh over the phone that she knows drives me crazy. *"Rien, rien, rien,"* she says. And then she pauses. "Unless . . ."

Ah hah! I think. Payback time. "Yes?"

"No, nothing. It would be an inconvenience."

"Tell me, my little ferret. What do you desire?"

"Well, I was just thinking . . . Perhaps some cheese?" she replies, phrasing it as a question.

That's it? I'm going to Paris and she wants a wedge of *fromage*? Meaning to be generous, I suggest something special. "Pepper roll, perhaps? Cranberry-flavored *Neufchâtel*?"

"Epoisses," she growls. Of course, this is before I know what it

is, so to me it sounds like she's just said "I pass" with a Brooklyn accent.

I ask her to repeat herself. *"Ay-pwoss,"* she cries, and I have to admit it is the sexiest thing I've ever heard her say.

"But of course," I say, having no idea what she's just asked for. "A little Ay-pwoss."

Two weeks later. My wife, Jan, is sitting in a bathtub drinking Veuve Clicquot. She is in total heaven. She loves the antique stores around Carré Rive Gauche, the wild strawberry sorbet at Berthillon, and the silk underwear at Sabbia Rosa, but mostly she loves lounging in the oversize tub in our hotel room sipping champagne and admiring the Eiffel Tower, which juts up into the cloudy sky just blocks away.

I am sitting shirtless and shoeless on a green couch in the Hôtel Lutétia's Opera Suite, eating a nougat bar, wedge by wedge, speaking on the phone with Diane Mincel, an extraordinarily beautiful and charming (aren't all French women?) *jeune femme* from the hotel's marketing department who, during our three-day stay, has done everything but walk our dog — and I'm sure she would have done that if we'd had one. I have waited until the last minute to secure Elaine's cheese, but we are leaving tomorrow, early, so I have asked Diane where, *s'il vous plaît,* I might find a little "Ay-pwoss."

Diane makes that peculiarly French blowing noise, like giving the raspberry without sticking your tongue out, which, loosely translated, means either "Your guess is as good as mine" or "What a silly question." "Perhaps I can find out for you," she says. The French always qualify everything by saying "perhaps." This way they always look like heroes when they actually do something. "I will call you back immediately."

So now I am sitting in the Opera Suite, with its black-and-white photos of famous people I have never heard of — all French, no doubt — eating chocolate and waiting for Diane to call and tell me where I can pick up some cheese.

After half an hour, she rings me up. She is very excited. "I have found a place for you. Marie-Anne Cantin. It is not far."

I tell Jan I'm off to get *le cheese*. She doesn't care. She has half a bottle of the Veuve Clicquot left and the bathwater is still hot.

So, with Diane's meticulous but complicated directions in hand, I
head off in the general direction of the golden cupola heralding
Napoleon's tomb, which, evidently, is near the cheese shop.
Let's pause right here while I'm getting a bit lost wandering up
and down streets that, for some reason, all seem to end at the Parc
du Champ de Mars. I want to give you some information that, at
this point in our story, I'm unaware of but I'm about to discover.
It's about this cheese. Epoisses. Epoisses de Bourgogne, as it is officially called. Here's what I'm about to learn: in France, where
they make over five hundred different cheeses, and a good Brie is
as easy to find as a baguette, this particular cheese is rare and expensive. But in the United States it is more than rare. It is unavailable. It is unavailable because it is as illegal as Cuban cigars. You
see, this unassuming little round orange bundle, which weighs
about nine ounces and has something of a barnyard aroma to it, is
made from unpasteurized milk. And in the good ol' U.S. of A., raw-
milk cheeses are absolutely, positively forbidden unless they have
been aged for at least sixty days, which would sort of be like saying
you couldn't sell fresh fish in a grocery store until it had been aged
for at least two months.

There is a very good reason for this decree from the U.S. Food
and Drug Administration. Bacteria that can cause diseases can be
transmitted in raw milk. Nearly a century and a half ago, the
French microbiologist Louis Pasteur figured out a process to elimi-
nate bacteria in wine by heating it. Later the process was applied to
milk and came to be called, as every schoolkid knows, "pasteurization." Before Pasteur's process was applied, all cheese was made
from raw milk. In France today only about half still is. But modern
pasteurization, in which the milk is heated to 161 degrees Fahrenheit for fifteen seconds, can give milk a "cooked" flavor. And the
whole point of having a fresh, raw-milk cheese, like Epoisses de
Bourgogne, is so you taste the distinctive flavors that come from
ripened, soft cheeses that have not had their rather pronounced
(substitute "smelly" here if you want) aromas "cooked" away by pasteurization.

In fact, in France, many of these cheeses have a season. What the
French call "*la meilleure époque*" — the best time to eat them. What
determines the best time to eat a particular fresh cheese? It depends on two things: the pasturage of the animal that is provid-

ing the milk to make the cheese and the ideal amount of time necessary to age the cheese. Take a nice artisanal goat cheese like Pourly. These goats graze on grass from the limestone plateaus of Bourgogne. The most abundant, flavorful grass is the new growth in the spring. And the cheese takes only two to four weeks to properly age. So the best time to eat Pourly is late spring to early summer. And if you are a true French cheese-geek, that is when you would buy it from your local *fromager.*

But I do not know any of this yet because I have not met Marie-Anne Cantin, who, in a moment, is going to tell me everything I don't know about cheese before she allows me out of her shop with forty dollars' worth of Epoisses. Let's meet her now, shall we?

Marie-Anne Cantin's *fromagerie* is inconspicuously tucked into a narrow little side street midway between the Eiffel Tower and Napoleon's tomb. She is sharp, perky, greatly opinionated, and reminds me just a bit of Debbie Reynolds. She is a second-generation *fromager,* having taken over the business from her father. I ask her if she has any Ay-pwoss, blowing out the second syllable as if getting rid of something nasty in my mouth, and she makes that same little raspberry noise that Diane made and leads me to one of her stunning little cheese displays where we stare, together, at four little creamy rounds that look like pumpkin-colored CDs. *"Voilà!"* says Madame Cantin, as if she had just produced photos of her grandchildren.

She carefully lifts one up to my face. I smile and sniff. It is . . . odoriferous. Seeing my reaction, Madame Cantin gives me my first lesson in French cheese appreciation: "The worse the cheese smells," she tells me, "the better it tastes." Then she shrugs and adds, "This is a hard thing for Americans to understand."

Since I'm not eating it, I don't care. I tell her it is a gift for a friend in California and ask if she can wrap one up. She asks when I am leaving. Tomorrow, I tell her. "Then I will deliver it to your hotel. What time do you leave?" When I ask her why I can't just take it with me, she sighs, looks at me sadly, and says it is simply not possible. That is when she delivers the bombshell: "You know, of course, this cheese is illegal in your country," she says. No, I tell her. I did not know.

And then she sees the problem: I am a dupe. A rube. A cheese mule, as it were. I have been asked to carry nine ounces of an illegal substance, something I know nothing about. So her mission is clear. If I am to go through with this, first I must learn what I'm dealing with. Before she will sell me the Epoisses, she insists on giving me a crash course in French cheesemaking (most of which I have already revealed to you).

Madame Cantin puts on a smart laboratory smock and leads me down some dark stairs at the rear of her shop to the cellar. Here she has two dark rooms full of stinky raw-milk cheeses. One room for goat cheese, another room for cow cheese. We enter the goat cheese room. There are hundreds — no, thousands — of little white slabs of cheese on trays stacked from floor to ceiling being aged to perfection. The Fort Knox of chèvre. For the next hour or so, I learn everything there is to know about curds and whey. I learn about rennet and mold and brine. I learn about washed-rind cheeses, like Epoisses, which, as they ripen, are brushed with marc, a French alcohol. But mostly I learn about the joys of making cheese from unpasteurized milk.

Madame Cantin is a high priestess in the religion of raw-milk cheeses, and she works hard to convert me, putting out a large tray of different raw cow- and goat-milk cheeses, any one of which would be illegal to sell in the United States. Seeing my trepidation, she says, "How can you be afraid to eat my cheese but not be afraid to eat a McDonald's hamburger?"

It is a question for which I have no answer.

I sample her cheeses. They are magnificent. She sees the look in my eyes and knows: I am a believer. Praise the lowly goat! Now she will sell me the Epoisses.

The next morning, as we are checking out of the Hôtel Lutétia, a messenger arrives from Madame Cantin's *fromagerie*. He has a very large bundle for me. Two vacuum-packed parcels wrapped in tissue paper. About twenty pounds of unpasteurized cheeses, including all four rounds of the Epoisses Madame Cantin had in her shop. I also have Camembert de Normandie, Langres, Vacherin Mont d'Or, and a dozen different fresh chèvres, some covered in ash, others rippling with a pale blue mold, all completely and totally illegal to bring back to the States.

My wife looks at me with alarm. "What's that smell?" she says as I hand her the packages and ask her to carry them for me.

"It's nothing," I tell her. "Just a little cheese."

"Is it okay to bring back?"

I do my little French snort. "Of course," I lie. "It's nothing. *Rien, rien, rien.*" And then, as the taxi pulls away from the hotel, the precious bundles of cheese sitting prettily on her lap, I give her a kiss on the cheek. "Trust me, darling."

JESSICA MAXWELL

Inside the Hidden Kingdom

FROM *Audubon*

THE HIMALAYAS cut the lapis horizon like the mandible of the mountain gods. The Himalayas! I talked my way into the cockpit of our small jet to get a better look. "That is Everest," said our Bhutanese pilot. Like nearly everyone younger than forty in Bhutan, he speaks the Queen's English. "That is Kanchenjunga, the third-highest peak in the world. And that is our own Jhomolhari, only five thousand feet less than Everest. Right now we are over Bangladesh. But once we reach those mountains" — he smiled — "we're in Bhutan."

Those mountains. Waiting among them, fitted into a score of knife-blade river valleys as if by nature itself, lies a kingdom that has somehow managed to remain unspoiled for a thousand years. Bhutan is still blessed with wildlife species that are extinct in many other parts of the Himalayas, and humans coexist peacefully with them. Winging across a blue-silk sky toward this secret garden at the top of the world is enough to give any Westerner spiritual vertigo.

On a map Bhutan floats jewel-like and remote on the southern slopes of the eastern Himalayas. Tibet lies to the north. To the east and south is the Indian state of Assam; to the west, the state of Sikkim. Nepal lies just beyond Sikkim. The mountains have always played an impressive role in preserving Bhutan's rich native culture and its extravagant natural beauty. They made invasion nearly impossible, helping Bhutan maintain the distinction of being the last independent Himalayan Buddhist kingdom, the only one that has not been absorbed by China or India or colonized by Europeans. To this day the Bhutanese believe that proper daily worship of the mountain deities protects them from evil. Now the mountains and their swift, steep rivers have begun to provide Bhutan with the cash source it needs to enter the twenty-first century with minimal damage to its environment: more hydroelectric power than you can shake a cell phone at, almost all of it produced by "run of the river" projects that use instream pipes to funnel water through turbines, producing electricity without dams or reservoirs.

As our kamikaze landing would soon prove, the mountains still deter invaders. Even with jet-age transportation, the few tourists who venture here find traveling to Bhutan a royal challenge. I had flown nine thousand miles from Eugene, Oregon, to Bangkok, grabbed a crummy four-hour nap in an airport hotel, then sleepwalked to a crack-of-dawn flight. Now we were dropping through the clouds toward the town of Paro, swooping alarmingly close to a mountainside and turning in hawk circles toward an airstrip that looked like a 7-Eleven parking lot.

The Paro Valley is the only one in Bhutan long enough to accommodate jets. From north to south, pretty farmhouses sit astride concentric rings of terraced grainfields. To the east and west lie the mountains. Down the middle runs the onion-colored rush of the Paro Chhu River. The shriek of our turbines seemed a terrible insult to this ancient Buddhist settlement. I'd been in Bhutan just two minutes, and already I felt protective of its otherworldly peace.

I first heard of Bhutan in 1993, from Guido Rahr, director of Portland's Wild Salmon Center, who went to the Yale School of Forestry with some of Bhutan's future conservation ministers. "There were twenty-five countries represented in our class," he told me, "but we always turned to the Bhutanese for answers — we couldn't believe how advanced they were." In 1996 my neighbors Russ and Blyth Carpenter returned from a trek in Bhutan raving about its natural beauty and the graciousness of its people. I decided it was time to see Bhutan for myself. Now I was here, getting ready to spend two weeks driving across the country, looking for wildlife and interviewing those responsible for its preservation.

It is no overstatement to say that preserving Bhutan's environment should be one of the highest priorities of modern conservation. Bhutan is one of the world's hot spots — places that together constitute less than 2 percent of the globe's surface area but contain more than 50 percent of its biodiversity — says Kirk Talbott, senior director of the Asia-Pacific program for the nonprofit group Conservation International. And Mingma Sherpa, director of the World Wildlife Fund's Bhutan program for six years, says, "Bhutan is the only country in the eastern Himalayas that still has temperate old-growth forest in the middle hills. It has nearly eight hundred species of birds. It still has snow leopards, rhinos, elephants, and tigers. . . . It has incredible potential for biological conservation."

Bhutan's diversity stems from its vertical topography. In a distance of about one hundred miles, its altitude drops from 24,500 feet above sea level to 900 feet. Almost three-quarters of the country, which is roughly the size of Switzerland, is forested. Musk deer, red pandas, blue sheep (slate gray, actually), snow leopards, and takins (cousins of the musk oxen) inhabit Bhutan's cold northern forests. Its southern jungles are home to a host of endangered species: Bengal tigers, leopards, greater one-horned rhinoceroses, Asian elephants, golden langur monkeys, pygmy hogs, hispid hares, Himalayan black bears, pure-blooded Asiatic buffalos, sloth bears, and four species of hornbills. Rare black-necked, or Tibetan, cranes overwinter in the central valleys. Bhutan has more than two thousand varieties of flowering plants, including fifty species of rhododendron.

But even challenging terrain couldn't have protected Bhutan from the past hundred years of industrial assault. What saved it was something even rarer than a snow leopard: two environmentally enlightened kings. Jigme Dorji Wangchuck ruled Bhutan from 1952 to 1972; his son Jigme Singye Wangchuck took the throne at the tender age of seventeen and is still king today.

Considered the father of modern Bhutan, King Dorji brought his country out of isolation in the early 1960s. A careful student of developed countries, King Dorji dearly wanted Bhutan to become a modern, economically self-reliant country. Cheered on by forward-thinking young nobles, including his own prime minister, the king initiated huge internal changes. He established the National Assembly, codified the kingdom's laws, made the judiciary independent, and abolished serfdom. In 1961 he began constructing the country's first roads.

But King Dorji also foresaw the dangers that modern values

posed to Bhutan's cultural and environmental integrity. So he laid out the country's first conservation policies, including the remarkable Forest Act of 1969, which banned hunting, fishing, the felling of trees, and the burning of forest.

King Jigme Singye, now forty-three, continues his father's crusade to bring Bhutan gracefully into the new millennium. The young king's battle cry is "Gross National Happiness" — a serious governmental goal that is repeated over and over in newspaper headlines. King Jigme has made many hard-line environmental decrees. For instance, only about 5,000 tourists a year are allowed into Bhutan (Nepal accepts more than 400,000), and all visits must be arranged through government-sanctioned Bhutanese travel agencies.

The king is also strongly committed to keeping at least 60 percent of Bhutan's forests intact. A decade after the passage of his father's Forest Act, when numerous private sawmills were found to be logging indiscriminately, Jigme's government first restricted commercial logging, then nationalized the forests. The Forest and Nature Conservation Act of 1995 went further, creating strong reforestation programs and requiring permits for all trucks carrying timber. Last January Bhutan banned the export of unprocessed logs.

Land conservation is equally strict. Nearly 30 percent of the country has been set aside for a system of national parks and preserves that is designed to represent all of Bhutan's major ecosystems, including the formerly unprotected broadleaf forests of its central valleys.

Last summer, in order to move Bhutan toward democracy, King Jigme relinquished some of his powers to the National Assembly, including the power to elect members of the king's cabinet. He also created an impressive group of policy-making bodies run by passionate young environmentalists. For instance, the National Environment Commission, the nation's chief environmental body, has to approve any new industry.

But it is the nation's Buddhist traditions that have proved to be its conservation trump card. "Respect for the natural world is a central tenet of Buddhism," states the preamble to the 1990 Paro Resolution on Environment and Sustainable Development. Indeed, the Buddhist belief in reincarnation makes it imperative to protect nature in this life so that it's still intact for one's next life. Bhutan's representative to the United Nations put it this way in his keynote address at a UN meeting: "Man is just a sentient being, among other forms of existence. The assumption that man is on top of the chain of beings is misplaced, considering the mysterious web of interdependent relationships that is now being confirmed through scientific studies. Reality is not hierarchical but a whole, circular, enclosed system. Sustainable development is, therefore, in the interest of every being, every day, not just in the interest of future generations."

A government publication explains that compliance with environmental policies is further guaranteed by the belief that "wind, water, rocks, trees, lakes, and mountains" are inhabited by nature spirits who demand reverence — or else. They "are believed to punish, with death and disease, those who disturb and pollute their domain."

It all sounds too good to be true. Thus, my journey to the Dragon Kingdom, as Bhutan calls itself, felt a little like putting Shangri-La on trial. But if Bhutan is really as good as it sounds, perhaps this little Himalayan outpost can set the environmental gold standard for the twenty-first century.

"So do you think Bhutan can save itself from the Galloping Rot?"

Thus spoke Peter Beard, the renowned photographer who was assigned to record our Bhutan expedition. A part-time resident of Nairobi, Kenya, Beard has spent forty years documenting Africa's "environmental disaster," caused by poaching, drought, and habitat destruction. He and Peter Tunney, his manager and the owner of a New York City gallery, had just arrived from the Paro airport, Beard wearing a navy-blue crew-neck sweater — and a sarong. The Peters had been escorted by Ugyen ("Oo-gun") Rinzin, the dashing owner of Yangphel Travel, who had arranged our tour. They caught up with me and Tashi "T.G." Gelber, our guide, in the dining room of the Druk Sherig Hotel in downtown Thimphu, Bhutan's capital. We were enjoying a tasty supper of yak meat, french fries, fresh peas, and red rice, the delicious, naturally rosy national staple.

"Long flight," Beard announced. "Had a run-in with an elephant recently. Better go lie down." Two years before, in Kenya, an angry female elephant had crushed Beard's pelvis. It amazed everyone that he survived. Fortunately, so had his love of photographing big game.

Unfortunately, there would be no rhinos and tigers and bears on this trip. Bhutan's southern jungles are off-limits to tourists due to a dangerous political situation on its unfenced 450-mile border with India. There would be no snow leopards either. The big shy cats live at such extreme altitudes that even trekkers rarely see them, though they do routinely spot the silvery blurs of Bhutan's blue sheep — which would also be out of our range. And since it was November, the Himalayan black bears would be hibernating.

We did have the possibility of observing the mammals of the "cold temperate forest" (at 10,000 to 12,500 feet), including musk deer, the laboring takin, the mooselike jura, and my favorite, Bhutan's adorable red panda, which looks like a cinnamon-colored cross between a koala bear and a raccoon. We also expected to catch some interesting birdlife, and we were assured of viewing Bhutan's fabulous black-necked cranes, which had already begun to arrive in the marshlands near the village of Gamey, our final stop before returning to Thimphu.

"It is very difficult to see wildlife in Bhutan," Ugyen warned us. The reason is a happy one: the lack of roads. Due to the construction challenges of its mountainous terrain, Bhutan's villages are linked by a single, twisting, one-lane road. With 46,500 square miles of country to wander around in, why should a wild animal hang out by the road?

"We do have a fungus that you might find interesting," Ugyen offered. "It's half-plant, half-animal. Really, it's a worm that has a fungus growing out of its head. Eventually the fungus takes over the worm. It's called *Yarsagumba*, or 'summer plant, winter worm.' People pay a lot of money to use it in traditional Tibetan medicine."

On that note, we all retired to our rooms, hoping for continued health as we readied our weary Western selves for the upcoming road trip.

If you're from America's West Coast, you wake up naturally at 5 A.M. in Bhutan. This bit of international time-zone mojo offers you a magnificent collection of sunrises — framed by the twin canine skylines of whichever mountain valley you happen to awake in.

That first morning, dawn broke in a glossy magenta yak-tail pattern, flaring sideways across the sky.

By nine we were on our way to Punakha, the first village on our itinerary. Our Land Cruiser looped its way along paper clip curves expertly executed by Tsering ("See-ring"), our gentle driver. The few other vehicles we passed took each turn as cautiously as Tsering did. Given the alpine abyss just beyond the road, this was reassuring. It did not, however, remove the potential for motion sickness, which soon rendered Peter Tunney chartreuse and asleep in the front seat.

"Only beauty can save the world!" Peter Beard announced, glancing out at the deepening green around us. Then he too shut his eyes.

Abandoned, I scouted the territory for possible wildlife. Half an hour later I made our first sighting: "Wild boar!" Sure enough, a small, black, ridge-back pig of some sort crossed the road, then trotted up a hill. Within seconds, a barefoot Beard was on its tail, snapping photos as he went. The nervous little swine zigged and zagged in an effort to lose him, but Beard tracked his quarry's every move until it vanished in the underbrush with an annoyed grunt. We were thrilled with this fortuitous debut.

"I'm sorry to fell you," T.G. informed us once we were under way again, "but that was a domestic pig. We have many like it."

What a shame. Wild boars *are* a regular part of the scenery in Bhutan. They're also one of the country's more serious environmental problems. The cause is a predator-prey imbalance, according to Sangay Wangchuk, the eloquent director of the Nature Conservation Section of Bhutan's Ministry of Agriculture. "Twenty years ago there were no problems with wild boars," he had told me over dinner in Thimphu. "We had wild dogs, and the wild dog attacks the wild boar's young, so the population was kept in check. But we also had a wild-dog problem — they were killing the cattle. So farmers were allowed to poison them. Then suddenly we find we have a wild-boar problem — all over Bhutan."

How do they plan to bring the wild dogs back?

"We've simply stopped poisoning them." Wangchuk expects the wild boar population to stabilize in five to fifteen years.

Bhutan has other environmental problems as well. Overgrazing is a serious issue, which Wang chutes agency is addressing by urging farmers to replace fifteen of their native cattle and yaks with two Jersey cows. This, he says, "will improve milk production by a factor of ten to twenty and greatly reduce grazing pressure." Although Bhutan currently has little air pollution, the thin air of the Himalayas makes it a threat, since low levels of oxygen lead to inefficient combustion of fuel. The government is considering importing electric cars and is encouraging the use of bicycles in urban areas. Bhutan has one of the highest rates of population growth in Asia — 3.1 percent a year — so every village health clinic now teaches family planning. Mining is a threat, too. Bhutan has some mines already, mostly small ones in the southern foothills, and the quarrying of limestone for cement manufacturing is a concern. "No chemicals are introduced," assures Ugyen Tsering, Bhutan's foreign secretary, "but there is scarring. The National Environment Commission shut down a marble-mining operation opposite the Paro airport due to scarring."

A Canadian forestry consultant I met in Thimphu had his doubts about the country's ecological purity. He brought up the forest-grazing problem and also Bhutan's serious potential for erosion, which results from unstable subsoils' being continually crushed by tectonic movement in the Himalayas, then saturated by monsoon rains. "The government says the right things, and their attitude on tourism is just right," he admitted. "But there's still some illegal logging."

I asked him how he would rank the country's overall environmental performance. He pursed his lips. I expected the worst.

"Well," he said finally, "I would say that Bhutan is the one country on earth that's on the threshold of learning to do it right."

Any missteps were easy to forgive on the road to Punakha. Every few minutes a different sector of valley opened up like a system of colossal geodes, revealing by turns their thick green hearts. To me, coming from the U.S. Pacific Northwest, clear-cut capital of the world, Bhutan's endless runs of virgin forest seemed impossible, a bittersweet suggestion of what my own Oregon must have looked like two hundred years ago. In Bhutan, wherever there is elevation, there is forest; wherever there is flat land, there is a farm.

Signs of the Buddha were everywhere. Every few switchbacks, we'd pass roadside boulders painted gay colors and inscribed with prayerful words written in Dzongkha, Bhutan's lovely lingua franca since the 1960s. And always there were prayer flags, long banners in five colors representing each of the five elements (air, water, earth, fire, and sky), attached lengthwise to tall posts and streaming in the ever-present mountain zephyrs. Even a Westerner could understand why Bhutanese Buddhists believe that anyone who erects them gains merit, which helps earn a better life next time around. It was hard to imagine a place of greater peace.

It was easy, however, to imagine a place with more wildlife action. "Where are all the birds?" Peter Tunney asked. He had a point. We had seen almost no birds.

"Wrong time of year," I replied, sounding a little too defensive.

"Yeah, but there should be some resident species, right?"

Hard to say. Bhutan is only now completing its official wildlife inventories. Yet I had to admit that our journey thus far had been a little disappointing. Eight hours on the long and winding road had produced but one worthy wildlife sighting: a barking deer, standing in a fallow field on the far side of a hill. We'd also seen our first Bhutanese rodent: a wild shrew. Dead, but wild. Perhaps what we needed was a prayer to the gods offered up by someone with the spiritual authority to get their attention.

"Maybe in Bumthang," T.G. replied thoughtfully, meaning tomorrow's destination (which is pronounced "Boom-tong").

By the next afternoon T.G. had arranged for a special ceremony to be performed for us by the lama of Bumthang's famed eighth-century Kurjey Lhakhang, or temple. We sat on the floor of the temple; two young lamas sat on cushions to our right, at the back of the beautiful room. At the front of the room, a younger assistant tended the altar, lighting red incense and butter lamps, and pouring holy water into silver chalices. Soon the lamas began chanting, reading from narrow, well-worn pages, their words tumbling out in an astonishingly swift stream. The stream became a single sound that rose and lowered, then rose again, broken only by the occasional beat of a drum. It was mesmerizing.

Afterward the young head lama invited us into his home — a single, modest room. We sat with him on the floor as he served us butter tea, a salty, rich broth that tastes like soup to the Western palate. Speaking Dzongkha, translated by T.G., he invited questions. Before I could ask about the ceremony, Peter Beard's big hands flew out in front of him.

"Don't you tire of all that incessant chanting?" he implored the lama. "Wouldn't you rather do something for your own pleasure?"

We'll never know how T.G. actually translated this transgression, but the lama replied, "When I ask the deities to help you, I gain merit for myself." T.G. informed us that the lama had asked the Buddhist deities to show us wildlife and to protect us on our long journey home.

Half an hour after we left Bumthang, a strange black-and-rust-colored mooselike animal crossed the road right in front of our truck. I was riding in the front seat with Tsering, and we both saw it, bounding boldly, with Mount Jhomolhari gleaming in the sky behind it.

"Jura!" Tsering called out, meaning one of Bhutan's rarely seen native ruminants.

We pulled over and got out. We could hear it crashing down the steep slope below us, but we did not sea it again. After that, though, we did see birds. First a kestrel, hunting from its perch on a power-line. Then a Himalayan pied kingfisher, a crimson-breasted pied woodpecker, and, I believe, a wall creeper. Our pièce de résistance was spotting a whole flock of glorious cuckoo doves preening in the low shrubbery around a steep roadside creek and dazzling us with their fabulous long, square, gray-barred tails. I said a quiet prayer of thanks to the nature gods, and to the kindly lama who had so successfully intervened on our behalf.

T.G. smiled. "Prayer is everywhere, you know," he said. "In prayer flags, in every drop of rain, in every leaf — even the air is filled with prayer in Bhutan."

"Rubbish," Beard replied.

"Peter!" I half yelled. "Why can't you at least consider the Buddhist way? Or are you trying to corrupt T.G.?"

Beard grinned. "Of course!" he cried gleefully. "I am the Galloping Rot!"

By five-thirty the next morning we were picking our way down a yak trail through the forest behind the Gantey guesthouse — an exhausting activity at eleven thousand feet. We crossed the frosted flatlands of the Phobjika Valley, winter home of some two hundred black-necked cranes. Our destination was a distant wooden hut, now a bird blind and the only structure on this officially preserved marshland. We heard them before we saw them, their cries hovering in our ears like clarinet notes from outer space. The cranes!

Black-necked cranes were hunted in Bhutan until a decade ago, when killing one was made an offense punishable by life imprisonment. Now Bhutan is in the process of making crane watching an international draw. (Later that day the Royal Society for the Protection of Nature would hold its first annual Crane Festival, a festive fund-raiser for its save-the-cranes efforts.) By the time we arrived at the blind, it was already filled with bird-watchers from all over the world. The crane count was at 129.

Nothing can communicate the drama of seeing a black-necked crane in the wild — its sheer size, its elegant yellow eye circle, its flamboyant black tertial bustle, and especially its hopping, open-winged dance. In archery, Bhutan's national sport, when a contestant hits his target, his teammates applaud by performing an imitation of the crane's mating dance. The Gantey cranes did not disappoint us, despite rumors that they were due to take off "at any moment." They stayed for hours and called and huffed and fluffed and called and danced and danced and danced.

Eventually they took to the air in threes, blessing us with their strange symphonic absolutions as they became small black crosses in the sky. Standing there on that ancient glacial moraine, with the first twists of wood smoke curling heavenward from distant farmhouses, I wanted more than anything to believe the circle of the black-necked cranes would remain unbroken. It's what we always want when we manage to witness one of earth's grand migratory events. For what is migration but the eternal path of nature, made visible to us by the animals that faithfully follow it? The difference is that in Bhutan this path is a holy thing, the wheel of Dharma itself, a symbol of the fundamental teachings of Buddhism and the endless circle of life — which, miraculously, the government genuinely honors. For once I could go home knowing that the wild animals I'd seen and those I hadn't — the cranes and the snow leopards, the jura and the golden langur monkeys, the cuckoos and the tigers and the dear red pandas — all of them would probably be there for centuries to come. Because if wildlife has a chance of surviving intact anywhere on earth, it's in the secret Himalayan garden of Bhutan.

P. J. O'ROURKE

Weird Karma

FROM *Men's Journal*

I NEVER WENT to India in the old days, when people were going there to get mystical, meditate their heads off, and achieve the perfect state of spirituality that we see embodied even now in George Harrison and Mia Farrow. I guess I wasn't evolved enough to follow my bliss. And, come to think of it, I don't have the kind of bliss you'd care to tailgate.

I never went to India at all until this past summer, and then, instead of meditating, I took a daft, relentless road trip organized by Land Rover as part of an around-the-world test of its new Discovery sport-utility vehicle. Four journalists, three Land Rover employees, and a photographer were put into two vehicles and sent 1,700 miles over six days from Islamabad, Pakistan, to Calcutta, through the most populous part of the subcontinent at the hottest time of the year.

The equivalent would be to drive U.S. Route 1 from the outlet shops of Freeport, Maine, to downtown Miami in August. Consider if the driver had never been to America before. What would he think, after being Blockbustered, Safewayed, Chevroned, Shelled, Dodged, Nissaned, Wal-Marted, Dress Barned, Gapped, Burger Kinged, Dairy Queened, and Taco Belled? Would he have a good impression of the United States? No. Would he have an accurate impression? That's another matter.

Yet even the most accurate impressions may be deeply confusing. You can come back from India in tune with the godhead, I suppose, or you can come back realizing you know nothing about India — or, possibly, anything else. I attained reverse enlightenment.

I now don't understand the entire nature of existence. My conscious mind was overwhelmed by a sudden blinding flash of . . . oncoming truck radiator.

Nirvana, from the Sanskrit word meaning "blow out," is the extinction of desires, passion, illusion, and the empirical self. This happens a lot in India, especially on the highways. Sometimes it's the result of a blowout, literally. More often, it's the product of a head-on crash.

We did our driving mostly on the Grand Trunk Road, the "river of life" and "Backbone of all Hind" made famous in Kipling's *Kim.* The Grand Trunk begins near the Khyber Pass, ends just short of the Bay of Bengal, and dates back to at least the fourth century B.C. For the greater part of its 1,600-mile length, the Grand Trunk runs through the broad, flood-flat Ganges plain. The road is straight and level and would be almost two lanes wide if there were such things as lanes in India. The asphalt paving — where it isn't absent — isn't bad. As roads go in the developing world, this is a good one. But Indians have their own uses for the main thoroughfare spanning their nation. It's a place where friends and family can meet, where they can set up charpoy beds and have a nap and let the kids run around unsupervised. It's a roadside café with no side — or tables, or chairs — where the street food is smack-dab on the street. It's a rent-free function room for every local fête. And it's a piece of agricultural machinery. Even along the Grand Trunk's few stretches of tollbooth-cordoned "expressway," farmers dry grain on the macadam.

The road is a store, a warehouse, and a workshop. Outside Chandigarh, on the border of Punjab and Haryana states, a blacksmith had pitched his tent on a bridge. Under the tent flaps were several small children, the missus working the bellows, and the craftsman himself smoking a hookah and contemplating his anvil, which was placed fully in the right of way. The road is also convenient for bullock carts, donkey gigs, horse wagons, pack camels, and the occasional laden elephant — not convenient for taking them anywhere, just convenient. There they stand, along with sheep, goats, water buffalo, and the innumerable cows sent to graze on the Grand Trunk. I watched several cows gobbling cardboard boxes and chewing plastic bags. There may be reasons besides sanctity that the Indians don't eat them.

With all this going on, there's no room left for actual traffic on the Grand Trunk. But here it is anyway, in tinny, clamorous, haywired hordes — Mahindra jeeps made with machine tools used on World War II Willys, Ambassador sedans copied from fifties English models, motorcycles and scooters of equally antique design, obsolete Twinkie-shaped buses, and myriads of top-heavy, butt-spring, weaving, swaying, wooden-bodied Tata trucks, their mechanicals as primitive as butter churns.

India's scientists had, just before our arrival, detonated several nuclear devices, yet everywhere around us was Indian technology that seemed more akin to the blunderbuss than to the A-bomb. The Tatas, Ambassadors, Mahindras, and whatchamacallits were coming right at us, running all day with horns on and all night with lights off, as fast as their fart-firing, smut-burping engines would carry them. The first time I looked out the windshield at this melee, I thought, *India really is magical. How can they drive like this without killing people?*

They can't. Jeeps bust scooters, scooters plow into bicycles, bicycles cover the hoods of jeeps. Cars run into trees. Buses run into ditches, rolling over on their old-fashioned rounded tops until they're mashed into chapatis of carnage. And everyone runs into pedestrians. A speed bump is called a "sleeping policeman" in England. I don't know what it's called in India. "Dead person lying in the road" is a guess. There's some of both in every village, but they don't slow traffic much. The animals get clobbered, too, including the sacred cows, in accidents notable for the unswerving behavior of all participants. Late in our trip, in Bihar state, the car in front of us hit a cow — no change in speed or direction from the car, no change in posture or expression from the cow.

But it's the lurching, hurtling Tatas that put the pepper in the masala and make the curry of Indian driving scare you coming and going the way last night's dinner did. The trucks are almost as wide as they are long and somewhat higher than either. They barrel down the road taking their half out of the middle, brakeless, lampless, on treadless tires, moving dog fashion with the front wheels headed where the rear wheels aren't. Tatas fall off bridges, fall into culverts, fall over embankments, and sometimes just fall, flopping onto their sides without warning. But usually Tatas collide with one another, in every possible way. Two Tatas going in opposite directions ahead of us snagged rear wheels and pulled each other's axles off. And Tatas crash not just in twos but in threes and fours, leaving great, smoking piles of vaguely truck-shaped wreckage. Inspecting one of these catastrophes, I found the splintered bodywork decorated with a little metal plaque: LUCKY ENGI-NEERING.

In one day of travel, going about 265 miles from Varanasi to the border of West Bengal, I recorded twenty-five horrendous Tata wrecks. And I was scrupulous in my tallying. Fender benders didn't score; neither did old, abandoned wrecks or broken-down Tatas. Probable loss of life was needed to make the list. If you saw just one of these pile-ups on I-95, you'd pull in to the next rest stop — clutch foot shivering, hand palsied upon the shift knob — saying, "Next time, we fly." In India, you shout to your car-mates, "That's number nineteen! I'm winning the truck-wreck pool for today!"

As we drove from Lahore, Pakistan, to the Indian border, it was clear that we were approaching a land of mysteries. We went down the only connecting road between two large and important countries and, suddenly, there was nothing on the Grand Trunk. No one was going to or fro. They can't. "Pakistani and Indian nationals are only allowed to cross the border by train," says my guidebook. This utter lack of traffic has not prevented the establishment of fully staffed customs posts on both sides of the border.

Getting out of Pakistan was a normal Third World procedure. A customs official explained the entire system of Pakistani tariff regulation and passport control by rubbing his thumb against his forefinger.

"Fifty dollars," he said. I opened my wallet, foolishly revealing two fifty-dollar bills. "One hundred dollars," he said.

Things were very different on the Indian side. The rules concerning the entry of two Land Rovers and a trailerful of spare parts into the country occupy a book large enough to contain the collected works of Stephen King and the unabridged *Oxford English Dictionary*.

The Land Rovers had already passed the customs inspections of thirteen nations, including Bulgaria and Iran, without hindrance, delay, or more than moderate palm-greasing. The Indian officials, upon hearing this, clucked and wagged their heads in sympathy for the hundreds of brother customs agents from London to the deserts of Baluchistan who had lost an opportunity to look up thousands of items in a great big book. Everything had to come out of the cars and the trailer. Everything had to go through a metal detector, even though the detector didn't seem to be plugged in. And everything had to come back through an X-ray machine that the customs agents weren't watching because they were too busy looking up items in a great big book.

All this took four hours, during which the seven or eight agents on duty met each hint at bribery with the stare you'd get from an octogenarian Powerball winner if you suggested the twenty-five-year payout option. The fellow who was recording, in longhand, everything inside our passports did take two cigarettes, but he wouldn't accept a pack.

None of the cases, trunks, or bags — unloaded and reloaded in 105-degree heat — was examined, except for a wrench set. Perhaps there is one wrench size that requires a special permit in India. Our tire pressures had to be checked, however, in case the all-terrain radials were packed with drugs. The Indian-government tire gauge wasn't working, so we offered ours. We were halfway through checking the tires when we realized that nobody was accompanying us. I walked around behind the customs building to take a leak and found drugs to spare. I was pissing on a thousand dollars' worth of wild marijuana plants.

By the time we left customs it was late afternoon. The staggering traffic and whopping crowds of India materialized. We still had 250 miles to go that day to stay on schedule. A brisk pace was required. Think of it as doing sixty through the supermarket parking lot and the school playground.

This is the India ordinary travelers never see — because they're in their right minds and don't drive down the Grand Trunk. And we didn't see much of it ourselves. The scenery was too close to view, a blur of cement-block shops and hovels in unbroken ranks inches from the fenders. But my map showed only open country with occasional villages meriting the smallest cartographic type size. There are a lot of people in India, some 970 million. I don't know what they want with the atomic bomb; they already have the population bomb, and it's working like a treat. And yet India, with a population density of 745 people per square mile, is not as crowded as the Netherlands, which packs 940 people into that same space. But nobody comes back from Holland aghast at the teeming mass of Dutch.

Indian crowding is not the natural result of baby-having but the unnatural result of too many people tied to the land by tradition, debt bondage, caste, and illiteracy. Business and industry is pushed into the road by subsistence agriculture, which takes up a lot more room than making a living with a laptop, a phone, and a fax.

Life is jammed tight in India to keep it out of the picnic blanket–sized rice field that's the sole means of support for a family of ten. Every inch of land is put to purpose. At the bottom of a forty-foot-deep abandoned well, which would be good for nothing but teenage suicides in America, somebody was raising frogs. Public restrooms in Calcutta employ the space-saving device of dispensing with walls and roofs and placing the urinal stalls on the sidewalk. No resource goes to waste, which sounds like a fine thing to advocate next Earth Day, except in the real world of poverty, it means that the principal household fuel of India is cow flop. This is formed into a circular patty and stuck on the side of the house, where it provides a solution to three problems: storage space, home décor, and how to cook dinner.

Therefore, what makes a drive across India overwhelming (and odoriferous) isn't population, it's poverty. Except it's even more complicated than that. It always is in India. The reason for those ranks of shops and houses along the Grand Trunk — and for the cars, trucks, and buses bashing into one another between them — is the money from an expanding economy that people now have to buy and build these things. And the reason for the great smoldering dung funk hanging over India is that people now have something to cook over those fires. The chaos of India is not just poverty's turmoil, it's also prosperity's stew.

When India gained its independence in 1947, the nation's political elite instituted an economic system that combined the perplexities of the capitalist old-boy network with the intricacies of socialism and then added the extra something we'd experienced going through customs. (Britain has a lot of paperwork and is a rich country, so if India has a lot of paperwork, it will be a rich country also.) The result was known as the "license-permit-quota raj." *The Economist* once said, "This has no equal in the world. In many ways it puts Soviet central planning to shame." Indian industries were trapped and isolated by the government. Like an aunt locked in the attic, they got strange. Hence the Tata trucks, the Ambassador sedans, and the motorcycles that Evel Knievel would be afraid to ride.

But by 1992 India had begun to surrender to free-market reforms. Imports were allowed, foreign investment was encouraged, and customs regulations were (amazing as this seems after having been through Indian customs) simplified. The Indian economy has been growing at about 7 percent a year ever since. As many as 200 million people now make up the Indian middle class — a number roughly equal to the total middle class of the United States. There are plenty of flat bellies in India but few of the distended kind that announce gross malnutrition. And the beggars, whom Western visitors have been taught to expect in legions, arrive only in platoons. A kid selling trinkets in Agra was irked to be mistaken for such. "I'm not a beggar," he said. "You want to buy, you get. Eighty rupees."

The quaint, old India is still there, however, just beyond the clutter of the Grand Trunk Road. In West Bengal we visited a beautiful farm village full of amusing thatch architecture and cute peasant handcrafts. Here the handsome patina of tradition glowed upon lives that were quiet, calm, and as predictable as the lifelong poverty, semiannual famine, and the dowry needed to marry off the ten-year-old daughter.

The villagers were friendly enough. But what if carloads of French tourists pulled into my driveway and took happy snaps while I scrubbed down the barbecue? I preferred the messy hopes on the Grand Trunk.

Maybe — on a brief trip, anyway — it's better to make no attempt to understand India. Just go to the beauty spots like the rest of the international rubberneckers and stand agape, getting your tonsils sunburned. We tried that, too. (Land Rover needed PR photos with something other than wrecked trucks in the background.)

We took a side journey into the Himalayan foothills, to Shimla, the colonial hill station that was the summer capital of British rule. It's built at a higher elevation than Katmandu. The road up was like the Grand Trunk except at the same angle as your basement stairs and in the shape of used gift-wrap ribbon on Christmas morning.

Shimla is a mulligatawny of concrete and roof tin, with the only charming parts being the leftovers of colonial oppression. Along the Mall there's a row of dusty shops that the British — seeing mountains all around them and not knowing what else to do — built in Alpine style. The parade ground has views to die for (or die of, if you lean against the flimsy railings). Atal Bihari Vajpayee, the prime minister of India, was headed to town. Preparation consisted of a minor government functionary's loudly testing the PA system:

HELLO HELLO HELLO HELLO HELLO HELLO HELLO
HELLO HELLO HELLO HELLO HELLO HELLO HELLO
HELLO HELLO HELLO ONE TWO THREE FOUR FIVE
SIX SEVEN EIGHT NINE TEN MICROPHONE TESTING
HELLO HELLO HELLO HELLO HELLO HELLO HELLO
HELLO HELLO HELLO HELLO HELLO HELLO HELLO

For an hour. This was the crowd warmup. The speech must have been a dilly. Meanwhile, behind handsome batik curtains, tribal women in full native dress with nose jewelry the size of baby shoes were repairing the pavement.

Back on the Grand Trunk, we visited the Taj Mahal, an impressive pile built with public funds in Agra while a famine scourged the countryside. The Taj was commissioned by Shah Jahan to memorialize his favorite wife, who died in 1631 giving birth to their fourteenth child. If Jahan had really wanted to show his love, he could have cut back on the Viagra.

And we saw the holiest place of all, Varanasi, where millions of pilgrims descend the ghats into the Ganges, using its waters to purify themselves of sins, as well as to carry away the funeral pyres of friends and relatives. Everybody but me made a sunrise trip to see these sacred rites. I stayed in bed. No death before breakfast, please. Plus, there's the matter of barging in on other people's religious ceremonies: Yo, is that the Holy Eucharist? Cool! Can I taste?

And once you got started looking at religions in India, how would you know when to stop? There are Buddhists, Muslims, Sikhs, Jains, Parsis (Zoroastrians), Christians, Jews, and 800 million Hindus.

I am confused enough by the material surface of India without delving into its metaphysical foundation garments. Hinduism is said to have 330,000,000 gods, which is fine by me if folks want that many. But such multiplication of divinity can't help but add to the profound obscurity of Indian culture, as do the seventeen officially recognized languages and the intricate caste system that somewhat resembles American ideas about social class, except you can't touch Wayne Huizenga because he founded Waste Management, Inc.

Everything in India seems to be a brain-teaser. Just getting dressed is a riddle. This is how you put on a sari: Take a piece of cloth four feet wide and twenty-five feet long and tuck one corner into your underpants. Turn around clockwise once. Tuck the upper hem into your underpants. Make a pleat by holding the fabric between your thumb and little finger, spreading your hand, extending the fabric around your forefinger and bringing it back to your thumb. Do this eight times. Tuck the top of the pleats into your underpants. Turn around clockwise again, and throw everything that remains over your left shoulder. (And I still looked like hell.)

Each little detail of India is a conundrum. Painted above door frames you see the Sanskrit character for the sacred, meditative *om,* bracketed by a pair of swastikas. The swastika is really just a Hindu symbol for self-energization and the accomplishments of life (the Nazis swiped it for the Aryan look). Nonetheless, the message over the doors seems to read *"Sieg heil* inner peace *sieg heil."*

Which isn't too far wrong at the moment. The current coalition government in India — the one that likes atomic bombs — is headed by the Bharatiya Janata party. The BJP is avidly nationalistic and espouses Hindu fundamentalism — sort of like Pat Buchanan and Ralph Reed but with 330,000,000 Jesuses. And the BJP believes in rigid observation of the caste system, so it's like Pat and Ralph have gotten together with the people who do the Philadelphia social register. Or worse, because the most influential support for the B.J.P. comes from the Rashtriya Swayamsevak Sangh, the R.S.S., a secretive, hard-line Hindu brotherhood that was almost certainly responsible for the assassination of Mahatma Gandhi, and whose half million members wear matching khaki shorts to early-morning rallies and make funny, stiff-armed salutes. One reputed R.S.S. leader, K. S. Sudarshan, has said, "We don't believe in individual rights because we don't think we are individuals."

Modern India is, in ways, an unattractive place. But things could be worse. And the B.J.P. seems determined to make them so. The country has a population greater than those of North and South America combined. Its land area exceeds France, Germany, Great Britain, Iraq, Japan, Paraguay, and Ghana put together, and its citizens are that similar. They get along as well as everybody at the U.N. does. India is as complicated as the earth. Indeed, if a person were to announce his nationality as "Earthling," there would be a one-in-six chance that he was Indian. To all this, the B.J.P. responds with a slogan: "One nation, one people, one culture."

Just when you think you're not getting India, you start to get it even less. East of Varanasi, in Bihar state, we encountered a Communist rally. Hundreds of agitated-looking agitators waved red flags and brandished staves. We were a ripe target for the anger of the masses — eight capitalist prats in fancy Land Rovers with a trailerful of goodies protected by only a tarp. We were ignored. It seems the ideological fury of the Communist Party of India (Marxist-Leninist) is directed primarily at the Communist Party of India (Marxist).

The latter runs Calcutta. According to my guidebook, "They have somehow succeeded in balancing rhetoric and old-fashioned socialism with a prudent practicality. . . . Capitalism is allowed to survive, but made to support the political infrastructure."

Not that you'd know this by driving into Calcutta, where the infrastructure doesn't look like it could support another flea. Certainly the Howrah Bridge over the Hooghly River couldn't. It carries sixty thousand motor vehicles a day, and they were all there when we tried to get across at 5 P.M.

I spent the next four days trying to accomplish something in India. If you're going to be confounded by the country, you can't go as a tourist. Tourism is a pointless activity. Pointless activity is a highly developed craft in India. You could spend months touring the country, busy doing fuck-all. Meanwhile, the Indian government and business bureaucracies are busy doing fuck-all of their own. You could accidentally come back thinking you'd caught the spirit of the place. If you intend to be completely baffled, you have to try to accomplish something. Any task will do. For instance, the Land Rover Discoverys and the trailer had to be put into a cargo container in Calcutta and shipped to Australia. This should take twenty minutes. Adjusting the clock to official Indian Daylight Wasting Time, that's four days.

First, the port was closed. Well, it wasn't really closed. I mean, it is sort of closed because the port of Calcutta has silted in and is nearly useless. Only about three ships were there. This doesn't keep hundreds of stevedores, shipping clerks, and port officials from coming to work, of course. But there were city council elections that day, with attendant rioting. So the police had to suppress voters and weren't available for harassment at the port.

Then the port was closed because it was Sunday.

Then our shipping agents got into an argument about when to pick us up at the hotel the next day. Not that they disagreed with one another.

"We will go to get them at 9:30 in the morning," one said.

"Oh, no, no, no, no," said another. "It must be nine-thirty in the morning."

"How can you talk like this?" said a third, stamping his foot. "The time for us to be there is nine-thirty in the morning."

We had about ten shipping agents. There's no such thing as hiring an individual in India. In a Bihar village it took the services of two shops, four shopkeepers, and a boy running for change for me to buy a pack of cigarettes.

While I waited for the port to open, I wandered the streets of Calcutta. The city is a byword for squalor, but parts of Washington, D.C., are dirtier (Congress, the White House), and Calcutta smells no worse than a college dorm.

The poverty is sad and extensive, but at least the families living on the streets are intact — talking to one another instead of to themselves. I did see some people who seemed really desperate, addled and unclean. But these were American hippies getting mystical at Calcutta's Dum Dum airport. I was standing in the ticket line behind an Indian businessman, who stared at the hippies and then gave me a stern look, as if to say, "These are *your people*. Isn't there something you can *do*?"

Calcutta's pollution is more visible than it's fashionable for American pollution to be — smoke and trash instead of microwaves and PCBs. The food sold on its streets may be unidentifiable, but it's less likely than New York City hot dogs to contain a cow asshole. The crowding is extreme, but you get used to it. You get used to a lot of things in India — naked ascetics; one hundred sheep being herded through downtown traffic; costumed girls parading in single file linked by electric wires, one carrying a car battery and the rest with blue fluorescent tubes sticking out of their headdresses.

I was waiting to cross the busiest street in Calcutta when a four-story temple complex on wheels went by, complete with high priest, idols, acolytes, clouds of incense, blazing torches, and banging gongs. And what I noticed was that I hadn't noticed it. Imagine the pope (and quite a bit of St. Peter's) coming down Broadway at rush hour and you thinking, *Should I wait for the walk signal?*

There's a certain pest factor in Calcutta, caused mostly by roving market-bearers who double as shopping touts. But it's not without its entertainment value. Bearer number A49 from New Market told me to avoid the other bearers because they would get me into their shops and cut my throat. Lesser merchants, squatting on the street, sell everything from new Lee jeans to brightly colored pebbles and pieces of broken mirrors. The poster wallah's selection included photographs of kittens tangled in balls of yarn and a rendering of the goddess Kali holding a severed human head by its hair.

In the midst of this was the Oberoi Grand Hotel, its guards stationed at the gate with sticks to use on touts and beggars. At the Oberoi everything was efficient, crisp, clean, pukka (except when the electricity went out). The Indians inside seemed as perplexed by the India outside as I was. I told Alex, the restaurant manager, about the muddle at the port. "Oh, this country," he said. "There are no two ways around it."

We had parked the Land Rovers and trailer in the hotel's courtyard. The shipping agents came by to inform us that everything in the vehicles had to be clean and packed exactly as described on the customs documents. We set about amending 1,700 miles' worth of dirt and equipment disorder. It was one hundred degrees in the courtyard. Removing the trailer tarp, we discovered an ax had come loose from its lashings and punctured a container of beef stew and a can of motor oil. The trailer bed was awash in oil and what Hindus euphemistically call "brown meat."

On Monday we went back to the port, where the customs inspectors ignored everything about our cleanliness and packing except the ax. "What is this?" asked the chief inspector.

"An ax," we said.

The officials conferred at length and decided it was so. Then there was a seven-hour delay because of an engine serial number discrepancy. The customs inspectors were worried that we'd stolen one of the Discoverys from Land Rover. "*We're* from Land Rover," we said. "These are the only Discoverys in Asia, and they can't be stolen because they're both right here." The inspectors returned to their office cubicles to ponder this. We sat on the dock.

I asked one of our shipping agents why so many of the Tata drivers had decorated their front bumpers with one dangling shoe.

"Oh, for the heck of it," he said.

Finally, the Land Rovers were rolled into the cargo container. I stayed on in Calcutta for a few more days, in awe at a dundering flux of a place that seemed in total disarray but where I couldn't even get lost because everyone with a clean shirt spoke English. In the midst of the street stampede (not a figure of speech, considering the sacred cows), there are young hawkers with what look like shoeshine boxes. What's offered for sale, though, isn't a wingtip buff. The youths crouch in the hubbub, juggling the tiny wheels and springs of wristwatches, setting timepieces running again. There is a whole street in Calcutta lined with tiny stalls where artisans with soldering irons rearrange the logic on the latest computer circuit boards.

The Indian journalist and novelist Gita Mehta says her country produces five million university graduates a year. That's four times the number of bachelor degrees awarded annually in the United States. Yet nearly 48 percent of all Indians are illiterate, and almost two-thirds of Indian women are. It is the smartest country in the stupidest way.

You walk by a newsstand — a "newssquat," to be precise — and see the *Calcutta Telegraph,* the *Calcutta Statesman,* the *Asian Age,* the *Times of India,* and stacks of newspapers in Hindi, Bengali, and other languages. A *Telegraph* feature section contained a "KnowHow" pullout on particle physics. A *Statesman* op-ed page had an article on energy efficiency: "The heat rate of the power plant, in layman's terms, refers to how much kilo calorie of heat is required to produce 1 kwh of power." You think you're in a nation of Einsteins. Then you look up from your newspaper and see a man walking along wearing a bucket upside down over his head.

TONY PERROTTET

Zoned on Zanzibar

FROM *Escape*

I HAD NO SOONER arrived in Zanzibar than I was knee-deep in vampires. Not that this fabled isle needed any extra exotica. From my first glimpse of Zanzibar Town, known here as Stone Town, at dusk, with its maze of alleyways and mosques spilling down to the Indian Ocean and the sails of the dhows billowing across the horizon like white feathers, I felt as though I'd wandered into an outtake of Pasolini's *Arabian Nights*. Joining me on the roof of his lavishly restored Omani Palace Hotel was the American expat extraordinaire Emerson Skeen — who briefed me on vampire doings while knocking back gin-and-tonics.

"You can't imagine the panic," recounts Emerson, a born raconteur and entrepreneur who spends half the year in New York's Greenwich Village and the other half tending to business in Zanzibar. During last year's rains, he wanted me to know, a trio of dreaded *papabawas* threw this normally tranquil East African island into panic. Calling these indigenous spirits "vampires" may be a bit of a stretch, but they share some similar traits. They're believed to wander around invisible or take the form of bats — and to strike in their own offbeat, vampirish style.

"You see, instead of sucking their victims' blood, *papabawas* sodomize them," explains Emerson, pausing to let this sink in. "So all over the island, people were refusing to sleep indoors — because *papabawas* only attack in confined spaces."

The narrow streets of Zanzibar's hub, Stone Town, were soon lined with mattresses. Out in the countryside, work in the clove plantations ground to a halt. "For the first week it was like this big outdoor party," says Emerson, pouring more gin. "Everyone was staying up all night talking. But then things started to get out of control."

In one village, a half-naked escapee from a mental asylum was taken for a *papabawa* and beaten to death. Then an old woman announced that she'd actually captured one in midattack. At this point, the president of Zanzibar was forced to intervene — ordering that the creature be brought to the central police station in a cage. A crowd of thousands gathered along the roadways to watch. "It was like JFK's funeral," declares Emerson. "And you can only imagine the scene inside the station. Four police officers conducted an official interrogation — asking a caged animal a bunch of questions in Swahili." Apparently there was no defense attorney. "Then the president made a radio address, telling everyone that it was a false alarm. It was no *papabawa* at all — just your everyday African bat." Zanzibaris cautiously returned to their beds, but the tale is still repeated, with various embellishments, all over the island.

It was an apt tale on my first day here in Zanzibar — sitting high on the rooftops of Stone Town with the whole island spread out below like a mysterious, clove-scented buffet. Whatever else, it quelled any suspicions that, just by opening its doors in the last five years to the outside world, Zanzibar has lost any of its mythic charm.

For centuries, Zanzibar has been the very definition of the exotic and the remote. Like Kathmandu or Timbuktu, the name alone carries a weight of romance that most PR agents would kill for. I'd wanted to go there ever since I was about eight years old and heard a reference to it in a cheesy black-and-white *Sinbad the Sailor* movie. Later on, I was reminded of it by various bars named "Zanzi-Bar" (there are hundreds of them, all over the world). I would also sometimes recall the old Noël Coward song:

> Why do the wrong people travel, travel, travel,
> When the right people stay back at home?
> What compulsion compels them
> To drag their cans to Zanzibar
> Instead of staying quietly in Omaha?

*

Zanzibar's location, twenty-five miles off the coast of Tanzania, has been the key to its storied history — both a blessing and a curse. Situated at the eastern gates of black Africa, its fine harbor is within striking distance of India, Persia, and the Arabian Peninsula — but over the centuries it has attracted plunderers, "protectors," and explorers from as far off as East Asia and Western Europe. Sumerians, Assyrians, and Egyptians all had short-lived stakes here. So did the Indians and Chinese — and then the Dutch and the English.

By far the most influential visitors were the Omani Arabs, who by the seventh century were so impressed with Zanzibar's climate, fertility, and remoteness from Islam's endless wars that they settled in for good. By the thirteenth century, Marco Polo was already reporting it as a wondrous, semimagical place. ("The people have a king, elephants in plenty and whales in large numbers.") Oman would finally lay siege to Stone Town in 1698. And about 130 years later, Sultan Said moved his entire court and the Omani capital three thousand miles south to Zanzibar from Muscat.

These were Zanzibar's glory days, a time of fabulous wealth, silk-laden excess, and merciless exploitation. Under Omani rule, the island became nineteenth-century East Africa's trade hub and first port of call for explorers from Richard Burton to David Livingstone. The island's first clove trees, planted in 1818, soon grew to provide the world's largest supply — giving Zanzibar its lasting nickname, the "Isle of Cloves." Stone Town, meanwhile, was becoming a huge clearinghouse for black Africa's two boom exports — ivory and slaves — and the most important town on the East African coast.

By the mid-1800s, when European powers began to dabble in the Indian Ocean, Zanzibar's strategic location drew eager attention. The heady mix of Arab and African cultures inspired images of decadent Omani elite lounging in gold-lined palaces while hordes of subjugated black Zanzibaris sang Islamic chants. The British eventually decided to stamp out the decadence. Gunboats began hunting down Omani slavers, who often tossed their cargoes into the sea rather than give them up. When the trade kept thriving, the British set up the island as an "independent protectorate," separate from Oman, with the sultan of Zanzibar as head of state. It wasn't until 1890, after blockades, cajoling, threats and bombardments, that the lucrative slave trade officially died.

More recently, politics has kept Zanzibar's attractions well cloaked. After the British gave the island genuine independence in 1963, it descended into a bloody left-wing revolution. Some 17,000 Arabs were slaughtered by the black Swahili majority in a week, a grisly revenge for centuries of slavery. Arab officials were hunted down and tortured to death, their wives and daughters ritually raped and forced into marriages with Swahilis. Once the revolution slammed the doors shut on the island, Zanzibar unified with mainland Tanganyika to create the new state of Tanzania. And for the next thirty years, the island drifted along in a Marxist netherworld, evicting all *wazungu* (foreigners), refusing all entry visas, and sliding, slowly but surely, into economic ruin.

The Spice Curtain finally parted in 1993 — and few places have embraced change with such gusto. As in Cuba, Zanzibar's revolutionary government has seized on tourism as the quick fix for its development blues — banking on balmy weather, tropical reefs and mile after mile of heartbreakingly beautiful beaches to reel in stray travelers.

I woke up exhausted at 4:30 A.M., encased in a billowing mosquito net in one of Emerson's four-poster Zanzibari beds. A sea breeze pushed through the open latticework. Antique chaises sparkled with tiny mirrors. Bathed in orange light, the room looked like a caliph's love nest, floating above the town like a crimson-lined cocoon. Then the sounds of Stone Town started busting up the dawn — wails, whistles, and chimes, women sweeping and roosters crowing, pigeons taking flight and the startling muezzin call to prayer blasting over a loudspeaker: *Allah Akbar! Allah Akbar!*

It's possible to reach Zanzibar by boat from Tanzania's capital, Dar es Salaam, but I'd actually flown from New York City "direct" — a euphemism for a forty-eight-hour odyssey via London, Nairobi, and Mombasa. Flattened by jet lag, I had to struggle just to get myself up — and then down Emerson's eighty-one steep steps to explore the dizzying maze of Stone Town.

Bounded like a bow between Creek Road (one of Zanzibar's only straight streets) and a small protrusion of western seafront midway down the island, Stone Town is a labyrinthine puzzle. Alleyways of the historic port sprawl in a crumbling brocade, too narrow for cars to enter. Mansions of former Omani slave traders lurch drunkenly on either side, so that tenants of opposite buildings can practically shake hands from their balconies. Wooden doors sprout bronze horns, once designed for deflecting elephant attacks. Veiled women whisk by with averted eyes. A man carrying a giant tuna on his back stumbles past, followed by a few guys dragging prehistoric-looking stingrays to the Creek Road market by their tails.

Though Stone Town isn't huge, inside the crooked lanes it feels that way, as if you need a trail of bread crumbs to find your way out again. F. D. Ommanney, an American traveler who spent time in Zanzibar in the 1950s, noted in *Isle of Cloves:* "It's easy to get lost. One walks on and on, twisting and turning this way and that, always hoping, but never quite sure, that one is heading in the right direction. One becomes drenched with sweat and apprehension. Are we here forever?"

The look of Stone Town is Arabic, the faces African, but the smells are definitely from India, pungent bouquets of curry and fermenting fruit hanging in the air like Calcutta during a garbage strike. Somewhere in the hive, I pass the most spectacular mansion of all, once owned by one of Zanzibar's most influential and notorious figures, Tippu Tip, a trader and slave kingpin who in 1895 owned seven clove plantations and ten thousand slaves. Tippu was known to argue with missionaries that God sanctioned his trading — since Abraham and Jacob were both slave owners themselves. These days, his spread is inhabited by a bunch of postrevolutionary families, a house described by one author as "the most magnificent squat in all of Africa."

Like a student of the absurd, I try to seek out relics from Zanzibar's fabled past, the voluptuous Omani world that was ousted by the revolution. Down by the waterfront, a half-asleep attendant lies sprawled along a bronze cannon just outside the sultan's old residence, the Beit-el-Sahel ("the House on the Coast"). After the bloodbath of 1964, it was turned into the People's Palace, and it recently reopened as the Palace Museum. I peek inside. Every room is still packed with velvet furniture and Baroque mirrors. Next door is the sultan's old ceremonial palace, the Beit-el-Ajaib (or "House of Wonders"), which looms above the town like a stale wedding cake. It was bombarded by the British in 1896, during an attempted coup that lasted precisely thirty-eight minutes (the

Guinness Book of World Records lists it as the shortest war in history). The doorway has long since been chained up with a lock the size of a coconut — so I slip the drowsy guard a few shillings for a quick look. There, in the dank courtyard, sits the sultan's official vehicle, a tiny Morris Minor, covered in dust.

To complete the colonial trifecta, I swing by Africa House, once the British Club, now a shabby bar with slashed vinyl chairs and dazed bartenders serving sticky beer. I find my new pal Emerson holding court with a few moth-eaten expats.

"I just couldn't stand the goddamn American winter," he booms, when I ask why he moved to Zanzibar. "So I packed up and traveled around Africa for a while — and spent about two years living in a shack in the Serengeti." Emerson ended up in Zanzibar in the early nineties. "Back then, virtually nobody was coming across from Tanzania. I really liked the freshness of it here — but it was one helluva job setting up Zanzibar's first real hotel." Now Emerson is expanding — restoring ancient palaces at a pace that mystifies many international aid agencies.

"UNESCO has spent one and a half million bucks and half restored a single house," he laughs. "I've spent a couple of hundred thousand dollars and restored six. Why? Because I don't have to fly in experts from New York every week to write reports."

Another member of Emerson's entourage, a plump little Englishwoman nursing a beer, spills her own story. She'd abandoned London to run a small restaurant in the Arab fortress. "I came here just for the hell of it, really," she confesses. "But it really is something telling people back home, y'know, that I'm living out in Zanzibar." Still, she was a little more wary of the place than Emerson. "I mean, the revolution was not much more than thirty years ago," she says, gazing out over the shimmering Indian Ocean. "Sometimes I look at these men I've got working for me, and I have to wonder. What were they doing in 1964? I guess some of them could have been murderers back then."

Zanzibar's union with Tanzania seemed like a pretty good deal on paper. The island got to keep its own president and parliament and was granted 20 percent of the national budget, even though Zanzibaris were outnumbered twenty-nine to one by mainlanders. But these days, many islanders have grown worried that Zanzibar is losing its identity as a result of the union — a sentiment that has caused its share of civic tension. While the opposition party is pushing for complete independence, Zanzibar's ruling party, the Chama Cha Mapinduzi (C.C.M.), led by President Salmin Amour, has in turn become heavy-handed in crushing dissent. Police raids and political harassment are on the rise. And when the opposition won a by-election last year, sixteen of its members were put on trial for treason.

The opposition has set up an office in a plaza garlanded with faded bunting from the island's first rigged elections, held back in October '95. I start talking to a man named Mustapha while he fixes a TV set that the party bought to lure supporters to meetings. The incentive for tonight's meeting, Mustapha tells me, is a Jean-Claude van Damme video. But he's none too optimistic about the coming elections, scheduled for 2000.

"My brother was a teacher, very active in the opposition," he recounts, fiddling with the knobs. "But the police arrested him with the school's English teachers. They beat him, broke two fingers, and shaved his head with broken glass. They made him consume his own excrement, then threw him from a car."

Mustapha sighs with admirable understatement. "He was very unwell for a considerable time."

Stone Town, it appears, harbors more than just benign oddities and enterprising expats. And after a few days here, I start feeling a certain uneasiness — a jumpiness — that may be my antimalaria tablets acting up. At any rate, my condition takes a turn for the worse when Diwali, the Hindu festival of light, suddenly commences. Without warning, the temple next to my hotel erupts into relentless fireworks all night. Whistling rockets explode only feet from the open latticework of my room. As I stare at myself in the mirror, the bombardment turns my drawn face green and red.

Clearly it's time to get out of town. The only trouble is that foreigners need a special permit to drive a rental car. I head over to the police station, a mildewy hole-in-the-wall where four policemen preside at a desk in spotless white uniforms with gold epaulets and caps. A single fluorescent light flickers. Before them is a vast ledger, like St. Peter's at the gates of heaven.

I present my passport and driver's license, which the policemen all pass along, one by one, to examine and chuckle at.

"You request a permit for how long?" the sergeant asks in wonder.

"One week." They all laugh harder.

"Twenty thousand," he says, smiling indulgently.

"I heard it was no charge," I smile back. When their grins don't flinch, I offer them five thousand Tanzanian shillings — about thirteen U.S. dollars.

The sergeant takes my license and disappears, sitting me on a wooden bench. Half an hour later, he comes back, looking concerned. "The top boss, he will not do it for five thousand. Not even for seven thousand. Maybe — maybe — he will do it for ten thousand."

Idiotically, I ask for a receipt. The man disappears again.

More time passes, and I recall something Mustapha had told me back at his opposition plaza. "For thirty years, we Zanzibaris have concentrated on two industries — bureaucracy and corruption. Corruption and bureaucracy. That is all we are really good at." Outside, the sky is darkening. I start wondering if I'll ever see my passport again. To distract myself, I try to scribble in my notepad — until another officer spots me.

"What are you writing?" she barks. "No writing in the station!"

Great pellets of rain begin to splash through the window. And then a monsoonal downpour turns the streets into canals. A cool breeze wafts in — the first for days. All of a sudden, Zanzibar seems to breathe a collective sigh of relief.

By the time the sergeant comes back, even he's untroubled and cheery. He presents a shred of paper with a few Swahili remarks on it, and I'm grateful just to pay up and run.

Less than an hour later, I'm accelerating out of the Old Town, weaving through droves of bicyclists, zigzagging from one pothole to the next, out past the New City's rows of enormous Stalinist apartment blocks flaunting their indifference to the tropical climate. Then I hit the countryside, and the tension evaporates with the rain. The "highway" toward the east coast becomes a shady alley of trees. Within an hour, the Indian Ocean appears across the horizon. I drive past a couple of Italian-owned "bungalow resorts" where honeymoon couples loll in hammocks, watching the wind blow through the palm trees. I turn down a path toward a smaller beach and plunge into the warm, placid waters here, the claustro-phobia of Stone Town receding into the distant past.

Out in Zanzibar's fragrant rural world, the roadways are mostly empty, save for the local women walking by in their vivid *kangas,* which drape like dhow sails in yellow and crimson — welcome re-lief from Stone Town's favored garb of funereal black. Ruined mosques covered in moss lurk by the roadside. Running in neatly combed lines, the trees in Zanzibar's famous clove plantations ex-plode with pink flowers. Most of the clove trees are more than a century old, but few farmers even bother harvesting them these days. The main market for the spice used to be Indonesia, where clove oil was used to flavor cigarettes. Since the economic collapse, Indonesians are now smoking their tobacco spice-free. Zanzibari farmers have since turned to harvesting seaweed for the Far East, and at low tide women can be seen wandering the beaches, filling wicker baskets with ingredients for miso soup.

Zanzibar isn't a big island, only sixty miles by twenty at its widest point, but getting around can be entirely baffling. There are no road signs anywhere in the countryside, and only one gas station. I hire a fastidious young student named Haji Ali Haji to help in navi-gation, his high school English, French, and Italian making him eminently employable. Haji is part of Zanzibar's new generation. He still lives in a mud-brick hut with his mother, but he wears Reebok shoes and imported jeans and has Nike posters plastered over every inch of his room.

"I hope you are enjoying Zan-zi-b-a-a-a-a-h," he intones, lingering over the name and hopping in the passenger seat.

Within an hour, Haji proves himself invaluable at the first of many police roadblocks. Showing them my scrap of a license, he adeptly negotiates the proper "fee" (bribe) needed to get through — usually the equivalent of a U.S. quarter. He also knows the secret crannies of this remote island — most of which burst with scenes from the timeless past. Heading south, Haji directs me down an un-named sand road to a fish market, where an auctioneer rattles off the price of a giant swordfish before a crowd. A few yards away, teams of teenage girls draw water from a sixteenth-century well. Around the corner, I'm introduced to some of Haji's family friends, who are all busy forging iron nails by hand. Off in the back-ground, a local urchin keeps their furnaces hot, working the bellows on a contraption like a medieval Stairmaster, sweat pouring in rivers.

As we head farther south on the main road, Haji gives me the latest *papabawa* update. For Zanzibari men, the most terrifying thing of all is that, once taken by one of these vampires, you can't help but sodomize someone else. "But there's nothing to worry about now," he assures me, "because they have all flown west to Mombasa. And anyway, it's the witches who are the most dangerous in my village." Haji lowers his voice. "They walk the streets invisible. They have sacrificed their children to Satan for power." I nod, as if it's a routine warning.

Our grand tour of Zanzibar's south begins to unfold like a chapter out of Gerald Durrell when we hit the Jozani Forest, a nature reserve nestled below twin bays along the east coast. No sooner do we enter the forest than a pair of red colobus monkeys (unique to the island) leaps screeching from the branches above. A few others start dancing around our feet, while the rest of the brood spectates warily from above, tossing half-gnawed fruit at our heads. The Jozani Forest, I am told, is also the home of the fearsome "Zanzibar leopard" — which, I later discover, is an altogether made-up species. Haji leads me through the jungle, and soon we meet yet another odd specimen, an entrepreneurial teacher who's started up his own snake farm. Spitting cobras and black mambas glitter in their glass cages, along with several not-too-long-for-this-world rodents.

"I would not like to be that mouse," Haji comments, practicing his English verb constructions. "No, that mouse I would not like to be."

We reach the southern tip of the island at Kizimkazi, a tiny coastal enclave that served as Zanzibar's capital up until the seventeenth century. These days, Kizimkazi is mainly known for its ruins, particularly the Shirazi Dimbani Mosque, one of the oldest in East Africa. From the outside, the historic mosque looks about as imposing as a Long Island garden shed, armed with a new corrugated iron roof. But its dark interior is tattooed with mysterious Kufic script, one section dating as far back as A.D. 1107.

In Kizimkazi, we're catapulted into the present by teams of fifteen-year-old kids who have a lucrative cottage industry: running boat trips around the coast each morning at dawn. I sign on with one bunch for the day. Soon I find myself swimming with a pair of dolphins, stroking their porcelain flanks and listening to their melodious underwater clicking. Beside us, flying fish leap from the water in silver waves, while schools of minuscule blue slivers dart through my fingers in the underwater reefs. On the way back, the kids effortlessly pluck a blue snapper from the sea, then barbecue it on deck on a homemade grill. The only drawback during this Zanzibari idyll comes at the end of the day — when our antique outboard motor gives out. As dusk quietly settles, we begin drifting out into the Indian Ocean without a paddle — or life jackets.

The only other passenger with us, a Swede, scans the horizon. "How far away do you think is the next land?" he asks.

Haji offers a not-so-encouraging geography lesson. "The Seychelles are just there," he says, pointing into the void due east, "the Amirantes over there. The Agalegas there. Diego Garcia comes after that. Only one thousand kilometers — maybe one and a half."

We continue to drift as the sun sets, gazing longingly at the shrinking coast. Finally one of the teens rolls up his sleeves and gets to work — proceeding to take a good chunk of the outboard motor apart.

We drift some more while the crew watches their fix-it kid reassemble our ride home from a pile of prehistoric components. He gives the motor another shot, and we sputter back to shore.

Haji and I next aim for the northern tip of the island, where its most picture-perfect beaches lie — cove after cove of pure gold sand and crystal-blue waters. By some perverse twist of cultural fate, though, most of them lie outside Nungwi, the most traditional Muslim village in Zanzibar. In the last few years, tiny bungalow hotels have mushroomed in every palm-fringed corner, along with a couple of scuba-diving shops. The former owners of this stunning slice of Zanzibari real estate are now as wealthy as sultans. But the villagers of nearby Nungwi are not impressed.

Nungwi's blindingly white coral houses huddle like a wagon train against the invaders, with residents who are trying to carry on their austere Muslim lives in an encroaching sea of Euro tourists. Every dawn, while the *wazungu* are sleeping off their forbidden-alcohol hangovers, teams of fishermen are slipping back to shore in sailboats, dragging their evening catch to be sold on the beach. While the foreigners are taking their first near-naked swim every morning, the dhow builders are planing their wooden hulls. And at dusk, as the faithful crowd into the mosque for evening prayers, the foreigners ritually gather for the sunset. "Why do they do that?" asks Haji that evening. "They sit watching every night, but it is always the same."

During a stroll along Nungwi's blindingly white beachfront, I watch teams of men building Arab dhows much as they have over the last five centuries. For about $25,000 at current exchange rates, you can pick up your own twenty-five-arm-length sailing boat (each arm length is eighteen inches). Not bad, considering that the work is all done by hand and takes six months from start to finish. The price does not include the hefty cost of the wild party when the dhow is launched. The whole village descends on the beach for a weekend to garland the mast in flowers and dip the prow in clove oil for good luck.

One of these master boat builders, a portly, tortoiselike man known as "the Fundi," seems perturbed less by the half-naked tourists than by the first English Coca-Cola sign. The Fundi's wiry son Ali, on the other hand, is clearly getting bored planing wood for his dad's dhows. He looks forward to a rumored megaresort that will soon be built near Nungwi — complete with ample employment opportunities. "Maybe we can take tourists out on the water," he says, a little uncertainly.

The conversation is suddenly interrupted by the sound of drumming coming from deeper in the village. "It's a Devil Dance," Ali explains — one of the island's traditional *uganga* ("white magic") exorcisms, which can last for several days. Ali leads Haji and me over to check out this grand social event. In clouds of sand and dust, villagers shuffle in a long line, singing and chanting. In the center, a shivering patient sits bolt upright with a white cloth over his head. Apparently he's from Stone Town and he needs a cure for madness. Stage-managing the event is a wild-eyed witch doctor, dressed in a long white shirt and waving a cow's horn that contains the nose of a dog.

Before I know it, Ali and Haji have thrown themselves into the line, singing to the offending demon in Swahili, "Who are you? Why are you making this man sick?" Quivering and rolling his eyes, the witch doctor looks as if he could do with some treatment himself. The aim of an exorcism, Haji explains, is to have the offending devil enter the body of the witch doctor so that the patient's relatives can ask him what's wrong. To achieve this, the witch doctor needs to discover the devil's "home." Every few minutes he runs back into the village. Soon he returns with some object — the branch of a palm tree, a kitchen plate — that may or may not contain the evil spirit.

But he's not having much luck with this demon. He tries again, returning with a trussed-up chicken. But no — wrong devil. Eventually, at sunset, the doctor calls his ceremony to a halt, telling everyone to reconvene tomorrow at 9 A.M. sharp.

Zanzibar's vampires may have flown into the sunset, but it seems the rest of the island's spirits are here for a spell.

Storming *The Beach*

from Salon Travel

Day Six: January 22 — Storming The Beach *(Prelude)*

It is three o'clock in the morning, and Lomudi Beach is possibly the only stretch of sand on Phi Phi Don island that is completely deserted. The only buildings here are small, sagging bamboo-and-thatch dwellings that probably housed Thai fishermen before the onslaught of sun-starved Europeans and North Americans turned those fishermen into bellboys and T-shirt hawkers. The high-tide line here yields a sodden crust of garbage — plastic water bottles, rubber sandals, cigarette butts — but this detritus is only evidence of the boaters, snorkelers, and sunburned masses who haunt the other parts of the island. Devoid of dive shops, pineapple vendors, and running water, Lomudi is quiet and empty.

Given the current development trends in this part of Thailand, Lomudi will probably sport a disco and an airport within a couple of months.

I hear the rhythmic thump of a longtail boat somewhere in the darkness, and I realize that my moment is at hand. Gathering up a sealed plastic bag of supplies, I wade out into the shallow waters to meet the rickety wooden craft that will take me across a small stretch of the Andaman Sea to the forbidden shores of Phi Phi Don's sister island — a majestic, cliff-girded island called Phi Phi Leh.

Phi Phi Leh island is not forbidden because of ancient tribal rituals, secret nuclear tests, or hidden pirate treasure. Phi Phi Leh is forbidden because it is the current filming location of a Leonardo

DiCaprio movie called *The Beach.* My sole mission on this dim night is to swim ashore and infiltrate the set.

I am not a gossip journalist, a Leo-obsessed film nut, or a paparazzo. I am a backpacker. The primary motivation for my mission is not an obsession with Hollywood, but simply a vague yearning for adventure. I wish I could put this yearning into more precise terms, but I can't. All I can say is that adventure is hard to come by these days.

Admittedly, I have a daunting task before me. In the wake of ongoing environmental protests, Leo's purported fear of terrorism, and the obligatory packs of screaming pubescent females, security on Phi Phi Leh has reached paramilitary proportions. Thus, I have given up on the notion of a frontal assault. Instead, I plan to swim ashore via Loh Samah Bay, change into dry khakis and a casual shirt, and — under cover of darkness — hike across the island to the filming location.

I'm not sure what will happen if I'm able to make it this far, but — summary execution excepted — I am prepared to cheerfully deal with whatever fate awaits me.

This attitude has much less to do with optimism than with the simple fact that, after one week of obsessive preparation, I don't really have a plan.

Day One: January 17 — DiCapritation

Thai Air flight 211 from Bangkok to Phuket has been taxiing around for the last twenty minutes, and there seems to be no end in sight. The European package tourists in the seats around me are getting fidgety, but this is only because they have not set foot on actual soil since Stockholm or Frankfurt. I, on the other hand, have been in Thailand for two weeks — and I've already faced the numbing horrors of Bangkok traffic. There, amid the creeping tangle of automobiles, buses, tuk-tuks, humidity, and fumes, one is left with two psychological options: nirvanic patience or homicidal insanity. Patience won out (barely) for me, and I am taking this present delay in stride.

In my lap sits a pile of notes and clippings about the movie production, most of it from Thai tabloid newspapers. Considering that culling hard facts from tabloid gossip is a challenge akin to discerning fate from sheep intestines, my mind frequently strays as I dig through the information.

I wonder, for instance, what would happen if Leonardo DiCaprio's teenage fans here were able to overwhelm his bodyguards. In every part of Asia I've visited, I've noticed how young girls act in the presence of their pop heroes, and it's somewhat unsettling. At one level, there is a screamy, swoony, Elvis-on-*Ed Sullivan* innocence to it all — but at a deeper level, I sense an intuitive desperation.

After all, not only is this part of Asia a survivalist bazaar society (where patiently standing in line is not part of the manners code), it also runs on a patriarchal system, where young girls simply have fewer options in life. If Leo's bodyguards ever fail him, I wouldn't be at all surprised by a frenzied display of grim, no-future pathos — a spectacle that, by comparison, would make punk-rock nihilism seem like a gentle tenet from the Sermon on the Mount. I keep getting this picture in my head of the handsome blond movie star being lovingly, worshipfully torn to pieces — of adolescent girls brawling over ragged bits of spleen and femur.

Several months before I came to Thailand, I read the Alex Garland novel on which the movie is based. In the story, a strange man presents the main character (a young English traveler named Richard) with a map that leads to an unspoiled beach utopia hidden in a national park in the Gulf of Thailand. The *Lord of the Flies*–style moral degeneration that results after Richard's arrival on the beach made for a thoroughly engrossing read.

After finishing the book, I toyed with the idea of emulating the plot — of finding some like-minded travelers, hiring a fishing boat into the restricted national park islands, and seeking out an unspoiled paradise. I ultimately discarded this notion, however, when I discovered that tabloid obsession with the film had already rendered my idea unoriginal.

When I arrived in Thailand and the tabloid hype still hadn't let up, a new idea struck me: Why not live *The Beach* in reverse? Instead of seeking out a secret, untouched island, why not explore the most scrutinized island in all of Thailand? Why not try washing ashore on the movie set itself?

The pure novelty of this notion has led to me this very point: seat

47K, Thai Air flight 211, which has now finally begun to accelerate down the runway. As the plane lifts off the ground and banks for its southward turn, a view of Bangkok fills my window.

Below, urban Thailand spans out around the Chao Phraya River in symmetrical brown-gray grids that, from this altitude, look like the outer armor from a 1970s sci-fi movie spaceship. For an instant, the earth looks artificial and foreign, as if it's been taken over by aliens.

The aliens, of course, are us.

Day Two: January 18 — The Hokeypokey

Although historically influenced by traders from China, Portugal, Malaysia, and India, the beach villages of Phuket island now seem to belong to northern Europe as much as anyplace. Western tourists abound, prices are steep, and miniature golf is readily available.

Since the cast and crew of *The Beach* sleep in Phuket, I came here with the intention of scouting out some information before I set off for Phi Phi Leh. Now that I've arrived, however, I'm a bit stumped on just how I'm supposed to scout out information. Mostly I've just been walking around and talking with other travelers, which is not much different from what I did on Khao San Road in Bangkok.

But talking with other wanderers is telling in and of itself, since nobody in the backpacker crowd wants to admit to even the slightest interest in DiCaprio or the filming of the movie. Instead, nearly everyone I've met talks about their own travels in wistful terms eerily similar to the characters in Garland's book. It would be difficult to characterize the nuances from each of my beachfront and street-café conversations this afternoon, but I can easily summarize:

Phuket, it is generally agreed, is a tourist shithole — best served for anthropological studies of fat German men who wear Speedos. For the ghost of Phuket past, try the islands of Malaysia or Cambodia. Laos, incidentally, is still charming and unspoiled, like rural Thailand in the eighties. The hill-tribe trekking around Sapa in Vietnam is as full of wonder and surprise as Chiang Mai treks were a decade ago. Goa and Koh Phangan still can't live up to their early nineties legacy; rumor crowns Central America the new cutting edge of rave. Sulawesi is, part and parcel, Bali ten years ago.

Granted, I have condensed what I heard — but for all the talk, you would think that paradise expired some time around 1989.

I am currently staying at the five-dollar-a-night On On Hotel in Phuket City, where a few interior scenes for *The Beach* will be shot in March. Since it is an official movie location, I had secretly hoped it would be brimming with an eccentric array of film groupies, security personnel, and rampaging Leo worshippers. Instead, the open-air lobby is filled with moths, mopeds, and old Thai men playing chess.

Earlier this evening, I spent a couple of hours here chatting and sipping Mekhong whiskey with Ann and Todd, a young couple from Maryland. Our conversation started when I heard Ann quoting a book review of *The Beach* from Phuket's English newspaper, which described backpack travelers as "uniformly ill-clad . . . all bearing Lonely Planet guidebooks and wandering from one shabby guest house to the next in search of banana pancakes, tawdry tie-dyes and other trash particularly their own." Since we agreed we prefer the Whitmanesque stereotype of backpack travel — pocketless of a dime, purchasing the pick of the earth and whatnot — this led to a discussion of what actually distinguishes backpack travelers from tourists.

On the surface, it's a simple distinction: tourists leave home to escape the world, while travelers leave home to experience the world. Tourists, Ann added wittily, are merely doing the hokeypokey: putting their right foot in and taking their right foot out; calling themselves world travelers while experiencing very little. Todd and I agreed that this was a brilliant analogy, but after a few more drinks we began to wonder where backpack travelers fit into the same paradigm. This proved to be a problem.

Do travelers, unlike tourists, keep their right foot in a little longer and shake it all about? Do travelers actually go so far as to do the hokeypokey and turn themselves around — thus gaining a more authentic experience?

Is that what it's all about?

The effects of alcohol pretty much eliminated serious reflection at the time, but now that my buzz is gone I can only conclude that the hokeypokey — whether done well or poorly — is still just the hokeypokey.

Or, to put it another way: Regardless of one's budget, itinerary, and choice of luggage — the act of travel is still, at its essence, a consumer experience.

Do we travel so that we can arrive where we started and know the place for the first time — or do we travel so that we can arrive where we started having earned the right to take T. S. Eliot out of context?

The fact that it's too late to know the difference makes my little mission to Phi Phi Leh less quirky than it sounds.

Day Three: January 19 — Lord of the Lies

Except for the fact that I met the producer of *The Beach* and some-how ended up stealing his Italian-leather screenplay binder, today hasn't been all that eventful. Mostly I've just been rereading Gar-land's novel. Tomorrow I leave for Phi Phi Don.

This morning's *Bangkok Post* featured a press statement from DiCaprio, who declared his love of Thailand, his affection for the Thai people, and his sincere concern for the local ecology.

The ecology comment comes on the heels of an environmental controversy that has been brewing since last fall, when 20th Cen-tury-Fox announced it was going to plant one hundred coconut palm trees on the Phi Phi Leh movie set. The reasoning, appar-ently, was that Phi Phi Leh didn't quite meet the Hollywood stan-dards of what an island in Thailand should look like.

The months following the coconut palm announcement have been fraught with protests, promises, legal action, threatened legal action, publicity stunts, and rumor. Thai environmental activists claimed the palms would disrupt the island's ecosystem; 20th Cen-tury-Fox responded by reducing the number of trees to sixty. When activists derided this as a meaningless gesture, 20th Century-Fox (perhaps misunderstanding the difference between ecology and landscape maintenance) paid a $138,000 damage deposit to the Thai Royal Forest Department and planted the trees anyway. Now environmentalists are claiming that producers flaunted their ear-lier compromise and brazenly planted no less than seventy-three trees at topsoil depths up to a meter deeper than had previously been agreed.

While the precise facts of this controversy would require a Warren Commission reunion, the fact remains that 20th Century-Fox's actions are a drop in the environmental bucket compared to the large-scale tourist development that has besieged southeast Asia's islands over the last decade.

Garland alludes to this phenomenon in his novel: "Set up in Bali, Koh Phangan, Koh Tao, Boracay, and the hordes are bound to follow. There's no way you can keep it out of the Lonely Planet, and once that happens, it's countdown to doomsday."

Countdown to doomsday. Kind of makes a person wonder if Garland was aware of the irony when he sold his novel's film rights to a media entity that makes Lonely Planet look like an obscure pamphlet publisher based out of the back of someone's Vanagon.

Protests aside, the real environmental impact of the filming won't be determined until after the movie appears in theaters and half a million starstruck teenagers in places like Nebraska and New Brunswick simultaneously decide that they, too, are going to buy a ticket to Thailand to seek out the last paradise on earth.

In a perfect world, I never would have had to sneak into the verandah of the Cape Panwha Resort Hotel and skulk around while the cast and crew of *The Beach* ate dinner.

Unfortunately, my more prosaic efforts at intelligence gathering (wandering around town, sending e-mails to friends of friends) had yielded little. Playing spy for a few hours was the only way to accurately gauge what I was up against.

Since I am the type of person who would rather hike eight extra miles than try to charm a park ranger into accepting a bribe, I was not filled with confidence as I took a motorcycle taxi out to Cape Panwha earlier this evening. I'd read on the Internet that the resort had hired extra security guards, and I was not looking forward to schmoozing my way past them.

Miraculously — despite my patchy beard, motorcycle-tossed hair, and sweat-salted backpacker attire — none of the hotel personnel gave me a second glance as I strolled past the reception desk and into the verandah area. I immediately spotted the cast sitting at a long table across from the restrooms. Leo was not among them, but I could tell from a glance that everyone there vaguely corresponded to various characters in the novel. Somebody in casting had done his job well.

Overcoming an innate, juvenile sense of dread, I moved to an empty table overlooking the swimming pool and ordered a Manhattan. I had never ordered a Manhattan before in my life — but since it cost more than my hotel room, I figured it probably contained lots of alcohol. I felt extremely out of place, and I needed something to calm my nerves.

I sipped my drink and tried to act aloof. It was easy to tell the film people from the other hotel guests. The movie folks ate and drank and laughed; everyone else peered around silently. I'm sure that half of the people there were waiting around on the off chance that Leo would walk through. I also suspect that — with the possible exception of a chubby little Japanese girl who kept standing up in her chair to gawk over at the cast — those exact same people would pretend not to notice if Leo actually showed up.

By the time Andrew MacDonald arrived and sat down at the table next to me, I'd washed my Manhattan down with a couple of Heinekens. My anxiety was mostly gone, and the only reason I hadn't sauntered over to schmooze with the cast was that it simply seemed like a stupid idea. Instead, I'd chosen the more conservative option of sitting around and doing nothing. I took the appearance of MacDonald — the film's producer — as a good sign.

Aside from DiCaprio, MacDonald was the only person from the movie that I could have recognized on sight. From one table away, he looked even younger and skinnier than he did in the newspaper photos. Sitting there — gangly, boyish, and pink-toed in his Birkenstocks — he looked like someone who was sullenly waiting to be picked last for a game of kickball.

Figuring it was the night's best chance, I feigned courage and walked up to him. "Excuse me," I said, "you're the producer, right?"

"I'm sorry, that's someone else you're thinking of," he replied, looking everywhere but at me.

"No," I told him, "you're Andrew MacDonald."

MacDonald seemed to cringe as he looked up at me. I wasn't sure if he always looks like this or if he expected me to sucker-punch him. Either way, I took it as my cue to keep talking.

I decided to take a neutral, vaguely journalistic approach. "I was wondering if I might interview some of your actors or spend some time on the set of your movie," I said to him. "Is that possible?"

"It's a closed set," he said wearily.

"What about the actors, do you mind if I chat with them a bit?"

"We're not allowing interviews."

"I don't necessarily want to talk to Leo; anyone will do."

MacDonald took out a pen and wrote a phone number down on a napkin. "This is the number for Sarah Clark. She's a publicist. You'll have to go through her if you want to do any interviews. But at most you'll probably just get an interview with me." He didn't look too thrilled by this possibility.

"So are you saying that there's no chance I can get onto the set, even if I swim there?" I said this as a kind of half joke, hoping it might scare up some clues on how to get past the security cordon around Phi Phi Leh.

"No chance on the island. You can apply as an extra, but that won't be until next month in Phuket and Krabi."

"I was once an extra in a movie called *Dr. Giggles,* but that was like seven years ago."

This utterly irrelevant trivia nugget seemed to disarm MacDonald a bit. *"Dr. Giggles?"* he said, smirking.

"Yeah, are you familiar with it?"

"No, I'm not. Sorry." He stared off at the pool, sighed, then absently checked his watch. "It's been a long day," he said, almost apologetically.

I didn't bother him when he stood up to go.

The events that transpired as I tried to leave the verandah make so little sense that they are somewhat difficult to recount.

First, I had a problem paying my bill, since the hotel staff assumed that I was with the movie crew. When I asked the waitress for my check, she just frowned and walked off. When she hadn't returned after ten minutes, I tracked her down to the cash register.

"I need to pay my bill," I told her. I figured it would be bad manners to sponge drinks after having already interrupted the producer's dinner.

The waitress gave me another strange look, then pushed a piece of paper in front of me. "Just write your room number," she said.

"Can I pay now in cash?" I'm not sure why I was being so insistently ethical; one Manhattan and two Heinekens pale in the face of a forty-million-dollar film budget.

The waitress shrugged, and I gave her the money. I turned to leave, and as I was passing the reception desk, the waitress came running after me.

"Your friend forgot this," she said, handing me a yellow cloth satchel.

Standing there in the lobby of the Cape Panwha Resort Hotel, the word "friend" caught me off-guard. I couldn't possibly imagine who she was talking about.

I opened the cloth satchel and took out a black Il Bisonte binder. Embossed into the leather cover were the words THE BEACH. And in the lower right-hand corner: ANDREW MACDONALD.

Putting the binder back into the satchel, I thanked the waitress and — just moments after my valorous display of Sunday school ethics over the drink tab — walked out the front door.

I spent the motorcycle taxi ride back into Phuket City trying to think of practical justifications for making off with Andrew Mac-Donald's screenplay binder. Since the binder was empty, I couldn't really think of any beyond using it as a kind of Hail Mary collateral if things got ugly when I invaded the film set.

Considering that the phone number MacDonald gave me turned out to belong to a confused Thai family in Yala province, the personally embossed keepsake was the closest thing I had to an asset.

Sitting in my hotel, I imagine myself on the shores of Phi Phi Leh, lashed to one of the illegally planted coconut palms and bleeding from the ears: I am being flogged with rubber hoses by a gang of vigilante set designers, dolly grips, and script supervisors. For the sake of reverie, they are all female, vixenlike, and dressed in bikinis.

MacDonald swaggers over. He is wielding a scimitar and has somehow managed to grow a pencil-thin mustache in the time since I last saw him.

"Closed set!" he bellows, fiercely raising the blade above his head.

About to lose consciousness, I muster one last ounce of energy. "I have your personally embossed Il Bisonte Italian leather screenplay binder, MacDonald," I sneer. "Kill me, and you'll never find out where I've hidden it."

A look of horror washes across the producer's face. "Not my personally embossed Il Bisonte Italian leather screenplay binder!" he screams, dropping the scimitar to the sand.

With a sudden look of resolve, he turns to the bikini-clad lynch mob. "Untie the intruder," he commands, "and tell that DiCaprio schmuck that his services are no longer needed." He turns back to me with a flourish. "I think we've found our new leading man."

A bit overdone, as reveries go — but I'll just blame that on the movies.

They seem to make a convenient scapegoat.

Day Five: January 21 — Heart of Dorkness

I'm starting in on my second day on Phi Phi Don island, but (for reasons that will become obvious) I didn't write anything yesterday — day four — so I'll try to cover both days in this dispatch.

To put it succinctly: things have gone sour in a way that I had not expected.

From a tactical standpoint, my mission is progressing nicely. The soaring cliffs of Phi Phi Leh stand just two and a half miles across the sea from my roost on Long Beach. A few casual conversations with some Phi Phi Leh dive-tour operators have provided enough physiographical clues for me to devise a landing strategy. I even found a deserted beach (Lomudi) where I can make a quiet departure in the dead of night.

The problem, however, is that I'm having trouble explaining why I want to go there in the first place.

I arrived here yesterday morning to discover that all the affordable lodging on Long Beach had been sold out. Welcoming the ascetic novelty of sleeping on the beach itself, I left my backpack with a friendly restaurant manager and set off to scope things out.

Technically, the island of Phi Phi Don is part of the same National Marine Park system that protects Phi Phi Leh from permanent tourist development. A person could never tell by looking, however, as an unbroken progression of bungalows and beach resorts lines the entire southeastern seaboard. Ton Sai — an old Thai-Muslim village on the isthmus that connects the two halves of the island — is clotted with luxury hotels, dive shops, restaurants, souvenir peddlers, and discos. The only evidence of Muslim heritage is that some of the women selling cigarettes and Pringles wear veils.

When I met a Danish pair on the longtail taxi-boat from Ton Sai back to Long Beach, I was immediately struck by their similarity to a couple of characters in *The Beach*. In Alex Garland's novel (and, I am certain, in the movie script), Richard travels to the beach utopia in the company of Etienne and Françoise, a young French couple he meets on Khao San Road. Granted, Jan and Maarta aren't French, but they certainly seemed graceful, companionable, and adventurous enough to merit a comparison. When I discovered that they, too, were being forced to sleep on the beach that night, I took this as a sign that I should invite them along for my adventure.

I pitched the idea over a pad-thai dinner on Long Beach. Since they were both familiar with the novel, I skipped straight into my plans to rent a boat and steal over to Phi Phi Leh. When I saw how this idea entertained them, I backtracked a bit and told them about my experience with Andrew MacDonald the day before. By the time I got to my fantasy about the bikini-clad lynch mob, I had the Danes in stitches.

"You Americans have wonderful thoughts," Jan said between gasps for air.

I saw this as my chance. "Why don't you two join me?"

"Yes," Jan said, still laughing, "why don't we join you?"

"Perfect," I said. "This is too perfect. Let's find a boat and leave tonight."

The Danes stopped laughing. "Are you serious?" Maarta asked.

"I am one-hundred percent completely serious. Let's leave tonight."

"But we thought you were telling, kind of, a joke."

This threw me a little. "Would you rather leave tomorrow?"

Jan and Maarta exchanged a raised-eyebrow look, which I took to mean either "This guy is really daring" or "This guy is a total dork." Judging from the exchange that ensued, I'd put money on the latter.

"If you really want to go to the movie," Jan said, "why don't you just wait until they finish on Phi Phi Leh and go to work as an extra when they film in Phuket or Krabi?"

"That's not the point," I insisted. "The adventure is in going to a place where you aren't supposed to go. The charm is in living the novel backwards — going to an exclusive and secretive beach that also happens to be famous."

"The island is guarded like an army," Maarta said. "You'll never make it."

"Even if you do," Jan said, "what will you do when you get there?"

By this point, I felt like whipping out the novel and showing Jan and Maarta that they were saying the wrong lines. The issue was getting unnecessarily complicated. In the story, Françoise and Etienne were much more agreeable.

"I don't know what I'll do when I get there," I said. "Walk onto the set, I guess. You know, see what happens when I violate their community. Like in the book."

Jan and Maarta conferred for a moment in Danish, then turned back to me.

"Why are you doing this?" Maarta asked, with a tone of concern.

Since I thought I'd already answered that question, all I could do was stammer. Ultimately I changed the subject — to the relief, I think, of everyone present.

In my own mind the reason why I'm doing this should have been obvious.

Or, even more accurately, the reason why I'm doing this should be irrelevant.

Now that I've had time to think about it, I'd say the motivation behind my mission has a lot to do with a kind of traveler's angst. I know I'm not the only one who feels it.

In his 1975 essay "The Loss of the Creature," Walker Percy attributes traveler's angst to the idea that our various destinations have been "appropriated by the symbolic complex which has already formed in the sightseer's mind."

In other words, the angst originates not in watching fat, Speedo-wearing German men defile once-pristine beaches — the angst comes from our own media-driven notions of how those beaches should be in the first place. We cannot hike the Himalayas without drawing comparisons to the IMAX film we saw last summer; we cannot taste wine on the Seine without recalling a funny scene from an old Meg Ryan movie; we cannot get lost in a South American jungle without thinking of the Gabriel García Márquez novel we read in college. It is the expectation itself that robs a bit of authenticity from the destinations we seek out.

Even the unexpected comes with its own set of expectations: in Garland's novel, Richard interprets what he sees at his beach utopia through the language of the Vietnam War movies he saw as a teenager.

Percy attempts to explain this phenomenon in his essay. "The highest point," he writes, "the term of the sightseer's satisfaction, is not the sovereign discovery of the thing before him; it is rather the measuring up of the thing to the criterion of the pre-formed symbolic complex."

The challenge this poses for the discerning traveler is that — here at the cusp of the next millennium — mass media has not only monopolized the symbolic complex of wonder and beauty, it has recently upped the ante by an extra seventy-three coconut palm trees.

Thus, by storming *The Beach* at Phi Phi Leh, I hope to travel behind the curtain, to break out from the confines of the consumer experience by attempting to break into the creation of the consumer experience.

In this way, I guess I could say that my mission is part of a greater struggle for individuality in the information age — an attempt to live outside the realm of who I'm supposed to be.

At least, that's what I would have told the Danes yesterday, had I had my wits about me.

Today I successfully managed to avoid the Danes entirely. After sneaking a shower at a poolside changing room in Ton Sai, I set off to find a boat that would take me to Phi Phi Leh. Since stealth is an important consideration in my mission, choosing the right boat was a painfully difficult process.

Actually, choosing a boat wasn't really a choice at all, since my only realistic option was to hire out one of the longtail boats that transport people and goods among the islands. Considering that these boats cut through the water as gracefully as bulldozers (none of them have mufflers), my only real option was in finding a driver who sympathized with my cause and wouldn't try to cheat me.

Just before dinner, I found a seemingly earnest boat driver who agreed to take me to Phi Phi Leh for 2,500 baht. We leave in a few hours.

It is already well after dark, and I have stashed my backpack under one of the old fishing huts here at Lomudi. In addition to dry clothes, I have sealed my passport and a few traveler's checks into my plastic swimming bag.

Andrew MacDonald's Italian leather screenplay binder, I'm afraid, was too heavy and will have to stay behind.

I pace the shoreline, killing time before the arrival of the longtail boat. Tiny bits of phosphorescence glow, star blue, at the edge of the waves, just as they do in the book.

Day Six: January 22 — Storming The Beach *at Phi Phi Leh, Continued*

It occurs to me that I don't know the name of the small, sun-browned Thai man who sits astern from me in the darkness. I hate to write him off as a minor character — "Boat Driver Number One" — so I have been thinking of him as "Jimmy." He just seems like someone who should be named Jimmy: trustworthy, average, unassuming. Even in the dark, he wears a wide-brimmed cloth cap.

Neither of us has spoken since I waded out and climbed into the longtail back at Lomudi. Both of us know we are breaking the law — that Phi Phi Leh is patrolled by police speedboats for the duration of the movie shoot. I am hoping that our drop-off site at Loh Samah Bay (instead of Maya Bay, where the film set is located) isn't patrolled very closely at three-thirty in the morning.

Unlike most of the longtail operators I met in Ton Sai, Jimmy is a quiet, introspective man. When we were negotiating the trip yesterday afternoon, he nodded silently as I took out a dive-shop map of Phi Phi Leh and told him where I wanted to go. At first I thought he couldn't speak any English, but he cut me short when I tried to use my Thai phrase book on him. "Three in the morning, Okay," he'd said. "I know Loh Samah Bay." I suspect he is working to support a wife and kids somewhere.

Twenty-five hundred baht — about $70 — is no small sum, but I have written it off as an inevitability. Edmund Hillary had to hire Sherpas; I had to hire Jimmy. Perhaps in an effort to accommodate me — or, just as likely, in an effort to conceal me — Jimmy has spread a rattan mat out on the ribbed wooden floor of the boat. Lying on the mat, clutching my plastic bag, all I can see is the bright wash of stars above me. Oddly, the thumping rattle of the outboard motor somehow makes the stars seem closer, as if they are a glittering kind of music video that hovers just over the boat.

My thoughts drift as the boat pushes through the water. I think about my first week in Thailand, when I was quick-dosing on an antimalaria drug called Lariam. Mild psychosis is a side effect of the drug, and — sure enough — on my second day of taking the pills I punched my fist through the door of my hotel room on Khao San Road. It was certainly one of the more violent acts of my adult life, and to this day I have trouble making sense of it. I don't know why I did it; all I remember was how I felt in the moments before security arrived to kick me out of the hotel. It was not a feeling of dread or shock, as one might expect, but rather a bemused, incongruent sense of wonder. Certainly Leonardo DiCaprio must feel the same way each morning when he wakes up and walks into a world that is staring at him.

"What the hell," I remember thinking to myself, "has happened to me?"

After about twenty minutes, Jimmy suddenly cuts the outboard motor. The silence leaves my ears ringing. I sit up on the mat uncertainly.

"Are we there?" I whisper. The boat rocks as Jimmy crawls up to join me on the mat. He pushes his face right up in front of mine, and I see that he is holding his finger to his lips. He rests a hand on my shoulder and peers past the bow into the darkness.

We sit this way for about ten minutes. Strangely, I am not nearly as nervous as I was on the verandah of the Cape Panwha Resort Hotel. Swimming and hiking are tangible activities — far more cut-and-dried than schmoozing and coaxing information.

But swimming and hiking are not the only obstacles that remain: Jimmy curses softly and moves back to the stern of the longtail. Only then do I hear it — the sound of an approaching speedboat. Before long, our wooden boat is awash in the beam of a spotlight. I try to hide myself under the rattan mat, but it's a useless gesture.

Embarrassed more than anything, I lie awkwardly in the bottom of the longtail while Jimmy and someone on the speedboat yell back and forth in Thai. I absently note that the sealing oil on the hull boards has a pleasant, cedary scent.

Surprisingly, Jimmy yells in his apologetic tone for only a couple of minutes before the speedboat cuts its spotlight and leaves.

"Okay," Jimmy says.

"It's okay?" I say, looking out from my hiding place.

"Okay," Jimmy says.

I crawl out and move to the stern next to Jimmy. He rests his hand on my shoulder. "Okay?" he says for the third time. I give him the thumbs up; he starts up the outboard and turns our boat 180 degrees. It's a couple of beats before I realize that we are headed back for Phi Phi Don.

"Isn't this where we just came from?" I ask, pointing my finger ahead into the darkness.

"Okay!" Jimmy says.

It takes me a good five minutes before I can undo the knot on my plastic swim bag. I'm not particularly proud of what I'm about to do, but I feel like I've come too far to give up now.

I crawl back over to Jimmy and I shove the traveler's checks underneath his nose. "Baksheesh," I say, gesturing back at where we last saw the speedboat. Actually, I'm not even sure if "baksheesh" is the correct word for "bribe" in this part of the world. I feel a little doltish as I say it, like I'm trying to speak Spanish by throwing out English phrases in a Speedy Gonzalez voice.

Jimmy puts his hand on my shoulder in what I now take as a wizened parental gesture. He looks down sympathetically at my traveler's checks. "Boat man, okay," he says. "Eye-land man, maybe okay. Movie man: no. Movie man not okay." He gently pushes my checks away.

"Yes! Okay!" I say, still waving the traveler's checks, but he just shakes his head.

The very trustworthiness that led me to hire Jimmy is now backfiring on me. Jimmy knows that, even if I manage to bribe my way past the various levels of Thai security on the island, a film crew with a forty-million-dollar budget will be less than impressed with my presence. Jimmy is simply trying to save me the money and stress of going through this whole ordeal.

I'm at a loss to convince him how that very ordeal is exactly what I want to experience.

Which Speedy Gonzalez catchphrases could make Jimmy grasp the pitch and moment that drive this enterprise? What can I say that will make Jimmy appreciate the intricate, shadowlike ironies of travel culture? How can Jimmy come to understand a moral world where it's somehow vital to avoid eating at McDonald's in Manila, virtuous to intentionally bypass the *Mona Lisa* while at the Louvre, and noble to sleep in a ditch in Africa?

How can I convince him that this "mission" is not merely another variation of the hokeypokey?

My tongue is ineffectual in its pivots; Phi Phi Leh recedes in the darkness behind us.

We go through strange rituals to prove things to ourselves in life.

As we near our trash-encrusted starting point, I insist that Jimmy cut the engine early, so I can jump out of the longtail and swim the last two hundred meters back to the abandoned fishing village.

Since simple epiphany doesn't screen well in the test markets, I will tell people that I swam those two hundred meters with a defiant sense of triumph. I will tell them that each small step wading ashore was a giant leap for mankind.

I will tell them that I walked through the Valley of the Shadow of Death, and that I feared no evil — for the Valley of the Shadow of Death will soon feature guided tours and a snack bar.

MARK ROSS

The Last Safari

FROM *Talk*

I can hardly remember a time when I wasn't in Africa's thrall. As a boy I lived on a wildlife refuge along the east bank of the Mississippi. Behind my family's house there was a big rock; my little brother Colin and I would sit on top of it, imagining that it was a Land Rover on the African plains. We'd bump along for a minute or two and then leap off. One of us, the designated ranger, would wrestle the other, the wildebeest, to the ground and give him an injection to stop the spread of some rampant disease. I had my own airplane, too. There was a mudbank in the woods nearby; I'd scratch dials, instruments, and levers into the dirt and fly all over my imaginary homeland. Then, when it was too dark to play outside, I'd disappear into books like The Lost World of the Kalahari, *a chronicle of the search for the Bushmen, the oldest aboriginal tribe in Africa.*

Conversation was rare in our house. So was sympathy. "Bleed outside," my mother used to say when I came home all scraped up from climbing trees. In the summers our family would head out to Wyoming or Washington for mountaineering expeditions that lasted anywhere from thirty-five to seventy days. It beat being around the house.

I finally made it to Africa in the fall of 1977 as a student. It was everything I'd imagined. One of my professors gave me the keys to his jeep, and I spent a day in the bush. Back then the parks were wide open and more or less free of visitors. You didn't even have to look for wildlife — it was all around you. I had read in a book that elephants could run twenty miles an hour, so I raced one. The book was wrong. My speedometer was showing 25 when the elephant caught up to me and smashed the back of the jeep. I flew home to Illinois a couple of weeks later to finish my degree, but I knew I'd be back.

In 1980 I moved to Africa and took a job as a teacher. Five years later, just before I switched to leading safaris full-time, I got an assignment from the New York Times. *They needed a photographer, one who spoke Kiswahili and knew how to get around in Africa, to accompany a group of reporters into Uganda, where a civil war was raging. At the time, you couldn't get into Uganda without an invitation from one of the country's warring generals, so we forged one and it got us across the border. Then, three hours after we arrived in Kampala, the capital, I was hauled away, tied up, and interrogated by an officer serving under one of the generals, Tito Okello. I lied and told him our team was in Uganda because we'd heard that certain atrocities that had been blamed on Okello weren't actually his fault. The general bought it and wrote us a free pass to go wherever we wanted. For weeks we roamed around Uganda chasing stories. We were never hassled again.*

This was my land.

March 1, 1999

It's early morning and I'm lying alone in my tent in the pleasantly cool darkness on the edge of the Bwindi Impenetrable Forest. The sun rises later here in southwestern Uganda than in Nairobi, where I live, and I relish the extra time before dawn, listening to the various sounds of the forest. After twenty-two years of leading safaris, I've learned to start paying attention early, before daybreak, when unusual noises stand out. A lion's roar or bushbuck's yelp can tell me where to find the animals later on. I'm also listening for my clients, two couples from Portland, Oregon, who are camped down the hill. Birds and the occasional rustling of the croton and olive trees. That's all I hear.

We're in one of five camps set up on the grounds of a sprawling national park situated near Uganda's border with the Congo. In addition to my group of four, there are some thirty other tourists camped in the park, all of them here to see a rare breed of mountain gorilla found only in this part of Africa. I assume that my clients are still asleep. Most tourists need a lot of rest on safari, particularly at this altitude. We are 4,500 feet above sea level, and they've had only two days to acclimate.

Rob Haubner and Susan Miller are in the tent closest to mine. They are Intel executives in their forties, and they've traveled with me twice before. Both are real wildlife lovers: they were married in the Portland Zoo and spent their honeymoon in the Maasai Mara, where I took them on their first safari. Susan's game for just about anything. Last night we asked some local women to do Ugandan dances for the visitors, and she moved along as if she'd known the steps since high school. Rob is more inclined to sit on the sidelines, but Susan gets him to push his limits. On our last trip he even joined in when I got into a wrestling match with a twelve-foot-long python.

The other couple, Susan Studd and Bob McLaurin, are roughly the same age as Rob and Susan, and they also work at Intel. I met them in 1998, when the Haubner-Millers brought them along for a trip into Kenya and Tanzania. Heavy rains put a damper on that safari, and Bob and Susan convinced the Haubner-Millers, who'd spent sixteen months planning the trip, to pack it in early. I was surprised and pleased to hear that Susan and Bob wanted to come back; they hadn't struck me as repeaters. They are sleeping farther down the hill.

It's well after 6 A.M. — time to get out of my tent. My coffee tray has already been delivered, and I eat a biscuit and watch dawn break. Then I hear a strange noise.

It sounds at first like a tree falling and crashing into other trees, snapping off branches as it pitches forward. But there's no final thud, just more cracking, Suddenly I realize that I am hearing gunfire, and repeated volleys, not a poacher's lone shot. My body tenses. The gunfire continues, flaring up, then fading. Determined to find out what's going on, I start down the hill toward the camp's central lawn, aware that I'm heading toward the shooting when maybe I should be running away from it. On the way I pass Rob, who is half dressed, standing by his tent. "Stay put and get under cover and I'll get back to you!" I shout.

Near the bottom of the hill a small-framed black man with a rifle appears in silhouette about thirty yards in front of me. His gun flashes and a bullet rips through the leaves to my left. I raise my arms and slow to a fast walk — I want to get close to him quickly to show him that I'm a tourist, harmless and unarmed. As I draw nearer I see that he is about twenty and is wearing gumboots and a fatigue jacket. Our eyes meet briefly and he motions for me to pass, but as soon as I do he hits me in the back of the head with the barrel of his rifle. I sway, my knees buckling. Then he digs into my pockets for money and tears off my watch. With his gun at my back he pushes me the rest of the way to the main camp.

As we near the central lawn I see maybe half a dozen heavily armed men surrounding a gray-haired American woman who joined us on a gorilla trek the day before. Her name is Linda Adams. She's in her fifties and was exhausted during the hike, wheezing and gasping for air. Now she looks worse, white-faced and terrified.

I am pushed toward her, my head throbbing, but before I can get my bearings, a man carrying both a machete and a machine gun grabs me. I see fear on Linda's face as he rips off my belt, along with the Buck knife I have hanging from it.

When I recover my balance, I count about ten men surrounding us, all of them dressed in random combinations of wildly patterned clothing. They're all armed, but they look like a ragtag group, with no obvious leader. I take them for thieves.

There are of course rebel armies in various parts of East and Central Africa: the Lord's Resistance Army operates to the north of Bwindi, and the notorious Interahamwe — the extremist Hum group responsible for the slaughter of more than 800,000 people in Rwanda and Burundi in 1994 — has a faction to the west. *Interahamwe,* translated from Kinyarwanda, means "those who strike together," and the group's members are known for their expertise with machetes. During the Rwandan genocide, they would often disable their enemies by severing their hamstrings or Achilles tendons. They'd leave their victims to suffer, then return to kill them hours later.

But southwest Uganda isn't the territory of the LRA or the Interahamwe. And besides, in all my years on safari I have never encountered rebels in the bush.

For a while Linda and I seem to be the only focus of our attackers' attention, but then I see Rob Haubner and Susan Miller being escorted down from their tent. They are shoved toward us and sit on the ground with Linda and me, too scared to speak. Susan gasps for air, while Rob strokes her head. I try to calm them down, reassuring them that the men will probably leave once they clean us out.

But soon there are more armed men around us. They seem to be pouring in from the road below, herding in tourists from surrounding sites. A gang of them leads a group of about twenty dazed-looking college-age kids toward us, some still in nightclothes. The lawn is now crowded, with forty or so armed men milling about and maybe twenty-five tourists. It reminds me of a refugee camp, and I can't help but reevaluate. There are too many of these men for them to be a team of bandits. I take a closer look at their weapons. Two of them have old-fashioned bolt-action rifles, but most are carrying AK-47's or other automatics. One in three has a machete dangling from his belt loop. It's starting to look like they may be the Interahamwe.

A small group of them starts interrogating us in broken English. "Where from?" they shout. "Where from?" They are uncomfortably close, their faces almost touching ours, their weapons bumping our bodies. I reply in Kiswahili that I was born in America but have been living in Kenya for years. They are surprised that I know their language, and I tell them that I teach science in a small village in Kenya, which I did, only many years ago.

As the barrage of questions continues, other rebels emerge from surrounding tents loaded down with loot: radios, cartons of food, clothes, a computer — anything they can carry. They look like people fleeing a house fire. One guy walks by wearing Rob's dark blue jacket. Another has a familiar tan backpack slung over his shoulder. It's Bob McLaurin's.

But there's still no sign of Bob or his wife, Susan. I crane around to look toward their tent, now out of sight up the hill. One of the men sees me looking back and asks how many we are. I tell him that we are just three.

After several minutes of waiting tensely in the chilly morning air our captors order us to stand. I'm shoved into a line with ten or fifteen others. Apparently some of us are going to stay, while the rest — including me — will be forced to leave with the rebels. Rob, Susan, and Linda are nearby, but it's hard to tell who else. A French-speaking woman who says she's Swiss is thrust in with us. Still no sign of Bob and Susan. I haven't heard any more gunfire, but what if they've been clubbed to death in their tent?

My group is ordered to walk. As we begin to move, I decide that I might as well tell Rob, Susan, and Linda what I now suspect: that the rebels are probably planning to bring a few of us with them to ensure a safe escape from Uganda after they rob the camp.

Our captors must know that the Ugandan police, stationed about twenty miles away, will hear about the attack and come up to the camp to investigate. The rebels' best shot at preventing a firefight will be to take hostages.

We are forced single file down a series of steps connecting the camp to the main dirt road that runs the three-hundred–plus miles from Bwindi all the way to Kampala. Rob and Susan are barefoot — the rebels have taken their shoes.

Once we're out on the road, the rebels begin to haze us — blaring music from boom boxes they've stolen, smashing bottles at our feet, and throwing fake punches at the men. I count fourteen of us and some sixty-five of them, mostly healthy, muscular men in their twenties. One of them pretends to knee the guy to my right in the groin. When the hostage, a stocky New Zealander named Mark Avis, doubles over to avoid the blow, the rebels howl.

The man who pretended to knee Avis is maybe twenty-five and squat, with a pointy, triangular face. He's wearing an unzipped pink windbreaker and has one of those loud laughs that get under your skin. He's not carrying a rifle — just a sidearm — but he's brandishing a stick and appears to be one of the leaders. When he pretends to hit me I manage not to flinch, and stare back at him. He lifts up his stick and smashes me across the face. I rock back, but remain upright, my eyes watering.

Soon they move on to other humiliations, forcing us at gunpoint to dance to singsong African music. I never dance and am not about to make an exception. The rebels overlook me, but they continue to goad and prod the others, joining in as if to show how it's done. They took ridiculous: awkward clowns moving gracelessly under their AK-47's.

Overall, the taunting lasts about ten minutes; it ends only when one of the rebels orders us to head up the road toward the Impenetrable Forest. We walk about a hundred yards along the main road before turning onto a grass trail that leads precipitously up toward the Congo border, which I suspect must be our destination. Huge trees rise around us on steep valley walls, their tops still patchy with mist. I've been here several times before, to visit a family of gorillas, so I know we have a hard trail ahead. I buckle down to the task of walking — breathing steadily, resting briefly between steps, holding my arms loose and low, conserving my strength.

The path is narrow, only a meter or so wide, and it snakes steeply up the imposing hill. The rebels are spaced between the tourists, and because there are perhaps five feet between each person and the next, the single-file line seems to stretch endlessly in both directions. Early on, Linda falls behind and I lose sight of her, but I make sure that Rob and Susan stay close to me. I'm worried about them. If we are indeed headed for the Congo, they'll be on this rough terrain, barefoot, for several grueling hours — enough to exhaust even an experienced trekker.

But there are even more pressing things to worry about. I notice some semiautomatics among the assault rifles, and catch sight of two hand grenades, one the classic pineapple type and the other a smooth bronze case with a seam running around it. The pineapple grenade's pin is held in precariously by an old piece of black inner tube.

We continue to walk in the low morning light. Under the canopy of the forest it's still quite cool, even cold. But in some places the equatorial sun breaks through, making us hot and sweaty. The rebels haven't given us any water.

Periodically the whole line comes to an abrupt halt, which gives me a chance to check on Susan and Rob. As I feared, they are both in bad shape. Susan is having a hard time breathing, and she crumples into my left shoulder, her eyes closed, whenever we stop. Again and again I catch her and lower her to the ground, standing behind her so she can lean back on my legs. Rob seems almost catatonic, barely able to focus. There's no chance that he'll be able to help me support or even encourage his wife. He seems completely unaware of her.

How brutally hard this must be for them, and Susan in particular. She retired from Intel just one day before the trip, and she must have spent her last weeks at the company frantically tying up loose ends. She worked hard, traveled often, and was always on the run. I don't have the heart to tell her that we'll probably have to hike at least as far as the Congo border, which is still a good four miles away, and that our usefulness to the rebels will probably end where the two countries meet. I also don't mention that by now I'm all but certain who our captors are — and that they're not known for acts of decency.

I'm still aching from the blows I suffered earlier, and the trail is getting steadily steeper. We stop often, sometimes for so long that it baffles me. During one break maybe an hour into the trip, I notice that Linda isn't with us anymore. I ask a few of the rebels where she's gone. From what I'm able to understand, she was allowed to go back down to camp because she has asthma.

Hearing that news starts me thinking about how to get Susan released. She's walking more sluggishly than ever, and every few steps she bends over at the waist, her eyes shut tight, barely able to stay on her feet. I tell a nearby rebel in Kiswahili that Susan has a heart condition and ask that she be allowed to return to camp. He looks at me skeptically but moves ahead to the front of the line. He comes back with good news.

"She'll be able to return," he says, stone-faced.

"I'm grateful," I reply. "She doesn't need an escort. She knows her way down." The idea of Susan walking back alone bothers me, but it troubles me less than the thought of her with one or more of these men.

Rob drops back in the line about fifteen places, and I watch him say good-bye to Susan. Their faces are blank. They don't hug or even hold hands. Then Susan steps off the trail and we go on. I can't tell whether she's going to be accompanied down or not.

We continue up the same trail, but it's getting narrower, rockier, and more overgrown. For those who were forced to give up their shoes, it must be especially difficult to negotiate.

We stop again. As we catch our breath, one of the rebels comes toward me carrying a laptop computer. He wants help starting it, but the battery is low and I can't get it going. Other stolen items are brought forward for explanation.

"*Hii ni nini, ni dawa, chakula, au mchezo?*" "What is this thing — is it medicine, food, or a game?" And so it goes for various kinds of medicine, lotions, makeup. The rebels' questions seem to relax some of the hostages — one man volunteers his computer expertise, others offer to give demonstrations — but the discussions irritate me. I want our captors to get to the goddamn point already and tell us what's in store.

The line of people ahead of me starts moving again, and we trudge on. I notice Rob, marching along with heavy steps, his head hanging down, arms swinging in useless, shallow arcs. I have to at least try to get him released.

So far I've noticed two commanders — the pointy-faced man who clubbed me on the road and another with a curly black beard.

But when I press a nearby rebel about Rob, a third man is brought down. His appearance is surprising: he's light-complexioned, about thirty-five, and wears a pressed long-sleeved blue shirt and belted, well-fitting pants. Like the others he's wearing gumboots, but his trouser legs are tucked neatly inside them. He must be a member of the Kikuyu, a prosperous tribe from Kenya. I also notice that he's wearing my watch.

I explain that Rob needs to go back to take care of his wife. He has to give her some medicine, I lie.

The Kikuyu goes back up the trail toward the head of the line, and soon another rebel returns with the answer: No.

Rob is watching from behind me, and I suspect he knows he is being discussed. Not wanting to worry him, I sneak him a thumbs-up. We continue on.

The trail steepens another notch. The trees up here are shorter, and butterflies the size of small birds flutter overhead. The morning mist has disappeared, and the sun is almost directly overhead, beating down on us as we walk silently, heads down. I catch sight of someone's watch: ten-thirty A.M. We've been climbing for three and a half hours.

About halfway up an incline I hear a woman's voice behind me. She's speaking to one of the rebels in French, and from what I can understand she wants to relieve herself. I look back. It's the Swiss woman. She's young — just over twenty — and vigorous and alert, all things considered. After a brief discussion, she leaves the trail with one of the rebels. I stop cold. Wet your pants or pee in front of us, I think, but don't give these guys an excuse to get you alone. In addition to being proficient with machetes, the Interahamwe are known as savage rapists. I'm sure that we are about to witness something horrific, and I feel helpless to prevent it.

A few long minutes pass. My mind races. I wonder whether I can wrest a rifle away from one of the rebels and take my own hostage. Then I hear a rustling: It's the Swiss woman reemerging. She looks all right. But my relief turns again to concern when I hear her and her escort engaged in what sounds like a casual conversation. No doubt she thinks that becoming friendly with our captors will improve our situation. I fear that nothing could be further from the truth.

We march on. The rebels don't seem to have a plan: sometimes they behave like thugs, but at other moments they seem to follow strict rules of conduct. What are they up to? Again we stop. Several minutes pass. We wait in silence. More time passes. What's going on? I glance at a rebels watch: it's eleven-thirty.

Suddenly, without any explanation, we are ordered to turn around and march back down.

As I start to head back, I come across Rob sitting directly in the path. Determined to keep him with me, I reach down and begin to pull him up by his upper arm, but a rebel steps in front of me and slams me in the stomach with his rifle butt. Just before I fall onto Rob, the rebel catches me, pulls me upright, and pushes me forward. I stumble about fifty feet before I am able to straighten up enough to look back at my friend, who is now surrounded by rebels. He's being kept behind. I look back in panic: he is sitting like a child, his legs drawn up, his arms wrapped around them, looking at me.

Whenever the trail opens up a bit and offers a view, I look back up the hill, hoping that I will catch sight of him. But I've lost him.

We continue to backtrack for maybe ten or fifteen minutes, then our captors turn right and start bushwhacking across a steep, slippery incline. We're now heading directly toward the Congo. The single-file order quickly breaks down on this new terrain, and I'm able to take stock of our group. The results are alarming: Just six of us are left now, out of the original sixteen. Have the others gone down ahead of us? Were some kept behind with Rob? Or are the rebels simply having their way with whomever they choose as I march on, oblivious?

I decide that the remaining hostages must stick together and so I introduce myself to the two captives nearest to me and manage to get their names. All of us are walking together now, flanked by the rebels. We speak in English, whispering, so as not to call attention to ourselves.

Michael Baker, the tall Australian who offered to help with the computer, is soft-spoken but clear-headed, and remarkably agile in bare feet. Mark Avis, the stocky fellow who was the favored target of the rebels' hazing, is awkward; he stumbles often and is prone to falling behind. (I learn later that the rebels stole his glasses.) His wife, Rhonda, is one of the people who started on the march but disappeared along the way.

Danja Walther, the Swiss woman, is athletic-looking and has a sweet face and short hair. (I eventually discover that she's a Swissair flight attendant who came to Africa to recover from another shock: six months ago she was on standby for Swissair flight 1 1 1 from New York to Zurich, which crashed off Nova Scotia, killing several of her close friends.) Danja sometimes stumbles, but she's able to keep up. She stays close to a guy named Gary Tappenden, a slight man with bleached hair and earrings. At the back is a Canadian, Mitch Keifer, who looks scholarly and has a quiet, careful manner. He too keeps falling back.

I tell the people in the group to remain close to each other, no more than a couple of feet apart. I believe that if we keep together we'll stay alive, though I'm not sure why. I also tell Danja, who continues chatting with the rebel who accompanied her into the woods, to cut it out — interacting with these guys is too dangerous. She is taken aback, but gets the message.

We continue to trudge along at the irregular pace dictated by the slope of the mountains and by the rebels up ahead. The next time we stop, water bottles are passed down from the head of the line. A rebel's watch reads 1 P.M. We've been hostages for six hours and haven't had a drink the whole time.

As I swallow the warm water, I think again about Bob and Susan. Most likely they were killed in their tent. I also recall a newspaper story I read about a tour group, four New Zealanders I think, who were captured by African rebels several months ago. One of them was released, but the other three haven't been seen since, dead or alive. Are we in for days, weeks, even months of this nomadic prison life? Or will we simply be killed at the Congo border, which is now no more than a couple of miles away?

The well-dressed Kikuyu rebel breaks in on my thoughts. "Do you know what this war is about?" he asks me.

I try to play dumb, but he's on to me.

"How could you live in Kenya so long and not know what we're fighting for?" he demands. "What would you say about our cause?"

"Tell me what you're fighting for," I reply.

Finally their purpose becomes clear to me. As I suspected, they are Interahamwe, Hums who blame America and Britain — and Uganda — for backing minority Tutsi rule in Rwanda after the genocide. Abducting us is a terrorist bid for publicity that will damage and maybe even destroy the gorilla tourism that is a mainstay of Uganda's economy.

"Write down your views," I suggest quietly, "and I will take the letter back to the U.S. ambassador and get it to the press." The Kikuyu says nothing.

During the next break we're allowed to drink again. We sit and Danja rests her head on my knee. One of the guards comes down the line and demands to know what's wrong with her.

"What the hell do you think is wrong with her?" I shoot back. "We've been stripped, robbed, and beaten, and we're scared, tired, and hungry."

Just moments later, as if I've worked a spell, a rebel brings me a loaf of raisin bread that looks moist and sweet. I divide it among the group, urging everyone to eat, especially Mark, who looks to be on the verge of losing his will.

The Kikuyu man appears again. "You shouldn't be afraid," he says stonily in Kiswahili. "You're going to be all right."

I wonder whether to tell the others, whether they would believe him or not — and which would be worse. When he goes back up the trail, I say nothing.

Of course, I am tormented by the real question: Do I believe him myself?

At the next break I am asked again what I will say to the world about the rebels and their cause. My heart quickens with hope. In Kiswahili, so the others cannot understand, I repeat everything I said earlier: that I'll take anything they write to the U.S. ambassador and make sure it gets to the international press. He tells me not to be afraid, that we will be released at 3 P.M. I look at his watch: 2:41.

I finally decide to let the others know what I've been told, reasoning that at this point even false hope is better than no hope. But no one seems to react to the news. Three o'clock comes and goes.

About forty minutes later we enter a burned-out clearing bisected by a huge, smoldering white log. Apparently local villagers have cleared the area for a farm plot. As we leave the clearing and head toward a ridge, I realize that we're virtually at the Congo border. I'm sure that our fate will be determined there. We will be killed, released, or — perhaps worst of all — held indefinitely as hostages.

I make a decision: if they want to take someone for further protection once they enter the Congo, I will volunteer. I have no wife or family waiting for me. I also tell myself that whatever happens I will protect Danja. As the only woman left among us, she's the most attractive target.

We stop at the ridge. The sky has turned gray, and a soft rain is coming down through the trees. A rebel kicks at Gary's shoes, motioning for him to hand them over. Gary is wearing no socks underneath, and his toenails are painted green — an incongruous reminder of another world. Just then a black man I take for a rebel comes forward and stands near us. His face is bloody and bruised. I mention that I know that one of his fellow soldiers has some ointment for his wounds.

"I'm a *hostage*," he responds, surprised. His name is Masindi and he's a driver at the park. Brought along as labor, he's been at the front of the line cutting trail all day.

Masindi and the rest of the group sit down, but I remain standing, surveying the hostages, with their mud-caked arms, badly scraped feet, and torn clothes. They hang their heads, their eyes downcast. But not even the arduousness of the day's journey has wiped the look of fear from their faces.

Then what I've been fearing all day happens. The rebel Danja was talking to makes his move. He reaches out and roughly takes hold of her chin, digging his fingers into her face. Grabbing her hair with his other hand, he pulls her up toward him.

"I'm taking this one on," he calls out in Kiswahili. He looks around, his eyes settling on Gary. "And that one, too." He must think that Gary — with his bleached hair, earrings, and painted nails — is a woman.

I grab Danja by both shoulders and pull. A brief tug-of-war ensues, then suddenly she falls back toward me. I brace for the rebel's attack, but he stands motionless.

For the first time, Danja's composure breaks. She bursts into tears. I lay her down, hold her close to me, and cover her with a jacket. A few rebels collect around us, jeering.

Then the Kikuyu commander approaches me with a few sheets of loose paper. I see they are in French and tell him I cannot read them.

"Then tell everyone this," he replies, and he begins to talk.

All of Africa is a war zone, he says, and his group has three or four units in this area, all originally based in Kigali, Rwanda. Next time, he warns, his army will take no prisoners. They will instantly kill everyone — everyone. Do we understand?

As he speaks and I translate for the group, I notice his men adjusting their weapons and cargo, as if preparing to move again. When the Kikuyu finishes speaking, I ask him for my watch. "Buy another," he says, laughing, then turns to go.

I look at my group, waiting, not knowing what to expect. Then slowly our captors begin to fade into the jungle. At first I can't believe they're leaving us. After all, we possess dangerous information: we can describe them in detail to the Ugandan army. But suddenly we are alone. No one says a word. Tentatively, we rise to our feet. I stare off into the Congo; I can hardly make out the path the rebels created in their departure. They are gone.

It's just after four o'clock and we still have to get back down to camp before dark. I'm worried about everything: more rebels, land mines, getting separated, accidents. I warn the group about the hazards, but not everyone listens. I chase Mitch and Masindi down the trail and convince them to stay with us.

We make it to a stream that I remember crossing an hour or so ago. Someone asks if the water is safe to drink and Danja and I can't help laughing out loud, given all we've just been through. Michael stops the group to hold hands and say a prayer of thanks. We hold hands. Someone else says something brief. I can't come up with anything. It feels either too early or too late for prayers.

It turns out to be too late. About an hour later, as we descend the hill in the fading light, I spot two bodies off the trail, below us. I fight a wave of nausea as I recognize the green pants and yellow shirt on the first body. It's Susan Miller. She's lying on her right side, covered in blood, with her left arm thrust stiffly into the air. Her head has been slashed with a machete. Her life must have ended within fifteen minutes of her brief good-bye with Rob.

I don't recognize the other body, also a woman. She's lying on her back, her shirt pulled up to her neck and her skirt gathered high around her waist. It looks as if she's been raped.

I back away and start to retch; then I drop to the ground in tears. I stare at my hands. I feel like I can't move them.

It takes forever to reach the main road that leads to camp. We arrive just as twilight turns to darkness, and a Ugandan army officer meets us at the entrance with bad news. Five tourists are confirmed dead, he says, and he wants me to help identify them.

Earlier, after discovering the bodies, we ran into some soldiers from the Ugandan army who had been pursuing the rebels. They brought the two dead women back to the camp. I am forced to look at Susan's body again. She and four others are lying out in a gravel parking lot near the camp headquarters. I glance at the other faces. Neither Bob McLaurin nor Susan Studd are there. I ask after them, and the officer says they are alive. They hid outside their tent and escaped; in fact, they are already back in Kampala. Then I ask about Rob. No one even realized that he was missing.

Masindi left with some friends as soon as we got back to the grounds, but I find the other five survivors at a camp a mile away that was left undisturbed by the rebels. They're huddled in blankets, sitting together in a large tent. We have tea and hot showers, and then the six of us lie shoulder to shoulder on thin mattresses on the floor. I'm in the middle, with Danja and Gary to my right and Michael, Mitch, and Mark to my left. Danja cries quietly, without stopping. A light breeze blows the flap of the tent.

Nearly all those who weren't forced to join our march survived. So did Linda, who had seemed so weak to me. Mark Avis's wife didn't make it. Neither did Rob. He was found hacked to death in the Congo, miles from where we had left him crouched on the hill.

Gorilla trekking in Uganda may have ended that day. All tourism to Uganda was suspended for a month. Now travelers are again allowed to visit, but very few are choosing to do so. Most Western countries maintain strongly worded advisories against traveling there. Tour companies in the region are having bookings canceled left and right. If the violence persists and the visitors stop coming, the landowners may raze the forests and plant over the places where the gorillas and other wild things live. The rebels will have successfully robbed the government they hate of a major source of revenue.

As for me, a couple of weeks after these tragic events I went back into the bush for a few days. When I crawled into my tent after sunset a feeling of terror washed over me. I had to dart back outside and sleep by the fire. It's not that I blame myself for what happened out there. I wish that I could have pulled Rob along with us when we doubled back. I wish that I could have protected everyone, but there was just no way of knowing what was going to happen that day. These rebels had killed hundreds of thousands of people. And our captors had so many guns. I was powerless against them.

I came to Africa for the adventure, but before long it became my home.

There was no place in the world like it. I depended on its honesty, its predict-
ability. A lion may be a killer, but he's not malicious; he's just doing what he
must do to stay alive. When a leopard hunts its prey, it has no ulterior mo-
tive. I've seen death in the wild and I've seen people die in accidents, crimes,
and war. I have lived a life of close call, been shot at half a dozen times, and
I have even saved lives. But I cannot get that day out of my mind. The faces
crowd in on me every night. I think of the last line in a letter Rob sent me be-
fore the trip, when we were discussing the hazards of the trek: "Gorillas or
not, this will be a fabulous trip." I think of the spell Africa cast over me.

For weeks I bled inside from the rifle jab. I am still sleepless, and still
bleeding inside. I know no cure for the horror and grief we all feel, for the
wars that split and ravage our land, for what has happened in Africa. The
continent has always been the love of my life. But now there is trouble be-
tween us.

Winter Rules

FROM *Sports Illustrated*

I

"I COULDN'T CARE LESS about Greenland," William C. Starrett II said with disarming candor shortly after arriving in the northernmost country on Earth. "I'm here for the golf."

Sixteen empty beer bottles were lined up in front of the retired California bankruptcy lawyer, so he looked like a contestant in a carnival midway game. It was the last week of March, and Starrett, two photographers, and I were passing a five-hour layover inside the modest air terminal in Ilulissat, a southern suburb of the North Pole, by systematically divesting the bar of its biennial beer supply. We began by drinking all the Carlsberg and then depleted the Tuborg reserves, and we were grimly working our way through the supply of something called Faxe, evidently named for the fax-machine toner with which it is brewed, when Starrett began recounting his life's memorable rounds. Rounds of golf, rounds of beer — the distinction was scarcely worth making.

"Livingstone was an interesting course," he said. "It's in Zambia, near Victoria Falls. The greens fee is thirty-five cents, and the pro shop has one shirt. At Rotorua, in New Zealand, the hazards are geysers. Sun City, in South Africa, has an alligator pit, and you don't play your ball out of that." This summer, Starrett said, he would rent a house in County Cork ("Walking distance to the Jameson's distillery") and travel from Ireland to Iceland for the Arctic Open, played in twenty-four hours of sunlight. He was, on the other hand, unlikely ever to return to the Moscow Country

Club. It has gone to seed, don't you think, after expanding hubristically from nine holes to eighteen?

I feigned a look that said *You're telling me* and shook my head world-wearily.

"It is said that once a traveler has seen the world, there is always Greenland," says the Lonely Planet guidebook *Iceland, Greenland and the Faroe Islands,* which only partly explains Starrett's presence here, 250 miles north of the Arctic Circle in Ilulissat, at the exact point at which mankind's appetite for golf exceeds the capabilities of fixed-wing aircraft.

Our profane party of golfers and journalists had flown five hours to Greenland on its national airline, Grønlandsfly, after first laying waste to the duty-free liquor shop in the Copenhagen airport so that its ravaged shelves resembled those of a 7-Eleven in the hours immediately following a hurricane warning. After alighting on Greenland, the world's largest island, we required two more northbound flights of an hour each to reach Ilulissat. This was the end of the line for the four-prop de Havilland DHC-7, and we now awaited the arrival of a Vietnam-vintage Sikorsky military transport helicopter to take us the last hour-and-twenty-minute leg north, to the frozen coastal island of Uummannaq, for the first — and possibly last — World Ice Golf Championship (hereafter known as the WIG).

The WIG was open to anyone with two thousand dollars, a titanium liver, and a willingness to spend a week 310 miles north of the Arctic Circle, in one of the northernmost communities in the world. Who could resist such a powerful come-on? Every citizen of planet Earth save twenty, it turns out.

Still, though the tournament was a sponsored contrivance designed to promote Greenland tourism — and a Scottish liqueur company, Drambuie — winter golf on Greenland promised to have singular benefits for the high handicapper. For starters, the island's 840,000 square miles are virtually unblighted (from a strictly golf-centric view of the ecosystem) by trees. Nor would water come into play, as 85 percent of Greenland is covered by a permanent icecap, which in places is two miles thick. Most significant, the Greenlandic counting system goes only to *arqaneq marluk,* or 12, after which there is simply *passuit,* or "many" — an idiosyncrasy surely to be exploited to my advantage on a scorecard.

The incoming Sikorsky at last set down in Ilulissat like a great mosquito of death. The vehicle was so old, a Dane living in Greenland told me with perverse pride, that its manufacturer wants the relic returned for display in a museum when Grønlandsfly retires it. At this news I signaled the bartendress for a final round of Faxes, but she gestured to her glass-fronted refrigerator, now empty, and said accusingly, "No more beer."

With growing dread, I returned to my companions in the waiting area. In the lounge chair facing me was a London-based sports photographer named Gary Prior. A janitor who moments earlier had been cleaning the men's room approached Prior from behind and began massaging his scalp, and a look of supreme serenity spread across his — the janitor's — face. Prior prudently avoided any sudden movement as he mouthed, "This bloke's gone mad."

So it was with a profound sense of foreboding that we boarded the Sikorsky, its belly filled with golf clubs, and set out to defy Robert Louis Stevenson, who wrote, "Ice and iron cannot be welded." Would this prove to be a prophecy? With a terrible shudder, the rotored beast rose above the icebergs, carrying us, its human prey, deeper, ever deeper, into a golfing Heart of Darkness.

II

I had first heard of ice golf two summers earlier, while traveling under the midnight sun in northern Scandinavia. "You must return in the winter," implored the deskman at the Strand Hotel in Helsinki, "when we play ice golf on frozen lakes and snow, in freezing temperatures, with balls that are purple."

"Yes, well, I imagine they would be," I stammered, but truth be told, the idea intrigued me. Greenland was among the last outposts — on Earth or in its orbit — to resist golf's colonial overtures. Man first walked on the moon in 1969, and within two years he was golfing there. Greenland was first inhabited five thousand years ago, yet it had only a nine-hole track near the main airport, in Kangerlussuaq, to show for it. Until two months before our arrival, the game had never been seen in Uummannaq, and when the Sikorsky touched down outside the village, I had an irresistible impulse to plant a numbered flagstick, as if landing at Iwo Jima.

A week before our visit, 200 of Uummannaq's 1,400 residents had turned out for a golf clinic conducted on a makeshift driving range: the frozen fjord waters that surround the island. "I think it is very difficult to hit this ball," said Jones Nielsen, a fifty-eight-year-old resident, after taking his hacks off a rubber tee. "But the young kids, they are very interested and would like to learn more about this game."

As well they should. Greenland's 56,000 residents, 80 percent of whom are Inuits (the word "Eskimo" is best avoided), are said to be temperamentally suited to golf. "One thing about Greenlanders," wrote Lawrence Millman in his Arctic travelogue, *Last Places*, "they tend to find misfortune amusing"

You have to, on Greenland or in golf. "When they contacted me many months ago to attend this event," said Ronan Rafferty, referring to the tournament's sponsors, "I thought it was a joke." Rafferty, a thirty-five-year-old native of Northern Ireland, was the leading money winner on the European tour in 1989 and a member of that year's Ryder Cup team. He was paid by sponsors to attend the WIG, but a wrist injury would prevent him from actually playing. Mercifully he had his own wines shipped to Greenland, and he was toasted at dinner by the mayor of Uummannaq as "Ronan Rafferty, the famous golfer which I never heard of."

Rafferty arrived the night before I did with another party of golfers and journalists. All told, twenty competitors and twenty noncompetitors, representing six nations, attended the WIG. From Holland came Lex Hiemstra, who won the trip in a contest and was often asked if second prize was *two* tickets. Joining me from the United States were Starrett and Mark Cannizzaro, a *New York Post* golf columnist who turned up some instructive literature on local customs. "The stomach of a reindeer is like a large balloon, and the green substance in the stomach has a very particular smell," read the section headed *Food and How We Eat It* in a Greenland publication. "It is neither delicious nor revolting, but somewhere in between." This would prove useful, as our menus for the tournament would include whale jerky, blackened musk ox, and battered auk.

Jane Westerman joined my table at the welcoming dinner in the Hotel Uummannaq. Westerman, a widow from England with a newfound love of golf ("I'm quite keen, really"), is a member of the Roehampton Club in southwest London. "We have bridge, croquet and golf," she said. "But hardly any ice golf a-tall."

Peter Masters, also English, asked Westerman where exactly the club was located. "It's near The Priory," she replied. "Do you know The Priory? The upmarket psychiatric hospital?"

Masters did not know The Priory, but soon enough, surely, we all would. Outside the hotel, hundreds of Greenlandic sled dogs — frightening creatures resembling wolves — wailed all night at the moon. A message posted in the hotel said that alcohol was forbidden in guest rooms. A man explained that a drunk once wandered out and lay down among the dogs. In the morning all that was found of him was a button. A single button.

"What's the saying?" Masters asked, with more portent than he could possibly know. "Mad dogs and Englishmen . . . ?"

III

It was fifteen degrees below zero when I rose to play a practice round with Starrett. On the course he stood up his stand-up bag, and its plastic legs snapped in half. The bag collapsed to the ice, legs dangling at odd angles, like Joe Theismann's.

My own legs buckled at the beauty of the layout. The course was constructed entirely of ice and snow, nine holes laid out like a bracelet of cubic zirconiums on the frozen fjord waters surrounding Uummanmaq. Fairways doglegged around icebergs ten stories tall. This is what Krypton Country Club must look like. My disbelieving eyes popped cartoonishly, and I had half a mind to pluck them from my face, plop them in a ball washer, and screw them back into their sockets to see if the scene was real.

The fairways were snow-packed and groomed and set off by stakes from the icy rough. The greens, called whites, were smooth ice, like the surface of a skating rink. No amount of Tour Sauce could get a ball to bite on these whites; bump-and-run, I could see, was the only way to play.

The hole itself was twice the diameter of a standard golf hole, and players were allowed to sweep their putting lines clean with a broom. Other winter rules were in effect: all balls in the fairway could be played off a rubber tee, while balls in the rough could be lifted and placed within four inches of where they landed, on a line no closer to the hole. My own balls, alas, were not purple, but rather optic yellow low-compression Titleists, replete with the WIG logo.

I discovered many things during my practice round of ice golf: I discovered that any given golf shot is 30 percent shorter in sub-zero temperatures than it is at seventy-two degrees. (The course was appropriately abbreviated, at 4,247 yards for eighteen holes.) I discovered that it's difficult to make a Vardon grip in ski gloves, to take a proper stance without crampons, and to find a ball that has landed in fresh powder. But mainly I discovered this: that with suitable clothes, no spouse, and no desire for country club indulgences — caddies, shoeshines, combs adrift in a sea of blue Barbicide — there is nothing to prevent you from playing golf anywhere on Earth, in any season, any day of the year.

That alone seemed a more worthwhile discovery than anything Admiral Peary stumbled on in the Arctic.

IV

The WIG had a shotgun start. Except that a cannon was used instead of a shotgun, and the cannoneer reportedly suffered powder burns on his face and had to be treated in the village hospital. The next shotgun start employed an actual shotgun.

I was playing with Masters, an editor at the British magazine *Golf World* and a seven handicapper. On the second hole, a 284-yard par-4 with an iceberg dominating the right rough, Masters uncoiled a majestic drive. As he did so, a team of speeding dogs pulling a sled abruptly appeared to our left, two hundred yards from the tee box. The ball was hurtling up the fairway at speed x, the dogs were sprinting toward the fairway at speed y, and suddenly, as the two vectors approached each other, we were witnesses to a complicated math problem sprung horribly to life.

With what can only be described as a plaintive wail, one of the dogs collapsed. The rest of the team kept sprinting, dragging their fallen comrade behind the sled so that he resembled a tin can tied to the bumper of a newlywed couple's car. The driver glanced back at the dog and, with barely a shrug, continued to mush. Greenlandic sled drivers, in sealskin jackets and pants made of polar-bear pelt, are not given to great displays of emotion, and the entire hallucinatory vision quickly disappeared into the white glare of an Arctic horizon.

Masters couldn't have anticipated this ludicrously improbable event, but a Danish woman following our foursome — she composed our entire gallery — repeatedly accused him of huskycide. "How could you?" she kept saying. "We are guests here." What the

sled driver made of this act of God — a single optic-yellow hail-
stone falling from the sky and smiting his dog — is lost to history.

The very next hole was a righthand dogleg — a word our foursome now studiously avoided using in Masters's presence —
around an iceberg. I sliced consecutive tee shots on top of the berg
and never recovered, especially as I had exhausted my one sleeve of
optic-yellow Titleists and was now playing with the most garish
range balls in my bag. Masters, shaken, carded a 40 on the front
nine but recovered his composure to post a three-over-par 75 for
the round.

At day's end the Englishman Robert Bevan-Jones, whose record
31 on the back nine gave him a first-round 70, held a one-stroke
lead over the Scotsman Graeme Biases. My first-round 99 left me in
eighteenth place and in a powerful melancholia, especially considering that the tournament lasted but two days. We had come all this
way, and it was already half over. Long after the mood ended, I remained on the fjord, seasonal affective disorder setting in, and lost
myself in the endless white.

I was wallowing in a profound silence, two miles from Uummannaq on the frozen fjord, when my driver, a Dane raised in Greenland, broke the spell. "Uummannaq means 'heart,'" said Christian
Dyrlov while tracing a valentine in the air with his index finger.
"Because the island is shaped like a heart, or like the back of a
woman."

Hours later, back in my room, I unfolded a map and concluded
that it would take the entire imaginative arsenal of a powerfully
lonely man, in a frigid climate, at a far remove from the rest of the
world, to see Uummannaq as even vaguely resembling a valentine.
Or the tapering back of a beautiful woman.

It was beginning to look like both to me.

V

Saturday night in Uummannaq began uneventfully enough. The
dinner was verbally hijacked, as usual, by the speechifying representative of Drambuie, who kept urging us, somewhat salaciously,
to *nose* his product. Two downs performed. Then a few of us walked
through the restaurant's kitchen. Which is to say, through the looking glass.

Behind the kitchen in the Hotel Uummannaq, should you ever find yourself there, is a disco. Greenland, I kid you not, is a hotbed of something called Arctic Reggae. Alas, the headliners on this night were not Bob Marley & the Whalers. Rather, two aspiring rock stars from Moldavia took the stage, and they introduced themselves as Andy and Andreas. One played keyboards, the other guitar. "Our band is called Tandem," said Andy, or possibly Andreas. "You know, the bicycle with two seats?"

Andy and Andreas, singing from a notebook filled with handwritten lyrics to Western pop songs, performed phonetic covers of such unforgettable standards as "Unforgeteble" ("Like a song of love that clins to me/How a follow you that stins to me") and "Country Roads" ("Almost heaven, Vest Virginia/Blue Ridge Mountain, Shenandoah River"). A toothless woman forced me, at beerpoint, to dance with her, while leathery Inuit fishermen watched our group of golfing toffs and scrawny scribes pogo to the music and decided — for reasons known only to them — not to kill us with their bare hands.

"Why do you laugh during 'Mustang's Alley'?" Andreas (or maybe it was Andy) asked as I flipped through his notebook at a set break.

"It's 'Mustang Sally,'" I replied, and a light bulb buzzed to life above his head.

"Ahh," he said, as if his world had finally begun to make sense. "Thank you."

Forget love and Esperanto: the only two international languages are music and sports. While Greenland has a home-rule government, it remains a province of Denmark, and just fourteen hours had elapsed since Denmark played Italy in a qualifying match for soccer's European Championships. The match had been broadcast live on Greenland's lone television network. This qualified as event programming; the fare on another day consisted principally of a travel agent riffling through brochures for tropical resorts.

I now understood why our gallery had been infinitesimal earlier in the day: oblivious to golf, Greenlanders are soccer obsessives. The only permanent athletic facility visible in Uummannaq is a soccer pitch. Every fifth child wore a Manchester United ski cap. Man United's goalkeeper is Peter Schmeichel, who is also captain of the Danish national team. Additionally, England had played Poland that afternoon, and Man United star Paul Scholes scored all three goals for England.

So wired Uummannaqana were not ready to retire when the disco closed at 3 A.M., and we all repaired to a house party, which is when things began to get surreal. Just inside the door was a pair of size 20 clown shoes. Fair enough. On a shelf were several impressive ivory souvenirs — swords, perhaps, or walking sticks — that are difficult to describe. An English photographer was twirling one like Mary Poppins's umbrella when the Faroese hostess materialized to say, "I see you found my collection of walrus penis bones."

The clown shoes belonged to a thirty-one-year-old American named Joel Cole, who was visiting Uummannaq from his native Shakopee, Minnesota — a town nearly adjacent to the one I grew up in. The odds against our meeting near the North Pole were roughly six billion to one, but by this time I had come to expect anything in Uummannaq. Cole was once the national track and field coach for the Faroe Islands and led them to a respectable showing at the 1989 World Island Games, a kind of Olympics among Greenland, Iceland, the Isle of Wight, the Isle of Man, the Faroes, Shetlands, Gilligans, and so forth. Cole now clowns — he used the word as a verb — in the world's underprivileged places for the real-life Patch Adams, whom Robin Williams portrayed in the film of that name. Indeed, Cole was the man who had clowned us at dinner just before we nosed our Drambuie. Said Cole, memorably, "I've clowned in Bosnia."

By 6:30 A.M. the evening was running out of steam, and I made my way back to the hotel with four journalists turned English soccer hooligans. As all 29,000 of northeastern Greenland's sled dogs howled in unison, we strolled the streets — or, rather, street — of Uummannaq and sang (to the tune of "Kumbaya, My Lord"):

> "He scores goals galore, he scores goals.
> He scores goals galore, he scores goals.
> He scores goals galore, he scores goals.
> Paul Soho-oles, he scores goals."

I was due to tee off in two hours.

VI

I neglected to answer my wake-up call. I neglected to request a wake-up call. And I certainly neglected to "spring ahead" one hour in observance of Daylight Saving Time. So I missed my tee time. Which is why in the final WIG results, listed in several international newspapers the next day — from the *New York Post* to *The Times* of London — my name would be followed by the ignominious notation WD. Which stands, I gather, for "Was Drinking."

Having officially withdrawn from the WIG, I was free to follow the leaders. The gallery pursuing the final foursome on this soccer-free Sunday numbered several hundred townsfolk, whose mittened applause sounded like a million moth wings flapping.

Ronan Rafferty emerged from the hotel to watch the tournament play out. "You can cut the tension with a knife," someone said to him when three strokes separated the top three players with three holes to play. "Not really," said Rafferty. "You could maybe chip away at it a bit . . ."

The improbable leader, by a single stroke, was Peter Masters, who had put his game and life back together after dropping a dog in the first round. When he finally holed a short putt to win the first WIG with a final round of 67, two under on the tournament, he was rushed by a jubilant gallery. An old woman thrust a napkin at him, and Masters, brand-new to Greenlandic fame, didn't know whether to blow his nose or sign his name. He signed with a felt-tip pen. "Being on the other side of that," said the journalist, more accustomed to interviewing golf champions than being one, "was surreal." There was that word again.

"What does Peter win?" asked Graeme Bissett, the Scotsman, who finished third, two strokes behind Masters.

"A ten-year exemption," I speculated.

Bissett chewed on this and said, "From coming back?"

On the contrary, returning is almost compulsory. Masters won an all-expenses-paid trip to defend his WIG title next year. Organizers were quite keen, really, to make this an annual event. Said a representative from Royal Greenland, the prawn-and-halibut concern that cosponsored the affair: "Bringing golf here shows we are not a static society." Imagine that. For the first time in recorded history, golf was a symbol of unstodginess: of forward-thinking, bridge-building multiculturalism.

Life is too often like the stomach of the reindeer, I reflected at dinner: neither delicious nor revolting, but somewhere in between. We had all come to the end of the earth to be delighted or revolted — be anywhere but in the everlasting in-between of daily life. In that regard Greenland — without sunlight in winter, without moonlight in summer — succeeded on a grand scale.

"There are many difficulties here," said the mayor of Uummannaq. "The difficulties are darkness and harsh weather." He paused and added, "But there are also many beautiful times. The beautiful times are days like this."

The men, women, and children of the Uummannaq village choir appeared from nowhere and began to sing a cappella in their native tongue. One didn't have to speak Greenlandic to recognize the hymn. It was "Amazing Grace."

In that instant it occurred to me: Uummannaq is a Rorschach test. It really does resemble a human heart, for those willing to look long enough.

PATRICK SYMMES

From the Wonderful People
Who Brought You the Killing Fields

FROM *Outside*

THE PILL IS what started it. The paranoia. The dubious notions. The sense of surrender. Round, white, sealed in foil: it was only 250 milligrams of mefloquine, but I had put it off for an hour now. It sat on the bar at the Heart of Darkness in Phnom Penh while the techno-scratch of Prodigy assaulted the house stereo, sticky ganja swirled on the monsoon breezes flowing in the door, and a collection of expats maimed the pool table. Antimalaria pills must be consumed on a full stomach (Castlemain XXXX in my case) at the same time every week (midnight Saturday in my case) and in the same way (Cedar Tavern in Greenwich Village last Saturday, Heart of Darkness this). Rituals are important.

Extensive self-medication has taught me mefloquine's long list of maybes: maybe stomach upset, maybe stomach pain. Maybe nausea, maybe vomiting, maybe lightheadedness and insomnia. And maybe — or maybe not — effective armor against the hybrid strains of Cambodian malaria. Mefloquine, I have decided, may also induce paranoia. I conclude the latter from the fact that every expat in Cambodia is on antimalarials, and every expat in Cambodia is paranoid.

"Fat lot of good that'll do where you're going," the Australian next to me says, adding a gleeful "Ha!" for emphasis. He is an aspiring photojournalist looking for rare animals, a brave kid, and totally stoned. He is of the opinion that, having signed my life over to a man I'd never met to make a motorcycle trip to a place I shouldn't go to find a tourism minister who doesn't exist, I am beyond medical help. He is deep into a practical explanation of what to do "when" I get robbed.

"Immediately lie down on the ground," he says. "Put your hands on the back of your head, and don't say anything or look at them. You speak, wham, they hit you in the head with a pistol, mate. And they really don't like you looking at them. Mostly it's police officers that'r robbin' ya, so they don't want to be seen. Just keep your head down, don't speak, and let them take whatever they want. Mostly they're not bad blokes — they usually leave you a thousand riel to get home."

He claps a nearby Cambodian on the shoulder. "This fella right here got robbed last night," he booms. "Ain't that right?" The Cambodian nods.

Phnom Penh is bad; out of Phnom Penh is worse. Other than to the ruins at Angkor, nobody goes out. There are the five — or is it ten? — million land mines. The vipers, the two kinds of cobras, the poisonous banded kraits. Also the bacteriological soup of Japanese encephalitis, typhoid, and malaria. Also the fact that the army and police have not been paid in four months and are getting hungry. Also that the roads are positively African, but with all the land mines and snakes, the first rule of travel in Cambodia is never step off the road. Also there are the Khmer Rouge. They killed roughly two million of their fellow citizens during the 1970s and, despite nominal peace, have been holed up in the Cardamom Mountains for almost twenty years.

Yet in three days, after renting a dirt bike and making a few practice runs around the nearby countryside, I will ride deep into the mountains to play tourist in Pailin, a former guerrilla stronghold my guidebook calls "perhaps the most forbidden city in the world."

My mefloquine-induced paranoia is dismissed by Wink Dulles, my guide and fixer on this journey. A dead ringer for Mel Gibson, and even shorter, Wink had dismissed my fears with a simple but eloquent argument. "It'll be cool," he told me. And so we are going.

Author of guidebooks on Southeast Asia, Wink wrote the book — well, the very fat Cambodia chapter — on what can go wrong on a trip like this. In *The World's Most Dangerous Places*, published by Fielding Worldwide, he detailed with encyclopedic relish the convoluted threats of this basket-case nation. Forbidden from entering

Burma, arrested twice in Vietnam (where his other Fielding guide-book, *Vietnam Including Cambodia and Laos,* is banned), Wink is a cousin of John Foster Dulles, who was secretary of State in the 1950s and still appears on an official Vietnamese list of enemies of the state. Unwelcome in two countries, Wink settled on a ranch in northern Thailand with his common-law wife.

Our plan is to rent two dirt bikes and ride into the Cardamom Mountains to find the remnants of the Khmer Rouge, whose main arm announced early last year to local journalists that it was now accepting outsiders in its Pailin stronghold. Only Cambodia could produce a joke as unfunny as a Khmer Rouge tourism offensive, but there it was: they claimed they would appoint a minister of tourism and opened their doors to the Westerners they had only recently stopped kidnapping. I was going with mixed motives. I felt a journalistic obligation to take the pulse of a nation unexpectedly emerging from its grave, but I also wanted a thrill; I wanted to see some ragged edge of life, to glimpse the Southeast Asia behind the headlines. To many Western travelers like me, the allure of danger zones is undeniable. I wanted to measure the character of my fellow vultures, to know if we were fools for believing there was something to be gained in a place of so much loss.

This plan was not quite as idiotic as it sounded. Much has changed in Cambodia over the last several years. It is still brutally poor, but as Cambodians proudly tell you, their country is seeing its best times in three decades. There is an economy, albeit a primitive one. The government is weak but increasingly stable. Tourism to Angkor is booming, hotels and restaurants are cheap, and anyone in search of authenticity will find grim buckets of it. The gritty capital is a shell filled with squatters and beggars, but trips up the Mekong and Tonle Sap Rivers unveil a countryside out of an Orientalist's fantasy: slowly moving water buffalo, electric-green rice paddies, saffron-robed monks. The shooting is over, major roads have been cleared of mines, and backpackers from Australia and French *flaneurs* on postcolonial nostalgia trips are probing the interior again, bragging in the capital about who went where first.

But all the joys of adventure travel in Cambodia are of the queasy, that-can't-really-be-true kind. Travel here straddles the smudged line between the blackly ridiculous and the revoltingly tragic: you can spend a morning at a gun range outside Phnom

Penh, firing something called a "shoot airplane gun" and blowing up water buffalo with grenade launchers (fifteen dollars for the grenade; the bovines start around seventy-five). Then you can spend the afternoon stepping on teeth at the killing fields or touring the Tuol Sleng genocide museum. Of the sixteen thousand people who passed through this building when it was Security Prison 21, only seven survived.

The book (Conrad's *Heart of Darkness)* has become the bar, and the movie (*The Killing Fields*) has become the merchandising opportunity. (Pay two dollars to tour the killing fields; then buy a DANGER — MINES T-shirt.) Tourism here feels somehow profane, like traipsing through 1948 Poland with a beer in hand.

Sitting in the Heart of Darkness an my first night in Cambodia, I add "K.R. minister of tourism" to a kind of mental tally I continually update. In the positive column, Pol Pot is dead and the K.R. have "defected" to the government by making a kind of treaty. The last guerrilla holdout — the one-legged fanatic known as Uncle Mok — has been carted off to jail in Phnom Penh. Two years have gone by since the last kidnapping and killing of foreigners, one and a half years since a coup brought a kind of terrorized stability. In the negative column, the treaty's basic stipulation is, you leave us alone, we'll leave you alone. Positive column: The K.R. are weak and afraid of prosecution for war crimes. Negative column: They still have two thousand of their most hardened troops, plus vast profits from illegal logging and gem smuggling, and many of the same leaders as when they killed those maybe two million. Positive column: They aren't expecting us.

On balance, 250 milligrams of mefloquine seems quite irrelevant. I choke the pill down.

"Up and down like a whore's knickers," the Irishman says of the road out of Phnom Penh. He is standing beside it in the middle of nowhere — nowhere here being only sixty miles from the capital — supervising a crew of seven hundred Cambodians digging a trench for a fiber optic line. The telecom project is part of the slim economic recovery largely funded by French and Japanese corporations and international aid agencies. Every now and then one of the workers is blown up by a mine, but Cambodians need jobs and so they keep digging. The Irishman's rude metaphor for the road

politely conceals the truth: it is a nightmare of clay, dusty when dry
and slick when wet, pocked with craters. It is also Cambodia's major roadway, running 180 miles from the capital to the second-larg-
est city, Battambang.

After only a few hours Wink and I are excruciatingly butt-sore.
Our dirt bikes are ghastly, seven-dollar-a-day jokes that shed pieces
as we progress. We wear scarves and goggles to keep the pervasive
red dust from choking and blinding us, but when Wink is lightly
rear-ended by a car it becomes clear that the main danger we face is
the Cambodian driver. The only traffic laws are the laws of physics:
we lurch up and down, dodging the surprisingly dense traffic heading both ways in either lane. The typical Cambodian vehicle is a
scooter bearing multiple passengers; the typical car, a white Toyota
Camry, stolen in Thailand, with 200,000 miles, nine passengers, no
shocks, and the steering wheel on the wrong side, which creates
some problems when passing. Once in a while there is a truck or a
cart pulled by water buffalo. The countryside is flat as a dance
floor, dotted with palm trees, low huts, and children fishing in
muddy ponds. Their parents hoe and plant in batik sarongs; an
old, gentle Southeast Asia lurks behind the bloody recent history.

It is a hopeful scene, but placing too much trust in Cambodia's
appearance can be fatal. From 1991 to 1993 the United Nations
poured money and 22,000 people into Cambodia in an effort to
end decades of fighting. The U.N.-sponsored elections put a coalition government in power, and tourism began to pick up. Then
in 1997 the three-way government broke apart. By chance Ted
Koppel was in Cambodia during the coup, and a panicky ABC
turned to Wink for help arranging an evacuation flight. Over the
years, some Westerners weren't so lucky. In 1994, the Khmer
Rouge kidnapped and later killed three backpackers — a Brit, an
Australian, and a Frenchman — on the train from the capital to
the southern beaches. The next year bandits seized and executed
an American nurse near Angkor, and in early 1996 a British
demining technician and his translator were taken from the road
to Battambang — the same road we are about to travel. Neither has
been seen since.

As part of their last offensive, the Khmer Rouge shelled Battambang heavily, and as we wheel into the city the next day, after a
night in the village of Pursat, some fine noodles by the river, and

another gruesome five hours of dodging bottomed-out Camrys and bomb craters, the closeness of war is evident. Cambodia's second city is a low dump with a few rotting colonial buildings and a branch of the Mines Advisory Group. Its members work without body armor (one officer today is wearing a sarong and a cigarette), and I've seen better metal detectors at the beach; last year a man in the squad lost three fingers and an eye to a 72 Bravo. When we ask about the roads, a sergeant tells us that while there are "many" mines between here and Pailin, the road itself is clear. "Side of road not clear," he says. "Road okay, side of road not okay."

Our hotel is one of the comfortable ones constructed during the glory days of the U.N. occupation. There is a staff of twenty-five, one other guest, and a sign on the back of the room door that advises me, DO NOT ALLOW TO BRING THE EXPLODES AND WEAPONS INTO THE ROOM. Wink and I head out to the town's main bar, where the floor show is a rock band treading the increasingly familiar line between comedy and tragedy. Eventually Wink cannot stand it and charges the stage. He plugs in an electric guitar, waves at the keyboardist to join in, and launches into a long blues riff, growling out "Yeah!" and "Baby!" every so often. He's quite good, especially by Cambodian standards. By the second song he has filled the dance floor.

Watching him, I can't shake my dread of tomorrow's trip to Pailin. Wink has thrown in the idea that, along with finding the alleged minister of tourism and gleaning what we can about Pailin's safety, our visit should also include an interview with Ieng Sary, one of the century's ranking madmen, the intellectual author of the Khmer Rouge terror, and the official who orchestrated Pailin's uneasy peace with the government. Known in the anonymous hierarchy of the movement as Brother Number Three (though I find myself thinking of him as Butcher Number 3), Ieng Sary doesn't come into the sunlight much, so it would be a scoop.

We use a Thai cell phone number (go ahead, 011-66-1-217-1617) to call Brother Number Three at home. His son, Ieng Vouth, answers and in good English tells us that we cannot interview his father because he is ill, as the various disgraced Khmer Rouge leaders often are when journalists call.

"Don't come," he says, and hangs up.

There are two kinds of magic in Cambodia, a young Cambodian

warns me the next morning in Battambang. There is weak magic and there is strong magic, he says, pantomiming the difference between the two with agitated hand gestures involving bullets and triggers and guns. If you have weak magic, he says, either the gun aims the wrong way or the bullets go around you. But if you have strong magic, your enemies can't even draw.

I ask which kind of magic I have. He looks confused. Obviously I haven't understood the point of the story. "Foreigner have no magic," he says.

It is fear, not magic, that improves the road to Pailin. After a few hours, the dirt begins to smooth out, losing its bumps, potholes, and washboards in testimony to how few cars come this way. The people in villages confirm this by staring. We pass marked minefields and unmarked ones, too, as we were warned by the demining team. An armored personnel carrier lies dead by the side of the road. I dismount and inspect it — a neat hole in one side where the K.R. shot a rocket-propelled grenade into it. There are fewer and fewer huts, and as we begin climbing into the Cardamoms the first ruinous bridges appear, chaotic scraps of metal and wood thrown over deep ravines.

There have been checkpoints all along, but following Wink's instructions I have driven through them all with a fat grin and an open throttle. Now we come to the border between government territory and what is in effect still Khmer Rouge country, despite the treaty. A dozen soldiers are blocking the road. They order us off the bikes and indicate that we should "sign in." Wink converses in Thai with the sergeant in charge, who obviously wants money. Wink tells him we have five dollars. With a smile, the sergeant calls him a liar. Somehow we bluff our way through, grinning, saying "Yes, of course" and "Good-bye," and walking slowly toward the bikes.

Half an hour later we stop to relieve ourselves. "Whatever you do," Wink says, "do not step off the road." We stretch our legs, check for oncoming traffic — nothing — and wander to discreetly separated stretches of the shoulder. I stand on the last set of tire tracks and am staring into space when I notice a big antitank mine right in front of me. Olive drab and utterly fatal, it was probably left as a warning that the field is filled with mines. Wink comes over. The mine is only about three strides away.

"I wouldn't walk over there and pick that up if you paid me one million dollars," he says, lighting a cigarette. (Three days from now, two farmers and a pair of water buffalo will be killed by a mine about six feet off this road.)

I am still in first gear when a five-foot-long snake shoots out of the bushes, toward my front wheel. I briefly consider and reject the notion of throwing the bike to the right and crashing into the minefield. Instead I jam on the brakes, nearly going over the handlebars. My front wheel misses the snake's tail by inches.

"Christ," Wink shouts as he pulls up. "Did you see that? That was a krait."

My frayed nerves stretch tighter as we aproach Pailin. At an unmarked fork in the road a glowering K.R. soldier in a Mao cap cradles an ax and eyes us with unconcealed disgust. Foreigners were once worth as much as ten thousand dollars apiece to anyone who captured one. Now we're just big uncashable checks.

"Pailin?" I ask, pointing to the right. He ignores the question. We go right anyway and roll hesitantly up the main street in second gear, shopkeepers and kids turning to gawk as we pass two-story houses and furniture shops. Because of its proximity to Thailand — just twenty kilometers from the border — Pailin is not only an ideal refuge for war criminals and defeated guerrillas, but also a prosperous center for the smuggling of gems and lumber. We turn left and stop at the central market, a tent bazaar stuffed with food stalls, sneaker vendors, and emerald traders. Resting on the bikes, we collect hundreds of empty stares, neither hostile nor welcoming.

"Everybody in the place is K.R.," Wink says.

"Everybody except us," I correct him.

The town's guest house is two stories of cinder block occupied by a passel of Thai smugglers with topo maps. We check in and then ride back down the main street to a restaurant, where Wink orders us some delicious flat noodles with water buffalo and exchanges information with the matron in market Thai. As she speaks, a fat man in an orange polo shirt on a motorcycle — that is to say, a rich man in Cambodia — pulls up, orders a beer, and begins to sing karaoke. More men join him, encouraging his singing. I am in a state of advanced mefloquine paranoia now and conclude that he is spying on us. We label him Agent Orange.

Across the road, about a hundred K.R. soldiers are sitting on their haunches, watching a volleyball game. They wear bits and pieces of uniforms, sometimes with the new "government" shoulder patches they were issued after the peace treaty, sometimes not. Most are shirtless, and several of them have amazing scars. The game is played barefoot, four on four, and both teams are calling reverse sets with decoys, pump-faking spikes, and deploying the vertical stuff with discipline. I work up my nerve, join the crowd, and take a few pictures.

Slowly one soldier, and then another, begins to notice me. The game comes to a halt, and the ball bounces on the ground and goes still. We all look at one another. One fellow, the one with a beautiful touch as setter, begins pointing at me and addressing the crowd. I feign indifference, but the soldiers around me begin to laugh. I rise, smile broadly, and walk back to the restaurant.

Wink is waiting with a hazy grin on his face, the result of either too much MSG or the smug satisfaction of the journey-proud. "There are only a few places that I've been that are really the edge of the world," he waxes. "This is one of them. The lost outpost of a nation."

As lost outposts go, Pailin has some amenities: Khmer pop videos, telephone shops, monster trucks, a duty-free store, even an English school whose students shyly quiz us about our travels. The town is more prosperous than the rest of the province, mostly because of its proximity to Thailand, but the local people give credit to the Khmer Rouge for a law-and-order town.

As we try to locate the minister of tourism, the language barrier crops up; we follow pointed arms to the town hall, but it's populated only by chickens. At the police station, a barren cement hue, a young border policeman speaks some English. "No minister of tourism," he says, "because no tourists here." He adds, helpfully: "You can go walking in mountains."

Aren't there mines in the mountains?

"Yes," he says, enthusiastically.

We are taking in this information when a Mitsubishi Montero rushes past. "Mr. Ieng Vouth," the policeman says, pointing at the truck. The son of Butcher Number 3. At our urging, two teenage K.R. soldiers jump on their scooters, race out the driveway, and catch the Montero down the road. Then all three vehicles wheel back to the station.

The Montero pulls to a halt. Ieng Vouth is wearing a striped polo shirt and dark glasses. He takes a look at us. There is a rapid exchange in Khmer, and then he throws the Montero into gear and spins out of the driveway so fast he showers rocks behind him. He is out of sight in thirty seconds. So much for the interview.

Wink is unfazed. He spends the afternoon handing out the little grinning-skull stickers sold with the *Dangerous Places* book. "Are you Khmer Rouge?" he asks people. "Did you ever kill anyone?" He is enjoying himself immensely.

Khmer Rouge karaoke night gets under way most evenings at about seven in the Pailin casino, a sad, one-story building with a walk-through metal detector. It has just closed for the day when we arrive, so we sit down in the attached disco.

Our waiter speaks a bit of English. He is from Battambang and moved here only a few months ago, for the job. He doesn't like it. "Many bad men here," he says.

Soon they drift in. A few tough characters in military gear, and then a few more. Finally, Agent Orange enters with a large entourage.

"He is very big man," the waiter says. "He is major in Khmer Rouge."

In an hour the place has filled up with bar girls and men in flip-flops and uniforms. A few of the young ones are obviously aides to Agent Orange; they mutter into walkie-talkies while Orange and the rest tear into the hard liquor.

I lay my pill on the table. It is Saturday night again, the witching hour for self-medication. I open the foil packet and wolf down the tablet, washing its metallic taste away with beer. All day I have been picturing myself blown legless by land mines, or writhing in the grip of snake poison, or lying in a rice paddy with a Chinese pistol pressed against the back of my neck. At this point I am way beyond worrying about pills.

A disc jockey begins spinning the usual tragic Khmer pop, and different soldiers fight over the microphone and take turns singing the blues. They are all plastered, wobbling out the saccharine vocals. Fortunately there is no guitar on the premises, so Wink stays in his seat. I drink beer and watch, and after a while I decide that it might be a good idea to take a picture of karaoke night with the Khmer Rouge.

Immediately I see I've made the wrong choice. The two men I photograph notice the flash, of course, and begin seething. They glare at me, approach, shout angrily in Khmer, and then abandon the microphone and stalk back to their table.

"Let's get out of here," I tell Wink.

"Don't worry," he says. "Finish your beer."

We repeat this conversation every ten seconds for the next four minutes as I watch the far table. We never had any friends in Pailin, but now we have enemies. I'm smiling a lot; it's tense.

Then the two offended Khmer commandeer the camera. They snatch it, defiantly, and go back to their table. Wink goes over, picks up the camera, and brings it back. Most of the people in the bar are now watching the emerging confrontation, except for Agent Orange, who is facedown on his table, passed out. No one sings karaoke.

When they finally come for us, staggering over the dance floor with murder in their eyes, it is the longest five seconds of my life. We have crossed the border now, into that Cambodia which is beyond control. In that brief moment, it seems truly possible that I might be killed and that as I bleed to death on the dance floor of a karaoke palace in a pitiful town in the Cardamom Mountains, my last sight will be a mirror ball spinning overhead.

Just as they start in — I'm piling chairs between me and the pudgy sergeant who's trying to get close enough to hit me — the deejay cuts the tunes. Wink is in a face-off with a lean fellow in a white T-shirt, but when the music stops the whole bar freezes, and Agent Orange leaps up from his slumber. He sees the men threatening us and immediately rushes over and puts a stop to it. Our antagonists sulk back to their table.

Even Wink has had enough now. But our escape is blocked as Agent Orange stands over me and forces the terrified waiter to translate a long and drunken speech about international brotherhood and dutiful feelings of mutual respect. We exchange business cards with two-handed formality; his plastic card — jungle-ready — identifies him as the chief of police for Pailin. During the whole speech Agent Orange holds my right hand firmly. I'm sweating and trying to let go, but we are bonding, obviously, and whenever I try to stand up Agent Orange shoves me back down into my chair. He flips between hospitality and threats once a minute — my Cambodian experience in a nutshell.

Then he says he saw us on our motorbikes. "Pursat," he says, "moto," and he enacts riding a motorcycle. "Battambang, moto." The translator explains that by pure coincidence Agent Orange was also driving from Phnom Penh to Pailin and saw us bouncing up and down. He is impressed we have come through such difficult conditions to visit his humble town.

"Pailin," Agent Orange says, "no problem." It is his only English phrase. "Pailin no problem. Pailin no problem."

In the end I am kidnapped by the Khmer Rouge, but only to the dance floor. My hand is so sweaty he can hardly hold on to it, but Agent Orange drags me onto the floor and we spin in a slow counterclockwise circle, holding hands on the inside and using our outer hands to trace sinuous curves in the air. I'm proud to say that Agent Orange is almost as bad a traditional Khmer dancer as I am. After two minutes he walks off the floor, forcing me to keep dancing, alone, under the mirror ball. He orders his assistants to dance; reluctantly, they join me. He grabs bar girls, hauling them onto the floor, pairing up couples, culling strays, dragging Wink from a dark corner of the bar.

Like a petty dictator, Agent Orange stands in the middle, pinching the asses of passing bar girls, laughing like the petulant warlord in a martial arts film, and Wink and I spin around the dance floor slowly, surrounded by Khmer Rouge killers in flip-flops, exchanging fake smiles all around.

"Pailin no problem," Agent Orange crows at me every time I complete a revolution. "Cambodia no problem," I shout back. Finally it comes to me: Agent Orange is the Khmer Rouge minister of tourism, or at least the ambassador of goodwill.

Finally, after half an hour, he loses himself in a musical rhapsody, spinning at the center of the dance floor, his body bathed in blue and red diamonds cast off by the mirror ball overhead. Quietly, slowly, Wink and I slink out the front door.

I lock myself in my hotel room, but I don't sleep. All night I lie there, watching the mosquitoes spin overhead, and once in a while I sit up, sure that the banded krait has slipped from the drain in the bathroom floor. Partly it's the taste of the mefloquine metal that keeps me up; partly it's the fear.

But as I lie there, it sinks in that we will survive Pailin, that we will drive out of town and leave behind the Khmer Rouge, and that we will survive more days of even worse roads and even more insane drivers and even more minefields and even more snakes. Finally, drunk on Thai whiskey, Wink and I will lie on our backs at Angkor Wat at three in the morning and watch the Leonid meteor shower light the sky. Only then and there, amid nine-hundred-year-old temples crouched in the jungle, will I realize that there is no dividing the world into good and bad places, swept and unswept corners. We trouble tourists and samplers of disaster are neither vultures nor fools but both in equal measure.

JEFFREY   TAYLER

China's Wild West

FROM *The Atlantic Monthly*

IN   THE   HEXI   CORRIDOR, between the mountain ranges of
China's arid, north-central Gansu Province, the Great Wall crum-
bles to an end. The wall's decayed mud-and-stone ramparts outside
the town of Jiayuguan bear no resemblance to the grand other end,
more than a thousand miles to the east, near Beijing. Tellingly, the
territory of the People's Republic that is ethnically Han Chinese
ends at the wall. Beyond it, to the west, begins a Central Asian domain that is historically Turkic and Islamic — a land of terrible
desert and desolate massif that stretches to the Caspian Sea and in-
cludes the newly independent states of Uzbekistan, Kazakhstan,
and Turkmenistan, as well as the Xinjiang Uighur Autonomous Region, as it is officially called, in China itself.

During a recent visit I huffed and panted my way up a walkway
and from there to a watchtower overlooking the wall. I surveyed
Jiayuguan, to the south; against the dun-colored Gansu barrens it
looked less like a town than like an abandoned jumble of bunkers
on the surface of a lifeless planet. To the west I tried to descry the
beginnings of Xinjiang, where I was headed.

The region is China's westernmost and largest province, covering a sixth of the country. As a student of Russian history, I have
long been fascinated by this landlocked territory, which borders
what was for most of this century Soviet Central Asia. Xinjiang
seemed to belong neither to China nor to Central Asia: it was not
Russian, and it fell outside historically Mogul or Persian territory,
beyond even the farthest reaches of the Ottoman Empire. Xinjiang
was for me remoter than remote, alluringly enigmatic.

Troubling recent events had rekindled my interest. While China has been experiencing much-vaunted economic growth and social stability over the past decade, Xinjiang has suffered increasingly frequent bouts of separatist violence, much of it provoked by the spread of Islamic fundamentalism and Turkic nationalism (roughly half the population is Turkic), and at times the army has been called in to suppress revolts.

The stakes are high for Beijing. The region contains huge coal and oil reserves — its oil reserves are believed to be three times those of the United States — that are only now being exploited. Its size and contiguousness with the new states of Central Asia make Xinjiang a vital strategic arena and a valuable trade passageway. Finally, its sparsely populated expanses are providing lebensraum for the country's burgeoning population; unfortunately, some of these expanses have also served as convenient sites for nuclear testing and prison camps. Xinjiang, in fact, has been called China's Siberia.

I planned to cross Xinjiang from east to west, sojourning in the places where I could learn the most about the region: Turpan, a prospering but tense oasis town wedged between two deserts; Urumchi, reputed to be the capital of prosperity in western China; Ili, the Kazakh border prefecture, where, despite China's rapid development, prehistoric nomadic life was said to flourish still. I would end my travels in Kashgar, a medieval bastion of Turkic national identity so distant that until this century reaching it from Beijing took months.

I left the watchtower, and the wind followed me back to town. For millennia travelers, exiles, and merchants have said their farewells to China in Jiayuguan, and in a sense I did too. Lone cyclists wearing surgical masks against the dust dotted Gansu Highway, the main regional east-to-west thoroughfare; otherwise there was almost no traffic. The setting sun colored the roiling dust clouds orange and rust red. But it was the wind that set the mood, howling in from the desert, recalling a struggle that for eons has pitted men against their environment.

Xinjiang contains some of the harshest, most isolated terrain on earth. The Takla Makan, one of the world's largest deserts, has inspired dread in merchants and travelers since the establishment of the Silk Road, more than two thousand years ago: *Takla Makan* translates from the Turkic as "You go in and you don't come out." Temperatures hit 120 degrees, and sandstorms can last for days; in the past they frequently caused caravans to lose their way. North of the desert, across the Tien Shan, or "Heavenly Mountains," lies the Junggar Basin, a steppe of Siberian aspect where temperatures of minus sixty-eight degrees have been recorded. The Pamir, Karakoram, and Kunlun Mountains cut off the region on the west and south; to the north and east spread Siberia and the Gobi Desert.

The fortunes of Xinjiang were for centuries intimately connected to the Silk Road, which led from central China through the Hexi Corridor, and then forked around the desert and the Tien Shan to pass through oasis settlements and continue up into the Pamirs and the Karakoram. Two millennia ago the Han dynasty annexed Xinjiang and dubbed it the Western Region; possession afforded the Han a strategic advantage in resisting Hun invasions, and China profited from the Silk Road trade with the Mediterranean and Europe.

Although the Han dispatched soldier-farmers to settle the land, their hold on the Western Region remained tenuous. Around the eighth century, Turkic Uighurs poured in from the northern steppes, ousting the Han and establishing khanates. Sometime during the first millennium, the name Turkistan — "Land of the Turks" — was coined, and Uighurs today look to that era for affirmation of their claims to sovereignty over Xinjiang. In 1762 the Western Region fell to the Manchu dynasty; a century later it was renamed Xinjiang, or "New Frontier." Eventually the Soviets attempted to assert their influence in Xinjiang. Only in the early 1960s, after the Sino-Soviet split, did Xinjiang come completely under Chinese control.

The train was to take me from Jiayuguan to Turpan, along a rail line that follows what was the northern branch of the Silk Road through the charred gravel at the edge of the Takla Makan Desert, where topsoil temperatures can reach 150 degrees. By evening the sun, hanging low in a red-gray sky, was burning obliquely across salt flats and blackened rock barrens. In the villages women, scarved against the blowing dust, led camels loaded with water from the wells.

Turpan is the hottest, and lowest, place in China. Its population of 200,000 is three-fourths Uighur; the majority farm wheat and raise grapes in the irrigated suburbs. Beyond the suburbs stand majestic ruins dating from the Middle Ages, when Turpan thrived on Silk Road trade and was one of the region's most advanced centers of civilization. An awareness of past greatness enhances the Uighur sense of identity today.

Because of the heat, Turpan comes alive only at night. One evening I walked its main drag, Qingnian Street, with Yusup, a Uighur studying economics at the university in Urumchi, 115 miles away. With his square jaw, high forehead, and searching eyes, he had the relaxed mien of an aristocratic Turk and, in fact, was learning Turkish (we spoke in a combination of Turkish and English). But as we moved through the crowds, he spat at the ground after passing any Han, and he railed against the economic migrants arriving every day from the provinces to the south. In 1949 only 200,000 Han lived in Xinjiang, making up 4 percent of the population; now the number is approaching eight million, out of a total of eighteen million.

Yusup should have been the very model of the assimilated Uighur that the state-run media like to present as proof of China's unity; unlike most Uighurs, he speaks and writes Chinese fluently, and would thus have a good chance of finding remunerative work anywhere in China. Instead he seethes with resentment. "We have too many Chinese here — too many, and more keep coming," he said. "The Chinese have no religion; they are infidels. We look to Turkey and Iran and Arabia. We do not look to Beijing. Islam is our law."

But Islam is not the law in Turpan: we soon spotted a beer garden off the central square. I wondered if I would offend Yusup by suggesting that we stop for a soft drink, but before I could ask, he grabbed my arm and led me to a table. With an imperious snap he ordered two beers from the Chinese waiter. The place was filled, in fact, with Uighurs drinking alcohol.

"My parents are Muslims and don't drink," he said, gulping his beer. "But I drink only a little." He told me that his lifelong ambition has been to make a pilgrimage to Mecca to affirm his faith. After a moment of silence he leaned toward me, looked in both directions, and whispered, "This land is not Xinjiang, and it never was! This land is East Turkistan. But I am talking too much, and this is dangerous." He suddenly excused himself and took leave of me, though not before we had agreed to meet the next day.

Yusup was right to be cautious. For such talk — for using the term "Turkistan," laden with Islamic and separatist connotations — he could conceivably be arrested and dispatched to a labor camp without trial. The Beijing authorities have ascribed Uighur separatism to ideology born in mosques and private Islamic schools, and have closed many of both in the past two years. They are particularly sensitive about "Turkistan," which historically referred to much of Central Asia. With the exception of two short-lived rebel republics of Eastern Turkistan, in the 1930s and 1940s, there has never been a state by this name in Xinjiang.

Yet Islamic though Yusup's rhetoric was, most of his habits appeared to be secular. The next afternoon shopkeepers were hurrying to lower their awnings and fasten their shutters as I went to meet Yusup, on Qingnian Street. A fierce wind was blowing in from the desert — lashing at political banners, rattling windows and doors, knocking people off their bicycles. The sun was sinking in a sky turned ash-gray from the dust. We walked along holding handkerchiefs in front of our mouths and noses.

"In Uighur we call this the *boran*," Yusup said — a sandstorm wind. He paused to leer at a pair of passing Chinese women. "I don't like girls," he blurted through his handkerchief.

"What?"

"I mean, I don't like girls because I am ashamed of them. Islam does not allow us to have girlfriends. I must not have contact."

By the time we reached the basement karaoke bar to which Yusup had invited me, the *boran* had worsened. Drivers had switched on their headlights, and the wind was ripping vines from their trellises. Down in the bar a few Chinese teenagers horsed around in front of a video screen, howling out the lyrics illuminated at the bottom. Yusup looked at the group; Chinese women were *biaozi*, or "sluts," he said. He asked the disc jockey to play a Uighur tune. The languid Turkic melody drove the Chinese from the floor — the desired effect. Soon, beer in hand, Yusup had struck up a conversation with a young Kazakh woman, asked her for a dance, taken her phone number, and invited her on a date.

The rest of the evening served to emphasize something I encountered throughout Xinjiang: young Uighurs, educated in Chinese institutions, were following the Han in accepting Western pop culture and mores. Islam forms the basis of Uighur identity, to be sure, but modernizing, secular layers are gradually accruing. Xinjiang's Uighurs may well come to feel as torn between East and West as many Turks are today. Rent by the contradiction between Islamic traditions and acquired Western mores, and split along educational and generational lines, they will be more easily controllable by Beijing.

The *boran* had abated slightly by the time I left for Urumchi, the capital of Xinjiang, but not before taking its toll. In two days it had killed three people and five thousand farm animals, wiped out more than 66,000 acres of crops, and caused twelve million dollars' damage. Such losses were not considered extraordinary. *Borans* are accepted as routine in a region where the climate wreaks havoc as often now as it did a thousand years ago.

The *boran* had put a halt to all bus traffic out of Turpan, so I had to take the train to Urumchi from nearby Daheyan. I rode in a *yinzo,* or fourth-class car, like most of the approximately 300,000 Han who immigrate to Xinjiang every year. My train had originated in the central province of Shaanxi and had been creaking northwest for days, filled to capacity with Mao-jacketed proles dozing on their suitcases and thick-knuckled peasants nodding over baskets of cabbage and leaky sacks of rice. They were all on their way to Urumchi too.

In Jiayuguan I had met a young Chinese businessman named Shu, who earned a good living by buying up consumer goods in Urumchi and selling them in provincial towns. He traveled first class, wore a silk suit and gold rings, and frequently consulted his pager; he was exactly the kind of prosperous Han merchant that Uighurs love to hate. Uighurs have voiced bitter resentment that the immigrant Han benefit from China's economic reforms more than they do; envy as much as religion has sparked anti-Chinese riots across the region. Yet it was impossible not to have sympathy for the Han masses traveling in the *yinzo.* Poverty and overcrowding, not greed, were driving them from their homes to Xinjiang.

As we left the desert and climbed the slopes out of the Turpan bowl, the *boran* diminished further, and the spirits of the passengers lifted. Soon verdant mountains and pastures and flocks of sheep began to appear; the air rushing in from the open windows turned fresh and was free of dust. But a commotion arose at the end of the car: a white-smocked attendant was shouting *"Zou! Zou!"* ("Clear the way!") as she shoveled a two-foot-high pile of beer cans, plastic-foam cups, plastic bags, peanut shells, and wastepaper down the aisle, displacing passengers. A second attendant opened the car door, and the sudden draft sent a tornado of rubbish whirling back onto us all; the door was slammed shut and the rubbish recollected. Then the attendants shoveled the rubbish through the door on the other end into the pastoral idyll outside. Plastic bags blew into the cedars and caught on the branches. Cups rained onto the grazing sheep.

Minutes later there were shouts of the Chinese name for Urumchi: "Wulumuchi! Wulumuchi!" A teenager had sighted the skyscrapers and cranes of the capital. A half hour later we were rolling through shantytowns to the station.

Urumchi ("Beautiful Pastureland" in Mongolian) is now a boomtown, enriched by commerce in oil and coal and by Beijing's selection of the city as a trade zone spared normal taxes — a kind of landlocked port, and a city of dreams for the Han. Centuries after the Tang dynasty populated the Urumchi area with soldier-farmers, the Chinese state continues to sponsor immigration: the city's population has increased seventeenfold in the past fifty years, to almost 1.5 million. Han compose 80 percent of the citizenry, with Uighurs, Huis (Chinese Muslims), Kazakhs, and White Russians making up most of the rest.

With good reason Beijing has sought to anchor Urumchi firmly in China by means of immigration; if it had not done so, Urumchi might well have slipped into Soviet hands decades ago. After consolidating Soviet power in Central Asia, Stalin turned his attention to Xinjiang, where Chinese government control had never been strong. Uighur and Han warlords proved amenable to trading with and receiving military aid from the Soviet Union, until the Sino-Soviet split put an end to Soviet influence. Still, Russian signs hang from buildings in Urumchi, Russian is a common second language, and local Uighurs look back on the era of semi-Soviet rule with a moist eye, feeling more affinity with the Russians than with the Chinese.

From afar, Urumchi's construction cranes and skyscrapers dazzle the eye. Up close, one sees that the cranes are idle and the sky-scrapers stand half finished in mud lots without sidewalks. Jeeps, Audis, and Mercedes bustle through the streets, but many have tied-on fenders or cracks in their windows. Stores selling authentic Rolexes and Longines glitter — but are usually empty. Within sight of the Holiday Inn and the Rock'N'Roll Cafe, on prime downtown real estate, one encounters the kind of vendors that crowd the streets of any Third World city.

The popularity of the Russian Market, near the neighborhood of Min Yuan, serves as an indicator of the true state of the economy. Crowds pick through piles of fake Omega and Russian-made McLenin watches, imitation Ray-Ban sunglasses, sturdy military binoculars, Uzbek textiles — everything that can be made or counterfeited cheaply in the former Soviet Union. The Han migrants I talked to on average earn the equivalent of just over fifty dollars a month. Though this contrasts favorably with the twenty or thirty dollars they would earn in the poorer provinces from which they come, it is still far below workers' salaries on the prosperous eastern coast.

I walked the Russian Market and met Xinhe, a fleshy Russian-speaking merchant in his thirties. Xinhe was born in Urumchi, a few years after his parents arrived, in 1958, on the back of a truck from Gansu. He was doing relatively well as a trader, turning a profit of three or four hundred a month by shuttling between Almaty and Urumchi, taking clothes to sell in Almaty and using the money he earned to buy electric razors and tools for resale in Urumchi. He looked tired. Now more than ever, he said, he was living day to day, and recent murders by the Russian mafia of two Chinese merchants in Almaty worried him. Urumchi no longer inspired him, and he was pinning his hopes on starting up a business in Siberia. When, after glancing at the counterfeit watches in trays around us, I told him of the genuine Rolexes on sale in the city center for thousands of dollars, his jaw dropped. "I barely have enough to feed my family," he said. "Even with [Deng Xiaoping's free-market] reforms we just get by. I have no savings, nothing at all, and I have a daughter to feed and a wife. If one of my trips goes wrong, I'm wiped out." Only to those raised in the poverty of the central provinces could Urumchi be a city of dreams.

*

With a population of about 900,000, the Turkic and Islamic Kazakhs are the third most numerous ethnic group in Xinjiang; they have been granted three autonomous zones within the Uighur Autonomous Region. The officially recognized status of autonomy confers upon minority peoples such as the Uighurs and the Kazakhs a number of rights, the most important of which is the right to use native languages for purposes of education and broadcasting — though Beijing imposes restrictions on content. The largest of these zones is Ili, 167,000 square miles of steppe and mountain bordering Kazakhstan. Herdsmen have been driving their sheep, goats, and yaks across this land for millennia. The Kazakhs, unlike the Uighurs and the Han, are for the most part nomadic, migrating with their flocks from season to season, living in stone huts during the winter and in felt yurts in summer. China has for decades been officially discouraging the wandering life, deeming it unproductive and backward. Statistics are unavailable on how many still lead it, but figuring in the Mongols, one may hazard a guess of about a million people on the move.

I traveled from Urumchi to Sayram Lake, in the Tien Shan, to meet a few Kazakh people; I was curious to get an idea of how they differed from the Uighurs, and to find out how they regard rule from Beijing, in view of their proximity to independent Kazakhstan. Chocolate-colored mountains streaked with snow and riddled with glaciers jutted into cloud banks; in the foothills, where the bus left me off, stone huts hunkered over dun earth. Even here Han and Uighurs had set up roadside shops and restaurants. My self-appointed and unpaid guide, Chen, was Chinese, originally from Gansu, and the owner of a small general store I had noticed when I got off the bus. Chen was in his thirties, and though he spoke only Chinese (which I could mostly understand), he had emblazoned the walls of his store with Uighur and Kazakh advertisements in Arabic script.

Chen led me up a hillside from which I surveyed the lake, which was frozen; the early spring weather had not yet warmed, and the Kazakhs were still living in stone huts. Outside one we met Mapan, a Kazakh in his fifties. Shooing sheep out of our way, he invited us in. We sat cross-legged on carpets spread over a stone floor in a raised part of the hut; on the walls hung kilims blackened with soot from the wood stove. Mapan ordered his wife to serve us. She boiled tea and spooned in goat's milk. She had only a few teeth and was sinewy and solid. Mapan himself was leather-skinned. He sat lethargic in layers of wool clothing, his eyes half-closed under a wool cap.

His wife dumped a sack of petrified bread crusts on the table. Chen and I sipped our tea, sour from the goat's milk, dipping crusts to render them edible. In thick-tongued Chinese, Mapan told me about the seasonal movements of his sheep and oxen and about raising his seven children. The family had no radio, no television; time seemed to be standing still. Political issues apparently did not matter to people who lived with animals and roamed the hills.

One teenage son, ruddy and silent, came in and popped a tape into an ancient cassette player. The singer was Rozymbayeva, from Kazakhstan — a rare intrusion from the world beyond China's borders. I asked Mapan and his son what kept young people in the village. What did they do for fun?

"Well," Mapan said, "we have the [annual] Feast of the Sacrifice. We slaughter a lamb and, well, we eat this lamb." A silence followed. Many of the young, not surprisingly, are settling in the town of Ili.

Later, in Chen's general store, a concrete hovel that lacked the insulation provided by the stone and the carpets of Mapan's hut, I asked Chen how he got along with the Muslim Kazakhs. He shrugged cheerfully. He socialized little with them, content just to provide them with goods (liquor, sweets, clothes — especially liquor) that they would otherwise not have. His needs were as modest as those of his customers.

Genghis Khan once rampaged through Ili, heading west. Now, eight hundred years later, traveling across the great plateaus of the Tien Shan on my way to Kashgar, I saw his Mongol descendants, along with Kazakhs, still driving yaks up into the lairs of snow leopards and ibex.

I began my journey across Xinjiang at the end of the Great Wall. I finished it in Kashgar, a few hundred miles west of which stands another kind of wall — the natural barrier formed by the Pamir and Karakoram mountains, ranges of snowbound peaks that are the end of Xinjiang and of the People's Republic of China itself. Beyond this barrier lie the historical centers of Islamic civilization, in Central Asia, the Middle East, and North Africa.

Another *boran* whipped me along on my way to Kashgar. Clouds of dust browned out the noon sky as my bus rattled along the road bordering the Takla Makan Desert, prompting the driver to turn on his headlights and even, on occasion, to halt when the wind buried the pitted asphalt in sand. By the time we reached Kashgar, we were covered with dust and choking on it, shaking it from our pockets and wallets and hair.

Kashgar, 2,500 miles west of Beijing, seems more than anywhere else in Xinjiang to belong to a different country. Though the Han controlled the city two thousand years ago, for much of its history it has been dominated by Mongol and Turkic khans. In the nineteenth century Kashgar became a focus of the Great Game — the clandestine struggle between the British Empire and Russia for Asia. Since then Beijing's authority has been firmly established, but the Chinese have never caught up demographically: 75 percent of the 200,000 Kashgaris are Uighurs. Uighurs in Xinjiang consider Kashgar a bastion of tradition, the most Uighur of Uighur cities. Islam-inspired Uighur separatists in Kashgar have set off bombs, rioted, and murdered government officials.

Kashgar's main event, the Yekshenbe Bazari, or Sunday Bazaar, dates back two thousand years. It is a gathering of medieval aspect, a hurly-burly of trade conducted by 100,000 Uighurs from surrounding villages.

Well before I reached the bazaar grounds, by way of a bridge across the Tuman River, I could see the dust kicked up by legions of donkeys, rickshaws, and customers. Soon I came upon rows of stands where villagers were buying clothes and selling peppers, doling nuts into sacks, sampling spices. Pyramids of apples stood next to piles of figs. Men haggled over goats, women over cloth. You could find someone to break a horse or geld a stallion in the market; you could buy a sheep whole or assemble a slaughtered one from its component parts; you could have a molar pulled by a toothless dentist with iron tongs and blackened fingernails.

I walked farther into the melee. A boy was selling a brown drink of sorts from a bucket at his feet. An ox ambled over beside him and, sniffing a pat of dung, released a powerful stream of urine into the dust; it splattered copiously into the drink, and the young vendor scrambled to find a lid to cover the bucket. Later I watched him sell cups of the brew to villagers.

The more I saw of the market, the more I became convinced that tradition will work against the separatists. Illiteracy and fatalism render effective mass opposition unlikely. Riots and political murders cannot do the work of the sustained, sophisticated political campaign — both domestic and foreign — that would be necessary to force the Chinese to withdraw from Xinjiang. Well organized and in possession of powerful military and internal-security systems, they will do all they can to hold on to the region, and will go on creating facts on the ground by settling it with Han. There is no one to stop them.

Yet the roots of Xinjiang's trouble do not derive entirely from Chinese rule. History and geography have slighted the region, leaving it on the periphery of Islamic as well as Chinese civilization and far from the invigorating, progressive influence of the West or the developed East. Xinjiang's very remoteness — the quality that had drawn me to it — will effectively assure its continued status as China's vassal.

Later, as the call to prayer rang out above the market, I made my way back to the center. A *boran* was rising once again, and it would soon blot out the emerging stars and moon.

JEFFREY TAYLER

Exiled Beyond Kilometer 101

FROM *The Atlantic Monthly*

FOR THE PAST three and a half years I have found myself traveling regularly to Ozyory, a small town ninety-seven miles southeast of Moscow, to check in on the apartment of my friend Svetlana, to pay the accumulated heating and phone bills for her there, and to pick up her mail. Though I enjoy the respite that Ozyory provides from the churning pace of Moscow, Svetlana, now a Muscovite, is loath to return to her hometown, even for a day, and not only because it lies outside the zone of relative prosperity surrounding the capital, which has persisted despite the countrywide economic crisis. "Ozyory is full of exiles, criminals, and drunks," she says. "But what do you expect? It's beyond the hundred-and-first kilometer."

The lingering stigma associated in the new Russia with towns more than 101 kilometers (sixty-three miles) outside Moscow or other big cities reflects a perdurable Soviet legacy: the division of the land into favored urban areas and a neglected, poverty-stricken hinterland. This contrast has only grown more marked since the economic crisis began, in August. The bright lights of Moscow have not yet dimmed. Supermarkets are still stocked with goods unavailable elsewhere in the country; restaurants are still frequented, if less than before; and designer boutiques are still in business, though with fewer customers. A relatively small number of Muscovites kept their savings in banks, preferring to hoard cash dollars, so many have come through the collapse of the financial system with their money safe under the mattress, even if their salaries have been diminished by the devaluation of the ruble.

The geographic precision with which the city/countryside division was originally made bespeaks its police-state origins. To implement totalitarian governance, the Communist rulers zoned, rated, and regimented places and people to such an extent that Soviet citizens used to joke bitterly that their country was divided into *malyye zony,* or "small zones," a euphemism for labor camps, and *bol'shaya zona,* or "the big zone," meaning the rest of the Soviet Union, with *zona* here conveying the sense of a giant gulag. Peasants suffered a status equivalent to that of prisoners or serfs. By not issuing them the internal passports necessary for domestic travel, the Soviet government for decades forced them to stay on state and collective farms and, at the cost of their own impoverishment, to labor at providing the privileged proletariat with a regular and inexpensive supply of food.

The countryside was indeed demarcated along the lines of a gulag. For most of the Soviet era, criminals and other undesirables, including supposedly rehabilitated political prisoners returning from the labor camps after Stalin's death, were often banished beyond kilometer 101. (Presumably this was intended to keep disaffected elements away from foreigners, who were usually restricted to areas within twenty-five kilometers, or about sixteen miles, of city centers.) With the fall of the police state this practice has lapsed, but for many Russians mention of the land beyond kilometer 101 still connotes a pale of exile, a domain of reprobates and societal waste. Ozyoryans themselves assert that much of their population descends from former prisoners who had the words EXILED BEYOND KILOMETER 101 stamped on their release documents.

I began a recent trip to Ozyory from central Moscow, entering the metro a few steps away from Versace and Sandra Star boutiques near the Marriott Grand Hotel. I rode the train out to the southeastern suburb of Vykhino and boarded a worn-out red-and-white bus, which departed in a cloud of exhaust fumes and snaked its way through Mercedes-clogged traffic to Ryazan' Avenue. Twenty minutes later the driver was shuffling his documents into order; ahead of us stood the mud-splattered glass-and-aluminum police checkpoint marking Moscow's city limits. The flak-jacketed officer on guard recognized him, and motioned us through with an uninterested wave of his baton. At the checkpoint for the lanes leading into the city a half dozen cars had been pulled over; their occupants were showing papers and explaining what business had brought them to Moscow. Russians must register with the militia and pay a fee to stay in the capital for more than three days if they are not Muscovites. Leaving is easier.

After passing the checkpoint we rocked and rattled down the road amid flurries of snow. We soon left behind Moscow's neon-and-glitz environs and entered a somnolent realm of villages with ancient-sounding Russian names — Zhilino, Stepanshchino, Vokhrinka — where women gather at wells and goats scavenge for food among weathered wooden dwellings. We crossed over the Severka River, and the tarmac, now flanked by birch and fir groves, turned bumpy. Within a couple of hours we were beyond kilometer 101 and were passing the onion domes of cathedrals in Kolomna, where we picked up a side road to the south. Rusted signs along the way announced destitute state farms, decrepit factories, and then, finally, the county of Ozyory and the town itself.

After a brief tour one could be forgiven for concluding that Ozyory, with a population of 28,000, lies deep in the Russian hinterland. Many of its roads are tracts of mud, and hardly a car or truck engine breaks the whisper of the wind in its birches and aspens. Huge, crumbling concrete apartment blocks here and there tower over quaint but rickety wooden houses that hark back to the nineteenth century, when serfs who had bought their freedom from the landlords of surrounding estates began flooding into Ozyory to take up work in its burgeoning textile plants. The boom is over: today the town has a desolate, abandoned look that calls to mind broken lives, banishment, and poverty — in short, the lot of the Russian countryside and its people since the 1917 Bolshevik coup.

Svetlana's apartment is in the center of town, where Ozyory's main drag, Lenin Street, dead-ends at Soviet Square. Along the north side of Lenin Street stand a number of prerevolutionary wooden buildings, latticed and colorful, that now serve as stores selling a haphazard assortment of bread, knitwear, flowers, vodka, Kodak film, sausages, Rambo videos — and more vodka and more sausages. On the other side of the road are scattered tumbledown shops, adjacent to the bus station and the outdoor market, offering the same goods. A profusion of shabby kiosks skirts the edge of a foot-deep lake of mud fifty yards wide. This is the heart of town

— of the county, no less — after more than seven years of market reform.

Ozyory's economy collapsed with that of the Soviet Union. Its two textile factories (which suffered when the cheap supply of cotton from Uzbekistan ceased) and a defense-related optics plant (converted unsuccessfully to a chandelier factory) now stand idle. Many of Ozyory's kiosks, harbingers of the free market, have recently closed down. About all that still functions is a foreign-owned dairy plant. Reportedly, 40 percent of adult Ozyoryans are unemployed, most of those who work are paid late, and thousands more are pensioners whose stipends are months in arrears. Many survive only by farming their dacha plots; others have taken to small-time trading or have left to look for work in Moscow. In these economic straits a fierce power struggle has developed among local politicians: the regional branch of Vladimir Zhirinovsky's reactionary Liberal Democratic party is trying to overthrow the current (nominally reformist) county administration — which, it appears, does little more than preside over the town's decline. It is difficult to assess what a victory of the Liberal Democrats would mean for Ozyory, but one thing is certain: since 1991 the town has witnessed a tragic drop in living standards that makes the affluence of nearby Moscow, lessened though it may be by the economic crisis, look criminal by comparison.

Muscovites and residents of St. Petersburg refer to territories farther than 101 kilometers from their cities — that is to say, almost all of Russia — by a number of words roughly equivalent to "hinterland," the most common of which are *glubinka* (related to "depth") and *glush'* (deriving from "deaf" and denoting "a remote place of silence"). But Ozyory and other towns like it are not exactly dormant outposts lost to humanity. Ozyoryans evince a vigorous peasant heartiness that urbanites simply no longer need.

This is most apparent on market days. The Saturday morning after my recent arrival I wandered over to the market after Svetlana's neighbor, Vera, suggested that I do my grocery shopping there instead of in the foul-smelling stores across from the bus station. Fenced off and empty for most of the week, the market on Saturdays becomes *the* county hot spot, the place to see and be seen. Often it looks as if the entire town has turned out to slosh about in the mud under the rattling aluminum roofs, examining the unsteady tables stacked high with foodstuffs, cut-rate Turkish and Chinese goods, and secondhand bric-a-brac. When I walked in, a hale blond woman was hawking Turkish Lycra sweaters, a cherubic fishmonger was tending piles of salted herring from the Black Sea, and a lively Azeri woman, whirling like a dervish with two Romanian overcoats on her shoulders, was laughing and urging the crowd to step right up and try one on.

Nearby, a grandmotherly peasant with gold teeth stood over a pile of shriveled red peppers. I took one in hand and examined it.

"With that pepper there you can season a whole pot of potatoes," she said, flashing me a smile. "It's from my own plot."

"Is it hot?"

"Hot?" She raised her arms. "My God! It'll clear your sinuses and spice up your love life! Your wife will be happy tonight if you buy that pepper!" She and the women next to her broke into laughter that was all gold teeth and ruddy tonsils. I bought the pepper and moved on.

I drifted over to the tent area beyond the tables, needing to buy a plastic bag to put my pepper and other produce in. At one table I had a choice among bags emblazoned with likenesses of the Marlboro Man, Marilyn Monroe, the Golden Arches, and a half dozen interchangeable beautiful blondes stretched out under the sun on a half dozen interchangeable idyllic beaches. As I was paying for Marilyn, a declamatory voice rang out behind me.

"Ladies and gentlemen, there's a killer in our midst!"

Heads turned toward a young man standing behind a row of aerosol cans arrayed on a table under a blue tent. "Yes, it's Killer — the new nemesis of roaches," he announced, tapping a can. He sprayed a dose into the crowd. "No, Killer won't hurt you or your children if you don't drink it. And for those ladies whose hairdos fly apart in our stiff Ozyory breezes, how about this American hairspray here!"

"I'll take some Killer!" one woman shouted, forcing her way through the gawkers with a handful of rubles.

"Woman, here's your roach spray, but you might also want to remove that sweaty stench of yours with some of this German deodorant! And dear housewives, take those nicotine stains right off your teeth with this bleach paste!"

There were muffled laughs and a general rummaging in purses for rubles. The crowd pressed in around him.

Just beyond the tents middle-aged women were rifling through stacks of bucket-sized bras while the rave song "Encore Une Fois" blasted from a boom box nearby. Behind the women stood a cassette display marked RUSSKIY KHIT ("Russian Hit"), where a dozen crew-cut young men wearing track suits, black-leather jackets, and mud-caked wingtip shoes, and reeking of cheap toilet water, huddled around four or five teenage girls. As "Encore Une Fois" reached its climax, the young people began tapping their feet and singing along, adding distortions that turned the chic dance lyrics into a sort of Slavic burlesque — all the while glancing sidelong to see who was watching. They were, it appeared, the Ozyory *jeunesse dorée,* and the muddy market was their weekly venue.

My shopping done, I walked past the young people and started toward the apartment. Behind the kiosks, at the edge of the mud lake, an old woman bundled in a brown wool shawl sat hawking sunflower seeds in a weary treble. "Buy my seeds! Please, *please,* buy my seeds!"

Two young militiamen marched over. One prodded her with his baton. "Okay, Grandma, move along. You have no license to trade, and you know it."

The old woman looked this way and that. "Oh, I beg you, boys. I'm just trying to earn a few rubles. My pension is late."

"You can earn your rubles when you buy a license from the city. You heard us — move it!" The militiaman prodded her again with his baton. With a sigh of resignation, she grabbed her sack of seeds and hobbled away. Snow was falling. I trudged home along the embankment.

Vodka has served Russia's entertainment needs for centuries, especially in the hinterland, where there is often nothing to do but drink. There it replaces theaters, cinemas, operas; it binds men together in fraternal stupor and provides an escape from soul-numbing winters of darkness and slush. As a result, and not surprisingly, alcoholism has always been one of the countryside's most lethal afflictions. In Ozyory it is a scourge that nightly turns the elevator in Svetlana's building into a pissoir, provokes fights in the courtyard that often end bloodily, and, judging by the screams and plate-smashing one occasionally hears while walking around town, sparks domestic violence in kitchens up and down the otherwise placid lanes. It is only fitting that Russians have dubbed vodka — ever tempting, finally destructive — the *zelyonyi zmey,* or "green serpent."

During a previous stay in Ozyory, Vera had told me, "We call *pyatnitsa* [Friday] *pitnitsa* [drink day] here!" She was cheerfully foretasting the serpent's venom, it seemed, when I stopped to greet her in the stairwell one frigid Thursday. "You should go out and do the town tomorrow," she added.

The following night I took her advice and strolled over to Soviet Square. Blue-gray clouds of birch smoke hung in the icy air above the wooden houses. A militia car — the only vehicle on the road — chugged up alongside me and slowed down; the officers looked me over before accelerating. Time seemed suspended, hanging as still as the smoke, as frozen as the forest that came right up to the edge of town.

Soon I fell in behind the threesomes and foursomes of teenagers who were ambling up and down Lenin Street, carrying boom boxes and bottles of booze, swearing like stevedores, smoking and spitting and tussling and guzzling. I ended up across from a *pivnushka,* or beer bar. Strongly illuminated inside, the *pivnushka* was a cynosure of white light in the smoke and soft dark. I stuck my head in. Near the counter a fat woman was dancing on one leg, hopping around and hooting with drunken laughter. A teenage girl was slurping beer out of a murky stein and wiping the froth mustache off her upper lip with her sleeve. At the kiosk next door I asked the saleswoman what there was to do in town on a Friday night.

"You must be from Moscow. Our restaurant and café closed down after '91. All we have now on weekends is the Saturday-night dancing party in the Oktyabr' movie theater," she said.

I put off my outing for a day.

Saturday night the number 2 bus was jammed with excited teens heading down Lenin Street to the dance. The boys among them were already three sheets to the wind, and some of the girls had taken on the role of nursemaid, keeping their dates upright as the bus bobbed and bounced down the pitted road. *Mat* — swear-words — resounded all the way; it was as if the kids had just been released from reform school. Their lurching, expletive-filled horse-play had a vaguely threatening quality.

We arrived. Volgas idled in front of the movie theater; thick-necked *mafiozy* stood under a streetlamp with their fur-clad molls, smoking cigarettes and hawking phlegm into the snow. Inside, a sign reading NO ALCOHOL ALLOWED hung above the entrance to the dance, which was to be held in a hall above the theater proper. Taking Vera's advice, I had hidden two beers in my bulky overcoat. A nail-tough woman stood at the door and extracted from me and the rowdy youths what amounted to a one-dollar cover charge.

The hall was unheated — and it was twenty below zero outside. On the dance floor a legion of animated mummies — revelers in parkas and furs boogying to Euro-pop — puffed white breath into the red-lit gloom. Lining the walls were rows of wobbly seats that seemed to have been torn out of an Aeroflot jet. On the stage an Arizona license plate was nailed to a pole around which two women were doing a dance, running their hands seductively up and down their minks. Empty vodka bottles littered the floor. I sat down and took out my beer.

"Mind if I have a sip of that?"

A youth who looked no older than nineteen was standing over me. I handed him the can.

"Name's Sasha. Just got done with my army service. Two years on an island near the Kurils. They hardly had food to feed us. Almost starved."

He gulped some beer. He still had his service crew cut.

"So what are you going to do here?" I asked.

"What *can* I do here? Join the mafia."

Even in indigent Ozyory the underworld takes its cut from the few people who are in business, and its well-heeled thugs enjoy a measure of prestige among young people. Sasha took another swig. His friend Sergei showed up, staggering drunk and surly, and they both glared defiantly at the militiamen on duty. They had barely survived their tours, they said. No one in the military or the government gave a damn about them, and there wasn't a hope of finding work in Ozyory.

As I listened to them, a swarthy, petite woman walked past me, and our eyes locked; she looked to be in her mid-thirties, and was as out of place amid the teens as I was. With her mittened hands clasped in front of her and her head cocked coyly to one side, she introduced herself as Ilona. "Won't you invite me to dance?" she asked.

Saying good-bye to Sasha, I led her onto the floor. Among the patrolling militiamen and gyrating mummies we shimmied to "Scatman," our breath clouds mingling. After an hour or so we noticed that almost all the males in the place were slumped chin to chest in the Aeroflot seats, spent vodka bottles at their feet. We sat down; the boy next to us thrust his head between his knees and upchucked a florid stream of vomit onto his shoes.

Ilona winced with disgust and jumped up. "I hate all this," she said. "I can't stand it anymore. May I invite you home?" A fight broke out nearby: a pair of teenage boys in parkas and fur hats were swinging at each other, missing wildly in their drunkenness, and the militiamen on duty, brandishing their clubs, came running.

We walked out, picking our way through the crowd of lurching drunks, and then proceeded down Lenin Street, eventually turning up an unlit lane overhung with aspens, our boots crunching the fresh snow. The one streetlamp in the neighborhood was enveloped in a hazy white orb; the air twinkled with frost. Under the candy-striped tower of one of Ozyory's defunct factories we came upon a century-old green wooden house, and Ilona took me inside, to the room she rented there, where she seated me on the sofa. She worked for the city bureaucracy, she said. After clattering around in a credenza, she pulled out an album chock-full of yellowing black-and-white photographs.

"All that's left of my family is these photos. I was married once, but my husband turned out to be a drunk. I've long since lost track of him. I never knew my father — he left my mother and disappeared. My mother moved away and remarried."

She made tea and showed me the pictures. There she was: in her toddler's Octobrist uniform at camp on the Black Sea; at the May Day parade on Red Square in 1974; with friends in Abkhazia. She had no interest in politics, but the participation in political life that was obligatory under the Soviets had given her security and people to socialize with, and she reminisced volubly about the Brezhnev years. But then she dropped her eyes.

"I won't marry again — all the men here in the *glush'* are drunks or *mafiozy*. No one needs me anywhere else. The only place I could go would be Moscow, but you have to have friends to give you a job and papers there or you'll end up on a street corner. So I stay here and live out my time."

After tea we said good-bye, and I left. Snow had begun to fall, hissing as the wind swept it through the aspens. Rows of wooden houses stretched ahead of me until the murk absorbed them. Ozyory was only a few hours' drive from Moscow, yet a smothering pall of futility lay on the place. I found myself thinking that if anything sends Russia hurtling into anarchy or back to totalitarian rule, it will be despair bubbling into fury over the contradiction between what 10 million Muscovites see as the fruits of the new system, shriveled though those may currently be, and what 147 million other currently voiceless Russians see. In the same way that Lenin played on widespread discontent with czarist Russia to mobilize support for a revolution whose ideology the masses could hardly understand, in the same way that Pugachev could count on a reserve of serfs' rage in the countryside to fuel his devastating peasant uprising of the eighteenth century, so might a demagogue come to power riding the crest of the legitimate grievances of those residing beyond kilometer 101, impoverished and forgotten, now more than ever, by Moscow.

Whenever I arrive in Moscow from Ozyory, it is as if I am returning from a Lethean interlude. Invariably, as the bus nears the capital's outer districts, the visages of people from the countryside — set in a permanent cast of despondency and distrust — give way to the expressions of haste and preoccupation that might be seen on faces in any big city in the world. The deeper we penetrate the metropolis, the more we see garments of shining black leather, swatches of Day-Glo phosphorescence, gold and jeweled earrings glinting amid the flowing sidewalk seas of weather-beaten wool and flannel. When I reach the center itself, I often find something new being built — a boutique, a restaurant — that signals change for Moscow. Seeing this, I am reminded that I can count on the capital to continue growing steadily as much as I can expect Ozyory to remain depressed and silent — for now.

JONATHAN TOURTELLOT

The Two Faces of Tourism

FROM *National Geographic Traveler*

AT THE LIP of Batopilas Canyon, the Suburban van pulls off the narrow dirt track so that we can admire the view a mile down the road. Down, literally. The ponderosa highlands are behind us. In front, the land plummets away. Yucca, scrub, and raw rock line the giant gorge below. At the bottom, hazy with distance, a tiny, winding road leads, we've been told, into country you would hardly expect to find less than three hundred miles from the U.S. border — country long isolated from the modern world, where Tarahumara Indians race each other up and down canyons, and where a town straight out of nineteenth-century Mexico awaits. I'm aware, too, that I could be one of the last foreigners to see this road looking quite this way. Big plans are afoot.

Skip McWilliams had phoned a month earlier to pose the problem. "It's like being with a charming maiden. How do we enjoy her without destroying" — McWilliams, prone to heterosexual analogies, tried to finesse this one — "her maidenness?"

The maiden is Mexico's Copper Canyon country, and the threatened defloration is the government's new program to attract more tourists to the area. Lots of them. McWilliams, a Detroit businessman, wanted me to go see for myself what's at stake. It was a biased plea: he owns two unusual small hotels in the area.

Now I'm in this van, going from his lodge in the high country to his other one, far down in the canyon. The route is free of strip malls, lines of billboards, heavy traffic, tacky stands, and all the other trappings of "successful" tourism development.

Saving places from the ravages of mass tourism wasn't a major world issue until the late twentieth century. Now, with jet travel, superhighways, increasing world wealth, and exploding populations, tourism and travel are claimed to constitute the largest industry on Earth. The World Travel and Tourism Council predicts that people will be making one *billion* international trips annually by 2010. And, worldwide, four or five times as many domestic trips.

Try to imagine enough tour buses to hold a billion people. If parked end to end, the line would equal the length of every freeway in the 46,000-mile interstate system.

Triple-parked.

Hardly surprising, then, that tourism is transforming the world — in some ways for worse, in some ways for better.

As the Mexican government considers how to develop Copper Canyon country, it faces the classic dilemma confronting attractive places everywhere. Will the changes create a travel delight — or a tourism disaster? So far, indicators are mixed.

This region, in the sprawling state of Chihuahua, is known in the United States as the Copper Canyon. Actually, seven major canyon systems slice through this section of the Sierra Madre. The deepest part of one is indeed named Copper Canyon, but the seven collectively are called *las Barrancas del Cobre* — the Copper Canyons, plural. They carve up an area more than half the size of Switzerland and constitute one of the most dramatic complexes of gorges anywhere, dropping more than six thousand feet — deeper than the Grand Canyon. They offer splendid adventure hiking, and their many microclimates support a wide variety of flora and fauna for ecotourists.

They also support the reclusive Tarahumara Indians, which accounts for the region's other name, Sierra Tarahumara. Ever since the Spanish conquest four hundred years ago, the canyons' inaccessibility — limited until recent times to foot or hoof — has helped the Indians maintain one of the last semi-intact native cultures in North America. They have expressed little desire for company. Their own name for themselves, Rarámuri, is said to mean "runners." Famed for fleetness of foot, they now have nowhere to run.

*

My first view of the area was from the east, a long afternoon's drive up into the Sierra from the city of Chihuahua. Rolling hills, ponderosa forests, colorful outcrops — you would never suspect the hugely ruptured terrain that lies ahead. At eight thousand feet, the climate is cool even in summer, with hints of wood smoke in the air.

The dusty sidewalks of Creel, the main town, were busy: mestizo men in straw ranchero hats, Tarahumara women in traditional pleated skirts, European tourists in backpacks. Creel is becoming the regional tourist center — a needed boost, officials believe, for an economy too long dependent on logging, mining, and, in the back canyons, marijuana growing. The town is also becoming an architectural mishmash — new construction in stucco, cinder block, plate-glass. "Once the town was mostly log cabins," says Arturo Gutiérrez, who runs a mountain-bike concession. "Creel's identity is already lost. It is very sad."

In a valley a few miles from Creel, I checked out Skip McWilliams's Sierra Lodge — long, low, and, yes, all log. Each of the fifteen rooms has its own woodstove; there's no electricity, so illumination is by kerosene lamp; a sizable staff pampers guests with three meals, excursions, and margaritas. You can pay $250 per person nightly to stay there.

McWilliams, middle-aged and fit, was just in from Detroit, wearing his customary blue jeans and faintly mischievous expression, as if he finds life generally amusing and is capable of creative tinkering when it isn't. Fluent in Spanish, he's been in and out of the canyons for eighteen years. Of his enterprises, the Copper Canyon lodges are his favorite.

That's why he's been trying to persuade tourism authorities that less is more. "I'd never build a hotel with more than fifteen rooms," he asserts. "No atmosphere." And look, he tells them: he can charge more for *not* having electricity! Locals are often baffled: surely rich foreign tourists would prefer smart new fluorescents and Formica. "The next thing you know," McWilliams fears, "people will be opening water slides and miniature golf courses, and playing colored lights on the rocks."

As in much of the world, distant officials make the major tourism decisions. The Chihuahua state government and local groups play a role in the Copper Canyons, but overall policy is set a thousand miles away in Mexico City, by the secretary of tourism and by FONATUR (Fomento Nacional de Turismo), the federal tourism-development agency.

FONATUR's best-known accomplishment? Cancún.

Laid out on an uninhabited sand spit lined by a glorious beach, Cancún was planned as a utopian city of parks, low-rise hotels, and high-end tourists. But after the peso crashed in 1982, Mexicans desperate for foreign exchange relaxed the restrictions on Cancún. Hotel towers rose cheek by jowl; shopping malls sprouted; sewage flooded into the lagoon, and drug money into the economy. Cheap package deals brought in the rowdy spring-break crowd.

In 1995 the rise of ecotourism and adventure travel inspired FONATUR to turn its sights on the Copper Canyons, launching a program strongly backed by the Mexican president, Ernesto Zedillo, himself. The goal by 2010 is to raise tourism in the canyons sixfold, to over 400,000 visitors a year.

New roads are already punching through the countryside, augmenting what has been the only mechanized transportation in the canyons: the dramatic Chihuahua-to-Pacific rail line, which is how most foreign visitors experience the place.

The train makes a fifteen-minute stop at Divisadero, an overlook that provides passengers with their only good view of Copper Canyon proper. To reach the rim, tourists must thread through a gauntlet of craft and food vendors. Many visitors don't even make it to the overlook or to the pleasant two-story hotel whose glass-walled dining room commands a spectacular view. Outside, two pipes carry the establishment's septic runoff into the canyon, a watershed where several thousand people live. The manager told me matter-of-factly that the two other hotels on the rim do the same.

FONATUR nevertheless wants six hundred more hotel rooms up here, as well as some four hundred recreational-vehicle spaces in the region. Their idea, apparently, of what ecotourists and adventurers seek. "Enough to trigger it," FONATUR's assistant director, Mario de la Vega, told me. "It" being the tourist boom.

An American guide, Marsha Green, blanches at the prospect, especially of RVs: "With RVs, the place isn't remote anymore; it turns into Disneyland." But María Barriga, who co-owns a hotel just down from the rim, can't wait. "It's going to be wonderful," she told me, eyes sparkling. A FONATUR man had been by, she added, urging her to expand to one hundred rooms. A state tourism official had assured me earlier that no hotel was to have more than fifty rooms.

We climb back in the Suburban and descend into Batopilas Canyon. It is thrilling. The narrow track loops downward hairpin after hairpin. The canyon sides rise, becoming peaks high above. Deeper still, the road notches into the cliffs, edging vertiginously above the Batopilas River. Side valleys provide glimpses into other canyons, compounding the massive play of light and shadow — yellows, hazy blues, dusty greens — all on a gargantuan scale, as if Maxfield Parrish had painted the valleys of Brobdingnag. We are *descending* into a mountain range. No wonder this region has been so little known for so long.

In fact, startling discoveries are being made even now, largely by a balding, mild-mannered explorer named Carlos Lazcano, who has spent much of the past five years exploring the Sierra Tarahumara. In 1995, with the aid of backcountry locals, Lazcano identified Mexico's highest waterfall (at 1,486 feet the third highest in North America) in the canyons south of here. Just last year, up to the north, he found five-hundred-year-old, two-story Paquimé Indian cliff-dwellings containing six intact mummies. All discoveries you would expect to have occurred back when the conquistadors came seeking gold.

Of course gold is not what drives governments to fund expeditions these days. Carlos Lazcano works for the Chihuahua state division of tourism. We who tour are the gold.

Continuing our descent, we round a bend and encounter a surveying crew. Road improvements. McWilliams doesn't like it, fearing it would diminish the travel experience and make access tempting for those RVs that FONATUR wants.

The funky former mining town of Batopilas straggles along the river at the bottom of the canyon. Built by silver, Batopilas reached a zenith of sorts in the late 1800s under the American mining baron Alexander Shepherd, who had previously governed Washington, D.C. By the 1900s, Batopilas's heyday was over, the town population in decline, the elegant mining houses in decay.

Yet the town didn't die, the remnant thousand or so residents carrying on in their remote canyon, accessible only by foot and by mule until the road was chiseled through in 1978. Down here the ranchero world survives, complete with ten-gallon straw hats and the occasional shootout, often over a woman or, these days, over drugs.

Adventure travelers have already discovered the town, and government tourism people have plans for it, as a hiking center and historical site. The roofless, softly copper-toned adobe ruins of Shepherd's riverside hacienda form a major now-and-future tourist attraction.

There are already several small hotels in town, but none like McWilliams's. From ruins, he has built a dreamy re-creation of nineteenth-century Mexico: brilliantly painted rooms and passageways; garden courtyards; stenciled borders of blue curlicues on the walls; elegant kerosene lamps suspended everywhere; an eclectic collection of artwork and kitsch, antiques and knickknacks. In the big, eye-grabbing parlor, a faux-rococo painting covers the ceiling. The place is an *experience.* In the morning, you awake to the cooing of white-winged doves, the barking of town dogs, and the sight of sunlight touching the tips of the crags in that other world far above.

McWilliams wants to see the town not so much developed for tourism as restored for it. He's been urging locals to "return cobblestones to the streets, put back the old facades." He takes me into one of the abandoned, ruined houses from silver-boom days. Squatting over the rubble, he scrapes away a layer of grime on the wall with his penknife, revealing the same blue-curlicue stencil pattern now re-created in his hotel.

Being far from civilization, Batopilas lies close to unacculturated Tarahumara, often seen here in their traditional dress. For men, that's a billowy, balloon-sleeved shirt; a pale, triangular breechcloth called a *sitagora;* and a long-tailed headband. For women, it's brilliant, heavily pleated long skirts and full-sleeved blouses. Their clothes make the Tarahumara intensely photogenic. They do not like being photographed.

The forty thousand Tarahumara rank with Navajo and Cherokee as one of the largest native nations in North America. The tourism industry deploys pictures of Tarahumara everywhere. In Creel, murals and paintings of the Indians, ranging from skilled to atrocious, adorn hotel lobbies, shop signs, a motel water tank.

Ironically, Tarahumara value privacy even among themselves. They live apart, not in villages. They like silence, considering outsiders chatterboxes. They are loath to protest when wronged. It is through their lands that the envisioned legions of foreign hikers will pass.

I had to talk with them.

Her round, brown face small above the desk in the mission office in Creel, Felícitas Guanapani spoke hesitantly in the little-used English she picked up in a Jesuit school stateside: "When I was little, my mother told me to run and hide from a *chabochi*." *Chabochi*, whiskered one: any non-Indian. Trouble. Now, as a Tarahumara sophisticate, she could see the potential of tourism for her people, but she doesn't see it happening: "The white man takes all the money."

Except for crafts, especially violins. For over three centuries, the Indians have made violins to play at religious celebrations. Now there's a market for them. No varnish on them, though; the wood is left unfinished by tradition.

In Batopilas I buy one from Patrocinio López, considered by some the Stradivarius of the Tarahumara. By prearrangement, he jogs into town to sell it to me. The head is a delicately carved snake, a double loop. The Indians have found that this kind of embellishment boosts sales. Artistic corruption? Or advance?

López is an unusual Tarahumara; he enjoys slumming with *chabochis*. I ask about the prospect of many more tourists tramping through his country. Not so much a problem, he thinks. They come, they go. But most Indians make no distinctions among outsiders, lumping tourists in with evangelists — "*los aleluyas*" — who are a problem. "They stay, say we must wear pants, and change our ways. They marry Rarámuri women."

I think of a McWilliams wisecrack: "The main tool of cultural change is impressing the girls."

Hikers in the quantities FONATUR wants would become a permanent phenomenon, too. The mountain-bike man, Arturo Gutiérrez, also leads hikes but worries about crowds of independent trekkers. "What," I asked him, "if hikers had to have Tarahumara guides to keep them on acceptable paths?"

"Then it would not be the extreme experience that an adventure tourist wants."

Early one Saturday, the sound of helicopters drowns out the dogs and doves of Batopilas. Four times the choppers land, disgorging Mexico's technocratic elite. No ranchero hats in this lot. Crisp slacks, snappy weekend shirts, sunglasses. They are planners, architects, tourism specialists, officials, aides — yes, and even the governor of Chihuahua and the secretary of tourism for all Mexico.

The VIPs tour the town, then gather at McWilliams's hotel for a presentation by a high-powered Mexico City architectural firm. Handsome placards show the proposed restoration.

Not too bad, for Batopilas, at least. If — a big *if* — these plans come to pass, McWilliams would get almost everything he wants here, except the narrow road. Widened in some places, but not paved, they promise. In a region where tourism has tripled in just the last three years? "It's like a guy getting into bed with a beautiful woman and promising not to touch her," he grumped. "How long will that promise be kept?"

There's no mischievous look now. These canyonlands have carved themselves into Skip McWilliams's soul. He's not just protecting an investment; he's defending memories.

His own and those of his clients'. Memories of Batopilas inspired Cooper Young, a guest from Wichita Falls, Texas, to publish a story in the local paper when he got back home: See Batopilas now, he urged, "before electricity turns the stars off."

Some feel the tide of change need not be a flood. Electricity is spreading, but locals can mute the glare — especially if smart, revenue-bearing travelers request it. Tarahumara privacy is threatened, but there are ways to blunt the impact, like Indian cultural centers that provide visitors with museums, craft shops, dances, and events, located away from Indians' homes. North of the border several such centers provide models.

One, the Indian Pueblo Cultural Center in Albuquerque, provides a lesson, too. In the small museum there, a series of dioramas depicts Pueblo life over the centuries. In the last one, seated among several Indian figures, is a white man in casual shirt and sunglasses — the tourist. It's a frank acknowledgment of a growing worldwide truth: we visitors are woven into the fabric of the places we visit. The future of those places — and the quality of the travel experience — depends not only on how we comport ourselves, but also on how well tourism entrepreneurs sustain the character of what we've come to see.

My last night in the canyons, I stop in at McWilliams's Sierra Lodge. The gracious manager, Mara Carrillo, is supervising dinner preparations. I join a table with a woman just in from L.A. — a return guest, happy to be back. "I had a dream before I left," she's telling tablemates, "that when I got here, I found the lodge had become some kind of sprawling, stuccoed mega-resort. And to see Mara you had to make an appointment! But you could hear her voice on a loudspeaker: people with the red wristbands were to meet over there, and those with yellow wristbands over here . . ."

She turns to me, thinking I might need clarification.

"It was a nightmare," she says.

WILLIAM T. VOLLMANN

The Very Short History of Nunavut

FROM *Outside*

ON THE FIRST OF April, 1999, I had the privilege of watching as a new territory came into being, for most of the right reasons. The birth happened at midnight, in Canada's far north, with fireworks instead of bloodshed. I had just returned from Kosovo, and while I was watching the bright detonations over Iqaluit, the new capital of the new Nunavut, NATO bombers were busy over Yugoslavia. I could not help thinking of the faraway blossoms of those incendiary shells as I stood at the edge of the sea-ice that night when Nunavut became real, with Inuit children calling and roaring with happiness at each explosion. The fireworks hung like palm fronds around the full moon, offering green comets instead of leaves, and the silhouettes of gloved and parkaed people standing in the snow took on noonday life for a moment, until the light faded. Snow scuttered like gravel underfoot. There came more and more bursts, celebrated by fur-ruffed kids sitting on a high hillock of snow that had gone glassy with ice. With the windchill it was forty below; my face was numb; my pen froze. I'll never forget the dark figures on the pale snow, the rapturous cries, the fireworks' remarkable purity and clarity in that cold air. Every fiery star seemed as solid as a shard of glass in a kaleidoscope, and we could see its slowly dimming fall to the ice. Witnessing all around me the joy of the Nunavummiut, who had regained some control over their nation at last — after all, Nunavut means "our land" — I was moved almost to tears.

If you look at a map and take in the vastness of that balsamic paradise called Canada, you will quickly see why Nunavut, huge as it is,

remains outside the ken of so many Canadians, let alone the rest of
the world.

"Nunavut? What's that?" said a taxi driver in Montreal when I
passed through on my way north to Iqaluit. *"Le grand nord,"* I tried
to explain. *"Ile de Baffin, Ile d'Ellesmere, Ile de . . ."*

He shrugged. He didn't really care. Because Nunavut lies so far
away from almost everything! We're speaking of one-fifth of Canada's landmass, it's true — 730,000 square miles with one paved
road, only 25,000 people, and twenty-seven times that many caribou. But Canada, like Russia, can scarcely see and count herself
in her entirety. Two square miles or two million, it's all the same
to Canada. And so until now the conception, the *idea,* of Nunavut
has lain neglected, misunderstood. But the actual ground of
Nunavut itself? Well, for centuries explorers, whalers, merchants,
politicians, and soldiers have been coming here to the frozen edge
of the world — first only to where the ice began as they crept and
surveyed, clinging to the safety of water, the safety of summer's
final channels, dark blue and corduroyed with sunlight, with the
white cloud-puzzles overhead, past overhung ice-puzzles — and
then the white people calculated, gambled, stepped onto the ice.

Pretty soon some were doing well, like a Quebecer taxi driver I
know in Iqaluit who stops by the Navigator Inn late at night when
Inuit carvers sell their greenstone animal figures cheap because
they crave drunkenness; my acquaintance pays sixty dollars per
piece and sends them to his sister down south, who sells them for
four hundred dollars, keeps a 10 percent commission, and returns
him the rest, so he clears a tax-free ten grand a year from that
racket alone. Decades of cigarette smoking have awarded him the
voice of an Inuit throat-singer, and in those ragged tones he always
promises to lead me to the best carvers, or, if I don't go for that, he
can score me drugs, or anoint me a member of a top-secret club
whose purpose is to help me get *really close* to Inuit girls.

I rarely stay in Arctic towns on my visits north. I come with my
shelter on my back; I get off the plane and I start walking. Two or
three miles outside of town I pitch my tent. I come in a few times
and try to make friends. I go to church on Sundays and listen to the
Inuit pray for the Queen of England in Inuktitut. But mostly I leave
them alone. I am here to listen to wind and water.

What does Nunavut look like? This is difficult for me to say,
not only because deep down I don't want you to go to the Arctic,

and I feel guilty about going myself — Nunavut should be left to the Nunavummiut — but also because so many happy images and memories swirl behind my eyes whenever I think about this land. I wrote a novel set in the Canadian Arctic landscape, and I could write many more: pods of whales, polar bears, caribou running on ridge tops, summer moss, summer berries, mosquito crowds dense enough to blacken your face, cold that hurts, a sun that goes round and round in the sky like a clock without ever setting, long days and nights of winter moonlight bright enough to read a newspaper by (if you could stop shivering), the low elongations of the land, the blues and purples of the frozen sea, the sulfur-smelling crags of Baffin Island, waist- and shoulder-high rivers to ford, herds of musk oxen gathered (their spiked horns pointing out) in circles like immense wagon wheels, fossilized ferns and pine needles in valleys of icy shale, light, closeness to the sky, and above all, solitude.

I love that land, but it is not mine. It can never belong to me. When I was younger I once thought about settling here, in which case I would have become a member of the 15 percent of the Nunavummiut who aren't of Inuit extraction. Few of those people stay for long. So the land is truly not even mine to describe. To do so is to describe the Inuit themselves, because the Inuit are the land and the land belongs to them.

An Inuit woman named Elisapi has been my translator on several visits to the far northern settlement of Resolute; she is gentle, quiet, and plain, a serious, fortyish woman to whom I have always felt I could say anything. What word can describe her better than "pure"? But then I am always saying this about Inuit. To borrow from some idiot's remark about pornography, I can't define purity, but I know it when I see it. In Elisapi's case I think of kindness and patience and an unassuming spirituality. I hate even to write this much; I don't want to invade her soul with my conjectures and blundering definitions. Once, when I asked her what she thought was the most beautiful place in the Arctic, Elisapi looked at me in surprise and said, "Why, the land, of course. *All* the land."

What Elisapi loves above all else is to be "out on the land" — a phrase of almost mystic significance to Nunavummiut. *Out on the land!* On one of my trips to Iqaluit I met the wife of a carver, a slender woman who engraves brooches of walrus ivory. "I love to hunt anything," she said — the same words I'd already heard uttered by so many. "I've killed caribou, seal, walrus. I never killed a whale or a polar bear but my niece killed both already." She spoke with immense pride.

Elisapi, her husband, Joe, and their children have spent many a summer in a hunting camp on the ice. Even non-Inuit get infected. I've heard a Quebecer schoolteacher here use the same words: she was going to take her children out on the land for Easter, if the wind didn't prove too cold for the little ones. A young Anglo man I met in Apex, a little offshoot of Iqaluit, was always saying, "Man, I wish I were out on the land. Man, I wish I had a machine."

I remember the day Elisapi told me about the way she feels about the land. There was a strange light upon the hills and hollows, the armpits and throats of the white country, with the snow-covered sea pale blue like open water, and when Elisapi spoke, a feeling between love and sadness came over me, the same feeling I have year after year in the Arctic when I'm alone with mountains or musk oxen, far away beneath the sky.

Do I have your permission to compress the history of the Canadian Arctic into nine paragraphs? In 1576 Martin Frobisher sailed from England to seek the Northwest Passage. He anchored off Baffin Island, which now forms the eastern boundary of Nunavut, and loaded up his ship with tons of fool's gold while kidnapping other cargo: a man and an Inuit woman holding a small child by the hand. Frobisher's men carried them away from an elder, perhaps the child's grandmother, who "howled horribly." Perhaps it is no wonder that the capital, the only town of any size (population 4,500), which stands upon the site of the mariner's landing and which for years and years was called Frobisher Bay, changed its name to Iqaluit — "the place of many big fish." The locals would rather not remember him.

In Frobisher's time, Inuit families were self-sufficient, or else they starved. But then whalers from England and Scotland and elsewhere began to trade knives, needles, tea, rifles, and bullets for furs, meat, and ivory. Beginning in the late eighteenth century, subsistence hunting lost ground to the fur trade — although even now, as much as half of what some Nunavummiut eat remains "country food": caribou, seal, whale, ptarmigan, and the like, killed by relatives or friends. It was only in the second half of this century, when Canadian and American World War II air bases and then English-language schools mushroomed in the High Arctic, that the Inuit began to live in towns, twenty-eight little government-created settlements scattered over the snow and ice.

The growing dependence on trading with outsiders proved sometimes beneficial, sometimes pernicious. What happens if, instead of killing caribou to feed my family I hunt Arctic foxes to sell their skins for bullets? Then we earn a lot of bullets, provided that the price of fox skins stays high in the south and my caribou hunting is easy. But if the price falls, we just might starve, which dozens did in the 1934–35 central Arctic famine. We might also starve, or simply become idle and despondent, if hunting seals or whales were no longer acceptable, as happened in the 1970s and '80s, when Greenpeace and other environmental and animal-rights groups crippled the international sealskin trade. These do-gooders are accordingly hated throughout the Arctic; with varying degrees of justification, unemployment and suicides have been blamed on them. Many's the time in Nunavut and Greenland that I've been asked, "Are you a spy from Greenpeace?"

It was in part to protect the Inuit from a drastic boom-and-bust cycle that, in the 1960s, Canada's federal politicians began to encourage the construction of hamlets where people could enjoy medical care, education, warm beds, and an uninterrupted food supply. An old lady who'd been born in an igloo once told me, "In old days we had a very hard time. Government came, and it got easier." We sat on the sofa in her house in Iqaluit's tumble of old military hangars and prefab housing and unnamed gravel roads. I asked her, "If people wanted to live on the land again, would you go with them or would you stay in your house?" Sitting with her hands clasped in her lap, her head trembling, perhaps from Parkinson's disease, she peered at me through her huge and rimless spectacles, and then replied in high-pitched, glottal Inuktitut, "I can't stay in a remote outpost now. From the hospital they're giving me medicine, so I must stay in town."

And so, on southern Nunavut's green-mossed rock, painted oil drums, painted wood-and-metal houses, and garbage dumps rose up in the summer rain. In northern Nunavut, the colored houses appeared upon tan gravel banks. Of course, this new way of life further accelerated the very dependence which had already caused so much harm. I wonder if by then the future was already as evident as a yellow light bulb in Iqaluit glaring down on rock-hard snow. That future was mass welfare. Animal populations declined near the towns, making hunting less practical and more occasional. Dog teams sickened in the close quarters. More than one hunter came home in those days only to find that the Mounties had shot all his dogs in the interest of public health — for the white people, it seemed, always knew best. Could this have anything to do with the fact that Nunavut has six times the national suicide rate?

The most famous of these resettlement efforts took place between 1953 and 1955, when the government forcibly relocated some seventeen extended Inuit families from Inukjuak to new settlements at Resolute and Grise Fiord. Inukjuak lies way down in northern Quebec, nearly four hundred miles south of Nunavut as the Arctic raven flies. To me it is almost paradise. It is green, not white. In summer the tundra hangs thick with crowberries and caribou run everywhere. In winter the sun never disappears entirely. Elisapi's mother, Old Annie, who sewed my *kamiks,* the sealskin boots I wear on my feet, was born in a camp there. She never wanted to leave. But they shipped her north.

Some Inuit believe that the Canadian government wanted to assert sovereignty over the High Arctic islands in the face of the American air bases strategically placed there in World War II, and therefore settled them with the indigenous people most likely to survive. But it should also be said that Inukjuak was not so edenic in the late 1940s: the caribou herds were dwindling, the price of fur had fallen, the people were falling deeper into welfare addiction. The government figured, paternalistically, why not just move some Inuit to the northern ice and let them become the self-sufficient hunters of old. For good measure, they also relocated some families from Ellesmere Island's Pond Inlet — northerners to help the southerners settle in. But the relocations were accomplished against people's wills, with misinformation, and with appalling results. The people from Inukjuak were unfamiliar with the hunting strategies they needed to succeed on the Arctic pack ice; they didn't even get along with the Pond Inlet Inuit, who didn't even speak the same dialect. Look at a map of Canada to see how far away from home these people were taken. See Inukjuak on the northeastern shore of Hudson Bay? Now let your eyes sail north as the Canadian Navy sealift-supply ship *C. D. Howe* did, carrying those Inuit families: first three hundred miles into what is now Nunavut (we're out of Hudson Bay at last) and then perhaps one thousand miles farther north and two hundred miles west, almost to the magnetic North Pole.

The first time I went to Resolute, it was mid-August, around the same time the settlers had arrived, and it was snowing. By the time I left six weeks later, I had to chop up my drinking water with an ax. "When we arrived it was dark and cold," an old woman told me. "My child was really skinny from starving." The Inukjuak Inuit, who had never built igloos, constructed houses out of old packing crates and foraged for food in the garbage dumps of the whites, a sparse scattering of whom were stationed there with the Mounties, who oversaw a trading post in Resolute. For high prices, payable in furs, an Inuit hunter could obtain a scant few supplies, but sometimes there was an additional price — the sexual services of his wife. The results of the relocations: hunger, tuberculosis, lifelong bitterness.

The communities in Resolute and Grise Fiord survived, because Inuit are pretty damned tough. And in the more than twenty-year-long tale of the land-claims negotiations that created Nunavut, one reads a similar tenacity. What Nunavut gained — besides more than a billion Canadian dollars over the next fourteen years and valuable mineral rights — was a measure of self-governance. Nunavut is now a territory, exactly like the Yukon, exactly like the Northwest Territories it had been part of. What the Inuit gave up was the land. One of the only native North American groups who had never entered into a land treaty, many Inuit were anxious about extinguishing aboriginal title, and when the matter first came up for election in 1982, only 56 percent voted in favor of division. But what ultimately passed in 1993 — the Nunavut Land Claims Agreement Act — was the biggest land deal between a government and an aboriginal people in North American history. Suffice it to say that in the face of federal skepticism and infighting and bureaucratic foot-dragging and worse, a partition line was at long last drawn through the Northwest Territories. What lay east became Nunavut.

To me it was a miracle that this good thing was about to happen. And Iqaluit, which like so many Arctic towns is saturated with military-speak from the airbase days, seemed filled instead with joy-speak. Late in the evening on that last night of Northwest Territoriality, the bunkerlike elementary school filled with crowds come to hear the Anglican service in honor of Nunavut's birth. The stage was bedecked with figures in red and white robes, and the minister said, "We must remember that what we call Nunavut, our land, is in fact God's gift to us." In front of me was a little girl, half asleep in her mother's *amauti,* a parka with a hooded pouch in back for carrying babies. "We pray for our new commissioner," the minister went on, "for our new premier, for their families, for our new justices, who will be sworn in in a few moments, and most of all we pray for ourselves." In that cavernous, windowless gymnasium, built on concrete like a shop floor, they rose and prayed in English, French, and Inuktitut. "Now may the blessing of God Almighty be with us, both now and indeed forevermore. Amen." Then the minister smiled, checked his watch, and said, "Twenty-two minutes," and everyone laughed. In Inuktitut they sang "Now Thank We All Our God" in sweet and steady voices. A woman in a crimson vest embroidered with a white polar bear leaned her head upon her husband's shoulder as she sang.

A Nunavut for Nunavummiut — only some of the white cab drivers were sullen about it. Their taxi lights shone slow on the glassy night snow between the still, cold lights of the settlement.

The new territory purports to represent the interests of all residents, but the ultimate goal is to create a de facto self-governing Inuit homeland — not now, of course, but in twenty or fifty years. Today the non-Inuit 15 percent of the population holds a disproportionate number of the government, medical, and teaching jobs. Few Inuit are trained. Only a third of Nunavut's teachers are Inuit; there are no Inuit doctors; there is only one Inuit lawyer in all of Nunavut, thirty-four-year-old Paul Okalik, and he has been elected its first premier. A high-school dropout from Pangnirtung, a little village on the eastern shore of Baffin Island, Okalik wrestled with alcohol problems, jail, and his brother's suicide before going back to school on student loans. Despite his involvement in the Nunavut negotiations, he is as freshly minted a politician as Nunavut is a territory: he passed the bar and became premier within six weeks. The new territory's elder statesman — the father of Nunavut — is John Amagoalik, the journalist-politician who negotiated the land-claims settlement that created it and ran the Nunavut Implementation Commission that shaped its government. Sixteen of Nunavut's nineteen legislators are Inuit, too — a few former mayors, some businessmen, a snowplow operator. Starting on Nunavut Day, when a white person in the territorial government wrote a memo to his superiors, the reply might well come back in Inuktitut.

"They cannot just want to throw white people away," a Quebecer teacher named Thérèse, who works at the elementary school in Iqaluit, told me. "Not all of the Inuit are qualified." But then she added quietly, "I know some white people are afraid of losing their jobs, but gradually they should be replaced."

Plenty of Caucasians do fine in Nunavut: Elisapi's husband, Joe, for one, is white and as northern an individual as I have ever met. But many find living in Nunavut difficult. The language daunts them; the mores are so different. Thérèse had spent four years in Iqaluit, but she planned to return south. She had a few Inuit friends, acquaintances really, from work. But Nunavut was not hers.

Meanwhile, in northern Quebec, the Inuit region known as Nunavik (from which the relocations to Resolute and Grise Fiord were carried out) harbors similar, half-concealed aspirations to autonomy. And down in Ottawa, even as Nunavut set off its fireworks, Cree Indians were drumming and singing on Parliament Hill in protest of the new territory, on the grounds that 31,000 square miles of their land have been stolen to create it. And of course, many Quebecers long to secede from Canada and form their own Francophone nation. The white taxi drivers I talked with in Iqaluit are among this number. They told me that this whole Nunavut business was all *shit*. The Inuit weren't ready, one of them opined. Quebec should secede, but not Nunavut. Quebec pays too much in taxes, and Canada just called Quebecers *fucking frogs*. The prime minister was an *asshole*. This last cabbie was an angry, stupid man, but, like the Inuit themselves, all he really wanted was some kind of recognition.

Finally, from what now remains of the Northwest Territories comes talk of further partitions and ethnic homelands. There was a move to rename this region Denedeh because so much of it was Dene Indian land, but the whites (who'd become the majority after the partition of Nunavut) voted down the measure, after which a bitter joke went around the Northwest Territories that the only real way to satisfy them would be to call the territory by the Anglo name of Bob.

Given the desire of so many places to un-Canada themselves to varying degrees, I was all the more impressed when the prime minister of Canada, Jean Chrétien, who had flown up to Iqaluit for the Nunavut Day festivities, rated justice over expediency in his speech that night. "We have come to recognize the right of the people of the north to take control of their own destiny," he proclaimed. And everyone stood up and cheered, and I cheered.

It would be as pleasing as it would be false to end our tale with the close of that inaugural ceremony in one of the concrete military hangar bays, as tiny old Helen Mamyaok Maksagak, first commissioner of Nunavut, hugged to her heart the flag of her territory, presented to her by Inuit boys from Canada's Boy Scouts, the Junior Rangers. Or to conclude on Nunavut Night, the evening after the fireworks, where a heavy-metal band from Kuujjuaq was entertaining one crowd with noise and dry-ice vapor while two hangars down the little kids were jigging to banjo and fiddle, and the old ladies in parkas were nodding, smiling, clapping, and everyone was applauding, and Premier Okalik was wandering around in his sealskin vest, floating in a shyly happy dream.

The air grew hot with the fragrance of bubble gum, wet fur, human sweat. Dancers came out, circling and snaking to the repetitive melody; an old man in a red cap and a collar of wolverine skins with the claws still on jogged happily up and down, watching. So many people with Nunavut hats and T-shirts, so many with the new Nunavut sweatshirts! But finally it was time to go back out among the gray snowdrifts and glaring streetlights of April, back to the steep-roofed houses to sleep. And the next morning and forever the tale of Nunavut must continue, this time without miraculous ceremonies.

"I've already given you enough beer," the white waiter in Iqaluit's Komatik Restaurant told the Inuit grandmother and her toothless boyfriend. "So I'll just put your next beer in the fridge and give it to you next time."

At this, the boyfriend started crying out in Inuktitut, and the grandmother joined in, wailing, "How *come* you? How come?"

"You cannot drink them tonight because you don't need the beer," the waiter insisted. "You've had too much. That's the end of the conversation."

"Where's my beer?" the grandmother demanded. "Where's my

goddamned beer?" She wore a T-shirt printed in memory of a friend who'd died. Her eyes were lights glaring on ice; her words were breath-steam in the night. She was forty-four years old.

"If you keep this up," the waiter said, "there'll be trouble."

It was two nights after Nunavut Day. I'd seen her earlier that afternoon before she was drunk, a big, squat woman with cropped hair, upslanted eyes, and a downpouted mouth. She was pale and old; her arms were covered with cooking burns. One of her sisters had died of cancer, another of alcoholism, a brother in a car accident (the car ran over his head). The last brother had hanged himself "because he was crazy," she said.

Now, as the waiter refused to serve her and her boyfriend, I invited them back to my hotel, which stood almost within sight of the restaurant. The grandmother's boyfriend didn't want to come. He stayed on at the Komatik, wiggling his fingers, feebly bewildered.

So the grandmother and I walked and she whined and wept, because she was very cold. Her ancient parka didn't zip anymore, and the alcohol had only pretended to warm her, in much the same fashion that the low sun can gild a house's siding so that it glows and shines against the blue snow with spurious preciousness. I offered to let her wear my parka but she wouldn't. She kept crying: "Too cold! *Ikkii!*" She touched my hand and said: "You cold. Cold! You too cold! *Ikkii!* Better you eat like Inuk. Eat meat. Eat caribou, walrus, seal . . ."

Anytime I wanted her to smile, I only had to ask her what animals she liked to hunt. She'd reply: "Any kind!" and would commence counting off the different animals on her fingers, uttering the Inuktitut names. Earlier that evening, with the beer not yet raging in her, she remained a wise old huntress. Just as caribou are sometimes silhouetted against snow, especially on ridges and when they crouch down to graze, snowy-white-on-white, so her memories stood out or hid, browsing and drowsing within her, living their own life. She could scarcely read or write, but (or perhaps therefore) she could remember. And for her, animals were the most vividly numinous entities.

I said that I wanted to go hunting sometime with her or her family, at which she began to check me out very seriously and soberly, saying, "Okay, Bill, you got the mitts, you got the coat; you can come hunting. Your pants gonna be cold, though." Not having planned on hunting again this trip, I'd left my windpants back in America.

We were outside then. It was twenty below zero. Later that night, I wandered wearily through one of Iqaluit's arcade malls, my hood thrown back, my parka unzipped, wearing my *kamiks* since I had no other shoes, my mitts dangling conveniently from strings at my sleeves. A slender young Inuit girl, high or crazed, began mocking me and eventually came running down the hall and punched me and kicked me, shrieking: "Where are you *from,* Daddy-o? What are you doing with all that fuckin' stupid gear?"

She herself was dressed like a Southern California girl, and I wondered whether she had been among those serenely happy crowds on Nunavut Day, those people clapping grimy work gloves and sealskin mitts, while the fur ruffs of their parkas swirled in the wind. So angry and sad, did she care about Nunavut?

For her, the beauties of utility had given way to the beauties of fashion. Moreover, in so many young people's eyes, utility and fashion married one another in synthetic apparel. On a walk in Apex, I found myself promenading beside a young Anglo guy with dyed hair along the community's frozen shore, past rocks and trash cans protruding from the snow. He wore camouflage pants and a brand-name American parka. As we approached the frozen drifts on the frozen sea, with the wide, low domes of snow-islands ahead, he was telling me about one of his adventures over the winter. "We were fuckin' set up, man. We had fuckin' beer and the whole fuckin' nine yards. Then we got slammed with a 120-kilometer wind and, well, we lay down between our snowmobiles and we made it." He had no use for caribou-skin clothing, and neither did I.

In that mall, to be sure, I was ludicrously overdressed. My old huntress did not find me so. She was charitable and practical; she was gentle, open, giving. But later that night she was drunk; now she was crazy, too. A hundred years ago, she might have been better off — unless, of course, she'd starved to death. Now she could drink herself to death.

For her, perhaps, Nunavut had arrived too late; it would differ too painfully from her code of life. This new thing, Nunavut, is as beautiful as a woman's parka trimmed with strips of fur and strips of patterned cloth, as ugly as scraps of plastic dancing in an Arctic wind.

*

But who can foresee Nunavut's future even five years ahead? It's an experiment, full of vigor and nobility, the government resolutely, democratically local, with its ten departments housed in ten widely spread Arctic towns. And Premier Okalik is an Inuit leader, as bright and optimistic as the territory. No doubt he and the other young politicians will grow old; perhaps they'll fall into nepotism and inertia until the political landscape freezes like the laundry on a clothesline covered with Easter snow. But for now he seems committed.

On Nunavut Day, the elders gathered in the hangar bays cheered Okalik — he was *their* young man, homegrown. But precisely because he was theirs, they didn't have to stand on ceremony, and so their kids ran loudly in and out. Perhaps Okalik won the election because he exemplified the pragmatic modesty and moderation that has always served Inuit so well, the genial humility that had his colleagues in the territorial negotiations introducing one another's speeches with aw-shucks humor, insisting that at the beginning they didn't even know what a land claim was. Now, when Okalik came to the podium, he declared, "We have achieved our goal through negotiations without civil disobedience. . . . We hope we can contribute to the prosperity and diversity of Canada."

Here was no separatist poison, no threat to the sovereignty of the country at large. Nunavut remained Canadian — with a difference, of course. At the conclusion of the inaugural ceremony, they sang the national anthem, but this rendition of "O Canada" must have startled Prime Minister Chidden and the other federal politicians, for the Inuit decorated its melody at beginning and end with an ancient *ayah* song, performed by three women.

Nunavut remains her own place, an extended family even after all the decades of damage, the community a superorganism that tries to warm all in its bosom. But can the fresh new super-superorganism truly give itself to all Inuit? Almost 60 percent of the Nunavummiut are under twenty-five years of age. And the alteration of almost every aspect of material culture has occurred so rapidly that the elders and the kids riding their bikes in the April snow almost constitute two separate societies. Sometimes I think that the old huntress and the girl who kicked me had more in common with me than with one another.

*

At her house in Resolute, Elisapi's mother, Annie, takes a hunk of frozen raw caribou or seal from the freezer, sets it down on cardboard on the kitchen floor, and chops off splinters of meat with a hatchet. Annie says her favorite boarders are those who eat her "country food," and she always smiles at me because I fall to with relish. At community feasts, the Inuit drag in whole animal carcasses, and tear out raw intestines with their teeth; so the fact that I'll eat almost anything helped endear me to Annie, one linchpin of her culture being the sharing of home-killed meat. When by happy chance I found Annie and Elisapi living in Iqaluit not long after Nunavut Day, my hair was long, and Annie liked that too, because it made me look like a native. She told me this with Elisapi's help, because she cannot speak English.

For the people of Annie's generation, Nunavut is above all a vindication, a gift, a balm to wounded pride. Annie is entering her second childhood. Elisapi and the other sisters will take care of her. She's too frail to sew *kamiks* anymore. She'll never use a computer. She's already home. She'll die safe from the unimaginable changes now looming over Nunavut.

For Annie, and for so many Inuit, men and women alike, to be oneself is to hunt. Everybody hunts for survival: people raised on that basis know how to share, how to kill, and how to handle firearms responsibly. I once went out on a walrus hunt and watched a seven-year-old boy instructing his five-year-old brother in gun safety, with no adults in attendance except me. On that same hunt, I saw a seal killed with three shots and a walrus with one.

Many tourists from down south simply don't possess such attributes, but if the new territory of Nunavut gets what it wants, there will be more white hunters, more white visitors out on the land. The outfitters in Nunavut will soon be swimming in business, I imagine. They will take bird-watchers and whale lovers out to stalk their prey with binoculars, telephoto lenses, and watercolor brushes. They'll learn to pamper the ones who forgot their warm clothes. They'll learn that legal liability hangs over them at all times. They'll be treated to cries of amazed disgust when somebody from a city sees a hunter butchering a bloody seal on an icy gravel beach. It's all for the good, I suppose, as long as local people make money. Over time, Nunavut will be receiving a diminishing income from the federal government, so why shouldn't tourism make up the shortfall?

Today only about eight thousand tourists a year come to
Nunavut, most of them dogsledders, hunters, and wildlife watchers
bound for the remote interior or for Baffin Island, and its belu-
gas and killer whales. The adventurous few climb Mount Thor or
Mount Asgard, or sea-kayak the fjords of Baffin Island. But if it
weren't for the shiny glints of increased tourism and development,
why were corporate Canada's congratulations on the birth of
Nunavut so loud?

Elisapi and Joe were hoping to rent out their house to the rich
tourists who undertake expeditions to the North Pole. Elisapi had
come to Iqaluit, in fact, to enroll as a communications student. She
wanted to go into public relations or journalism. Since public relations is generally employed by businesses and governments rather
than by aboriginal hunters, her new career seemed fairly certain,
however indirectly, to further "develop" the land.

In that sense Elisapi reminded me of the carver's wife I met in
Apex; the woman liked Nunavut, she said, because there would
soon be more jobs. According to recent national census and provincial labor figures, 40 percent of the Inuit residents of Nunavut,
and 9 percent of the other residents, do not "participate in the labor force (wage economy)." Moreover, the remote Nunavummiut
must pay between two and three times more for basic goods and
services than southern Canadians do. So the carver's wife was worried about being left out in the economic cold. But she also hun-
gered for solitude, preferring Apex to Iqaluit because it was qui-
eter. Like Annie, she'd been born in a hunting camp.

There was a term for these new Nunavummiut: weekend hunters. Their philosophy was to let the new life come and to benefit
from it while living the old life as long as they could. But as new careers and tourism push the caribou back, where will their land be?
It made me worry about the next twenty years. I said as much to
Elisapi's sister Laila, but she cut me off. "Don't worry about us," she
said with an angry smile. "We'll survive."

And why shouldn't Elisapi learn to shape the world's understanding of Inuit? Other people have. One sardonic old Inuit joke
used to run that the average Inuit family comprises 6.5 individuals:
a husband, a wife, 3.5 children, and a nosy anthropologist from
down south.

"Objectivity" may be lost, but much else will be gained, when

Elisapi replaces the anthropologist. And if her public relations contribute to the development of Nunavut, who am I to say that's a bad thing? And as Nunavut increasingly caters to tourists, wouldn't it be excellent, given that many of those caterers will doubtless be capital-rich entrepreneurs from Toronto or Sydney or Los Angeles, if Elisapi could make her percentage? As Inuit culture becomes a commodity, can't Elisapi sell it better than I can?

But what is Inuit culture? Endless hunting for the sake of prowess, the sharing of killed food, a knowledge of Inuktitut, sexual easiness and earthiness, old stories, a reserved smile, tenderness with children and confidence in them, respect for family, cheerfulness in the face of physical discomfort, *ayah* songs and throat-songs, animal-skin clothes? I can buy the garments; can I buy the rest?

If in the future they open resorts in Nunavut, remember solitude, and let someone else patronize them. If you must go, expect discomfort, inconvenience, and high prices. If you possess less experience than you will need to survive on your own, by all means find a local outfitter who can help you, and be guided by his advice. Above all, if you visit Nunavut, take care that your actions don't transform the region into a mirror image of the place you left.

For the next three months, Elisapi, with her two sons and Annie, was going to be staying at her daughter Eunice's place, an immaculate house (too much so for Elisapi's taste) with snow-white wall-to-wall carpet. In a corner niche I saw a group photograph, taken by a social worker back in 1955, of Annie and her family waiting to be relocated to Resolute, sitting forlornly on the rocks of Inukjuak.

I'd met Eunice once or twice in Resolute, the first time when she was about thirteen. She drew for me a picture of a polar bear stalking a baby seal on an Arctic midnight. When I got home I mailed her some colored pencils. She moved down to Iqaluit a few years later, and now, at twenty-four, she has two daughters and is a famous throat-singer whose albums are sold to strangers across the Atlantic. She had performed in traditional dress at the Nunavut gala. She'd already been to Hawaii three times.

Fifteen minutes after I arrived, Eunice said she'd see me around. Her husband had just bought a new snowmobile; they were going for a ride out on the land. This was not rudeness on her part, but the habitual casualness of the Nunavummiut, who come and go as they wish. Eunice told me what I already knew, that I was welcome to stay for as long as I pleased, and indeed I visited with her relatives for another two hours before I went on my way.

Getting ready for their ride, Eunice had slipped her younger daughter into the *amauti,* because it was one of those cold days when breath-steam rose high above everybody's hoods. I had asked Eunice what kind of fur she used for her hood's unfamiliar ruff, and she made a face: "I don't know," she had replied. "Some ugly kind. I should get it replaced." But Elisapi and Annie both knew what kind of animal it came from, and they immediately told her — or told me, I should say, because Eunice wasn't interested. The ruff was coyote, from way down south, like her carpet and her snowmobile.

I never got the chance to ask Eunice if she still hunted, and in a way it doesn't matter. Her strain of Inuitness, like her mother's, will survive even after that hypothetical day when all the shores of Baffin Island have reared up their apartment forests in mocking imitation of the trees that could never have lived here. Fluent in both English and Inuktitut, and deriving both recognition and cold cash from her culture, Eunice seems likely to thrive. Maybe someday she'll be the Voice of Nunavut, emerging from radios and loudspeakers like the muezzins of Pakistan calling people to prayer.

What Nunavut will Eunice live in then? Perhaps the land will be changed, developed. Perhaps she and Elisapi and their family will live in a city of skyscrapers. Perhaps every seal will be tagged by then, transmitting its location and vital signs to wildlife officials, and Eunice's throat-songs will comprise their own signals in a realm of signal, human and animal equal. Why not? Which is to say, who knows? This spring, Nunavut was a promise. Now Nunavut will become a mystery as socioeconomic forces weave their half-blind ravelings.

On the last night of my trip, I stood on a snow ridge between Iqaluit and Apex, gazing up at the aurora borealis sprinkling itself across the sky like confectioner's sugar, mingling with the city's steam trails and smoke trails. After a while it began to ooze slowly downward like white fists and frozen white winds swirling between stars. Far away, the lonely headlight of a snowmobile rushed across the land.

DAVID WALLIS

One Man and His Donkey

FROM *The St. Petersburg Times*

As I MEANDERED along the banks of the cocoa-colored river where the animal traders set up alfresco showrooms, a bull-necked Moroccan in a flowing white jellaba and lavender skullcap grabbed my arm. "My friend, good mule, only 1,100 dirham [about $110]," he promised.

I have always been skeptical of strangers who call me "friend," but I followed him, enticed by his offer of a bargain. Of the dozens of mules for sale at the Marriage Moussem of the Aït Haddidou — a matchmaking festival and souk held every autumn in a field near the Atlas Mountain village of Imilchil — most cost at least three thousand dirham ($300), well beyond my budget. And unlike the rug salesmen and peddlers of pointy leather slippers, whose prices plummet every time they pour you a cup of mint tea, mule traders are not budged by debate, feigned anger, or outright begging.

Unfortunately, the much-touted mule looked ready for the *tajine* pot: listless eyes, dull brown coat, bloated belly hanging nearly to the ground. Despite my doubts, I climbed aboard for a test drive. At first he scampered along at an impressive pace, but within five minutes he was waddling and wheezing. Imagine riding Boris Yeltsin.

I had known my original plan to trek the Atlas Mountains by mule wouldn't be easy. Being a native New Yorker, I had no equestrian experience aside from riding the Central Park carousel; I spoke no Arabic or Berber (the language of indigenous Moroccans) and only a few words of French (a vestige of colonialism); didn't know where to unload a secondhand mule; and hadn't even figured out that a mule was a hybrid of a mare and a male donkey.

But mule power held great appeal: I felt an affinity for the animal, having often been compared to one, and traveling like a local would afford me a mule's-eye view of Atlas Mountain culture. A tribal people, Atlas Berbers are rugged individualists who earlier this century fended off French troops for twenty-one years longer than their sea-level brethren had done.

According to Berbers in the know, buying and then reselling a mule was the most practical, economical way to see the remote, predominantly roadless region. But short of stealing one, I was out of luck.

"How about a donkey? It will cost less than a mule and still carry your pack," suggested Nasser, an economics student from Marrakesh who had befriended me on the way to the Moussem. I trusted Nasser. He had volunteered to translate for me without payment, and when I offered him a few dollars he was almost insulted.

Still, I had misgivings about his proposal. Typically, only old men and children ride donkeys, which are scrawnier, slower, and require more rest than mules. And I had my heart set on a mule. But I saw no harm in browsing.

One donkey stood above the competition — literally. He was well groomed, about four feet tall, and had muscular legs. Exuding poise, he kept perfectly still when Nasser grasped his white snout and peeled apart his lips to examine his teeth. Nasser guessed he was about eight years old, not a colt but sprightly enough for a short expedition.

Nasser examined the donkey's eyes, checking for, believe it or not, drugs. To fool innocent customers, unscrupulous traders tranquilize their unbroken donkeys. Finally he launched a right jab inches from the donkey's face, which the animal dodged with aplomb.

"Good reflexes," judged Nasser, and urged me to snap it up.

I handed the donkey's owner three hundred dirham ($30). He pressed the three limp banknotes to his lips and kissed them; they meant two months of food for his family.

"What's the donkey's name?" I inquired, provoking howls of laughter. "No one names a donkey," scoffed Nasser, also chuckling. I soon understood why. Berbers think of a donkey as inanimate — like a wheelbarrow.

I vowed to respect my donkey. He got a fresh set of steel shoes, straw, balancing baskets to lighten his load, and a name, Stevenson

— in homage to RLS and his *Travels with a Donkey in the Cevennes*. "We are all travelers in the wilderness of this world," mused Stevenson, "all, too, travelers with a donkey; and the best that we find in our travels is an honest friend. He is a fortunate voyager who finds many. We travel to find them, they are the end and reward of life."

Striving to be the best possible donkey owner, I bought Stevenson a green apple from a tented fruit stand. But he didn't devour it. Nor the grain I spread on the ground. Was I saddled with an anorectic donkey? Nasser shook his head, dislodged the metal bit blocking Stevenson's mouth, and said, "My friend, you are in big trouble."

Since Nasser was returning to Marrakesh the next day and could no longer shepherd me, I had to find a licensed mountain guide. To earn accreditation, Moroccan guides complete a two-year course, covering geology, horticulture, first aid, mountaineering, and a foreign language.

Mohammed, a guide recommended to me by one of the Moussem's organizers, must have failed English. "What want?" he grunted. My goal, I explained, was to reach Tounfite, about seventy-five miles away, where I could supposedly sell Stevenson for a profit at the town's souk, then catch a bus to Fez. Mohammed agreed to guide me for two thousand dirham ($200), which included four nights' lodging at Berber homes and a daily picnic for me and Stevenson.

"We go tomorrow, eleven hours," said Mohammed, a spindly man with a shock of gray hair who had a bulky bandage speckled with blood on his right wrist. "What happened to your hand?" I asked. "Problem," barked Mohammed. "We go tomorrow, eleven hours."

Luckily, I hadn't given Mohammed a deposit, because he didn't show up. As a final favor, Nasser (and one hundred dirham) persuaded a local farmer, also named Mohammed, to accompany me as far as Imilchil, where a few official guides were based.

I could communicate with Mohammed II by hand signals only, yet he taught me much about donkey driving. Lesson one: Repeat a rhythmic tutting sound; the faster you tut, the faster the donkey marches. Lesson two: From time to time shriek *"Ra, hamare, ra"* — "Go, donkey, go." Lesson three: Ride the donkey only occasionally or risk more frequent grazing breaks.

For much of the seven-hour walk, Mohammed allowed Stevenson to amble at his own pace, only leading him by the reins when
trucks packed with human cargo, known as "Berber taxis," barreled down the dusty, narrow piste, forcing us to scramble to the
shoulder. At dusk, we arrived in Imilchil, a film director's dream
village dominated by a turreted casbah the color of a dried red
rose. It was the last place before Tounfite to shop, sleep in a hotel,
use a telephone, or catch a Berber taxi back to civilization.

Early next morning, after sleeping at the shabby but friendly
Hotel Izmal — Stevenson slept in the manager's barn — I tracked
down Zaid, the only English-speaking guide available. We sat cross-
legged on straw mats in his *bit diyaf,* part living room, part bedroom, where most Moroccans receive guests.

A lean, caramel-complexioned man who chain-smoked cigarettes, Zaid had a disgruntled expression that said, "I need the
money; otherwise I wouldn't be doing this." Yet, curiously, he
couldn't have been more hospitable as we plotted our course on
a map. "Eat, drink, my friend," he implored, as his wife appeared
with tea, shelled almonds, and warm sourdough bread with apricot jam.

After collecting Stevenson, we trotted to the Plateau des Lacs,
sandy flatlands surrounded by mountains that appeared to be cut
from Italian marble. We stopped for lunch by a vast lake, which, according to legend, was formed from the tears of forbidden lovers.

While I soothed my feet in the water, Zaid set Stevenson loose to
feed. A dreadful high-pitched wail, an animal's rebel yell, shattered
the calm. Stevenson was gone, in pursuit of a flirtatious female
donkey. Lesson four: When parked, tie down your donkey.

Zaid and I, both barefoot, gave chase. Zaid disappeared over a
bluff, not to be seen again until an hour later, when he hobbled
back to the lake, an unrepentant, even smug, Stevenson in tow.

Much ground had to be made up if we were going to reach
Anine village by nightfall. But Stevenson moved even more slowly
than before. Now I know why boxers swear off sex before a bout. As
we ascended a steep mountain pass, I often had literally to shove
him uphill while Zaid reeled him in from above. "Your donkey likes
to mate but not to work," grumbled Zaid.

We made it to Anine in time for dinner at the home of a shepherd — also named Mohammed. A widower, Mohammed III lived
with his four sons and daughter in a squat breeze-block house with

a flat log roof. No running water. Not even a Turkish toilet. Flies everywhere.

As custom dictates, the men chatted over mint tea while my host's teenage daughter feverishly prepared the meal: *tajine* of just-killed chicken with potatoes.

A gray fog blanketed the mountains when we left Anine the next morning. Mohammed III tagged along for a while, leading us up a boulder-strewn path with a deadly drop-off, barely visible on the right. At first Mohammed seemed affable enough, until he started whacking Stevenson's hind legs with a switch, drawing a trickle of blood. Before venting my outrage, I recalled another Berber proverb, "Praise your friend in public — reprimand him in private," so I complimented Mohammed III on his skillful donkey handling and asked him if I could take over, seeing as I needed the practice.

The onset of exhaustion intensified every sense, heightened every emotion. The tomato I ate for lunch was the juiciest and sweetest I had ever tasted; the mountain air fresher than any I had inhaled; the impromptu bath in a fast-flowing stream the most cleansing; my contempt for Zaid — who would say things like "Next time, bring California girls for the sex" — more vehement than ever. And the tribal drumming greeting us as we entered Arredou village was the most hypnotic.

That night, on the floor of another strange house, fever hammered my body. Every muscle throbbed. I had nearly no medicine left, having dispensed myriad pills and potions to local people who view travelers as roving pharmacists. Every parasite and microbe in the Atlas Mountains must have been namboing in my intestines.

Since the nearest doctor was thirty miles away, I resumed the march at sunrise, trudging to the top of another peak, a climb of maybe a thousand feet. By the time we descended into a valley packed with pines, I had to rest every twenty minutes or so, irritating Zaid. "What's wrong with you?" he shouted. "Berbers will think you are crazy if you walk like that. Be a man, have courage." Although I sorely yearned to flop on Stevenson, I stumbled on.

I collapsed on the threshold of the farmhouse where we bunked that night. My hosts — a middle-aged couple with a seven-year-old son named Hassan — took pity on me. They fed me plain couscous, helped me take a cold sponge bath, and enforced a no-talking policy. Even Zaid took pity, finding me aspirin and Coca-Cola.

In the morning, I checked on Stevenson. Hassan had covered

him with a blanket and given him a pile of alfalfa, caviar for donkeys. I knew then that these impoverished potato farmers, who readily showed me compassion, would treat Stevenson as family. Here he would never be abused or end up in a stew, so I gave him to Hassan — on two conditions: the boy would pet Stevenson daily and occasionally introduce him to girl donkeys. We shook hands on that.

Still, I faced a dilemma. Walking a mile, let alone more than twenty, to Tounfite was impossible. Zaid came up with a solution: mule rental. For the discounted price of one hundred dirham (about $10), a friend of the farmer's agreed to lend me his animal, which his cousin in Tounfite would return later. In minutes, my ride pulled up to the farmhouse. As I climbed aboard the powerful white mule I felt mixed emotions: satisfaction at fulfilling my original plan, but sadness too. I was leaving behind a loyal friend.

AMY WILENTZ

Marseille's Moment

FROM *Condé Nast Traveler*

JEAN-ROBERT, a fifty-year-old contractor and housepainter, lives in Bonnieux, a hill village in the Lubéron surrounded by farmers' fields, orchards, and vineyards. He spent many years in Paris and then ran a record shop in Avignon, not far from Bonnieux. Jean-Robert is hip and cosmopolitan. He has a gray buzz cut and wears a T-shirt, chinos, and very laid-back sneakers. He is sensitive to the nuances of cool.

But life in bucolic Bonnieux is not about cool. There is nothing cool about his neighbors, who are old ladies carrying shopping baskets and old men with pipes and berets. Except for one café-bar, there is nothing at all chic or new or fresh in Bonnieux. This is why Jean-Robert started going to Marseille. He drives down from his remote provincial hill, an hour and a half on country roads and the autoroute, and he's in another country, a place filled with recording studios and fashion ateliers, the best seafood in the world, and people from everywhere. Marseille is "supercool."

What he likes best about Marseille is how sometimes when you're there you can forget you're in France. If you're French, this is a positive attribute. Next to us, in front of the Bar le Maraichers at the Place Jean Jaurès, four men are sitting at a table with their heads together, drinking espresso and speaking Arabic. In the middle of the square, on market days, stall after stall is manned by turbaned men who converse in strange tongues. African women in brightly dyed robes and scarves push strollers down the streets near the Galeries Lafayette and the Virgin megastore. Gypsies live in the suburbs in high-rises. In Marseille, the burden of Paris and of being

French and of having to speak perfectly and be rich and brilliant and cultured and well dressed and thin is miraculously lifted. In Paris, liking football can be objectionable. But you can love soccer in Marseille — in fact, you have to. You can be unselfconsciously working class in Marseille. It is permitted to be of foreign origin in Marseille. In fact, almost the entire soccer team, the focus of extravagant city loyalty, is of foreign origin.

Marseille is a city of immigrants and nomads and fishermen, and you can see it in the faces of the Marseillais. It's like New Orleans, another water-gazing town known for its mixed stews and mixed music, another seaport not really affiliated with the mother country. FIVE GENERATIONS OF SEA PEOPLE, proclaims a sign over the Maison Falcone, a store in the fish section of the Marché des Capucins. Here they sell fish as various as the Marseillais themselves: *loup, labre, sardine, truite, pageot, grondin, daurade, carpe, maquereau, merlan, bonite, allache, anguille* — long and slithery and alive in their box — as well as *mange-tout* (nameless tiny fish), soup fish (more nameless tiny fish), five kinds of squid, and octopus. In shops around the square you can buy pizza and pita sandwiches, olives and *harissa* (the spicy red sauce that is used to up the gustatory ante of couscous). The merchants wear fezzes and skullcaps, scarves and kaffiyehs, and even the occasional baseball cap. Unmistakably, fishermen infest the place. Their hands are scarred and weathered, and they have the faces of pirates: a half-closed eye here, a scowl there, a scar across the cheek, sun-worn skin, a tooth missing (or a finger), gnarled knuckles. They carry sharp, shining knives to clean the fish, and they stick together in little groups, talking, gossiping, comparing prices fetched for different catches, feeling the fish.

Suddenly, at the edge of the market square, just in front of an undistinguished alabaster statue of Lady Agriculture that graces the end of the market's vegetable section, an older woman with blond highlights in her gray hair comes walking amid all the bustle with her head held high. Like some kind of Parisian apparition, she's wearing a Chanel suit and heels. In one hand she has a shopping bag from the Galeries Lafayette; in the other she's grasping the leash of an apricot toy poodle that follows her jauntily as she sails through the crowd of smokers and hawkers and gamblers and early-morning drinkers and sailors and fishermen like a figurehead of France. The spirit of France exists in Marseille in just the right dose: the lady and the poodle, café life, *escargots,* the morning carafe of wine, an old-fashioned candy store, the workers' blue *salopettes,* or overalls, the elaborate gardens of the Palais Longchamp, the three graceful Haussmann-era boulevards.

"Marseille is the unbeloved child of France," says Claude Bertrand, the blunt-spoken chief of staff for Marseille's conservative mayor, Jean-Claude Gaudin, who was elected in 1995 after a long stretch of leftists. "It's attached to France, but it has the collective consciousness of an Italian city-state, like Genoa or Venice. It faces the sea, and the hills behind it enclose it and isolate it from the rest of the country." You sense this isolation in the speech of the Marseillais, with its distinctive flutey Provençal intonation and broad vowels (M. Bertrand, by contrast, has a Parisian accent), but the history of the town also tells the same story. When I first arrived, I thought, understandably, that the splendid fortifications that stand facing each other at the narrow entrance to the Vieux Port had been erected to safeguard the city from maritime predators. But no. It turns out that the cannons of both the Citadelle St-Nicolas and the Fort St-Jean were built by Louis XIV and were more often turned inward by the forces of the king in order to keep the Marseillais and their economically lucrative boats under French control, thus ensuring France's security and seafaring preeminence. (Similarly, Marseille's seventeenth-century Italianate Hôtel de Ville, located on a Vieux Port site where the city's government has been housed for more than seven centuries, stands squarely across from the old royalist Arsenal. The two buildings still seem to glower at each other from either side of the slender waterway.)

Marseille was a power to be dealt with at the height of its prosperity: "During colonial days," says M. Bertrand, "the city derived great wealth from the sea, from shipping. But from the moment of decolonization, the city suffered a terrible degradation, because it was no longer the central port of an enormous empire. Decolonization meant the utter transformation of maritime traffic, from which Marseille has never really properly recovered."

Marseille has borne the consequences of being other and alien and always rebellious — Paris has always known how to exact its tithe in humiliation, as anyone who has ever visited the capital will attest. No wonder Marseille and its people have a chip on their shoulder. But they are Marseillais, so they carry the chip with defiance and pride. The city has been compared to the popular French drink pastis, the cheap licorice-flavored fix of the French masses. "Pastis has bad press, like Marseille. It's a troublesome drink. . . . No one forgives pastis for being the people's beverage," writes Olivier Boura in his book *Marseille, or A Bad Reputation*. "Pastis constitutes a real challenge to the codes with which the middle class, since the nineteenth century, has surrounded the consumption of alcohol. . . . Impossible, with a glass of pastis in hand, to speak of its legs, its bouquet, to evoke the history of its origins or ancient traditions. . . . You like it light, you like it cold. That's it. And that's Marseille."

Jean-Robert and I are having a pastis at a bar next to the Coquillages Toinou, a famous Marseille seafood restaurant. He's an old friend, and we're used to hanging out together in cafés and bars. "What is special about Marseille is that it is a city where people work and where they are not ashamed of working," he says. "That's why the Parisians look down on it. Here, there are still openly working-class bars, and you can go into a café at midmorning and find everyone having a quarter carafe of red wine or a café crème and discussing the mistakes the other team made in yesterday's game, no matter whether OM won or lost." OM is the wonderful acronym for Olympique de Marseille, the city's soccer team. "Marseille is hip, but it's real," says Jean-Robert. He gives a small smile. "A rare combination in France. *Les gens ici à Marseille aiment bosser et bouffer.*" People here in Marseille love to work and to eat.

Bosser et bouffer. We move on to the Coquillages Toinou. It's nine-thirty, and the landmark restaurant is a controlled madhouse. The lights are unbearably bright, but they seem like a good idea when you're eating huge platters of unheard-of shellfish and washing them down with carafes of unheard-of wine. Across two chairs at a nearby table lies a six-year-old, sleeping while her parents have a loud fight about French politics with their dining companions, leaning over her to pass one another the rouille and the aioli and the delicate vinegar sauce the French love to serve with oysters, because they believe — unlike the prudish Americans — that you should actually taste the slimy beast. Upon closer eavesdropping, I discover that the six-year-old's father seems to be a plumber and one of the women a dental hygienist. Not the kind of people you find doing Paris's finest dining.

Jean-Robert continues: "You can't live in Marseille if you don't care about race, about politics, and about fish and football." He laughs. "Not in that order, of course." The waiter brings out two vast aluminum trays covered with a mix of raw seafood, heavy on the oysters, clams, sea snails, and violets — not the tender love flower but some sort of lavender-colored oyster relative. Jean-Robert's twenty-three-year-old daughter looks at him strangely. She has always believed that her parents are cooler than most people's parents, but now her father is talking about fish and football? She loves Marseille for different reasons — for the fusion fashion scene, the music, the new-world outlook of its students and kids in general.

"What's great in this city is the sound," she says, shaking her head at her father. "IAM," she says, mentioning the fusion band that is one of the hottest things in France. "Akhenaton. Radio Grenouille." Akhenaton is IAM's leader. Radio Grenouille (Frog Radio) is the best station for listening to local bands. Bands like IAM, a Marseillais-Corsican-Neapolitan–North African fusion group, and the singer Khaled Sahra, who recorded the beautiful ballad "Oran–Marseille" (a song of immigration named after the Mediterranean crossing between the Algerian port and Marseille), have given the city a reputation, at least in France, as a world-music center. This reputation is furthered by the fact that more than twenty-five percent of Marseille's population is of North African descent, and the majority of these are young people who want to make, and hear, new music.

Back once again at the Bar le Maraichers, I'm speaking with Hassane, a big, handsome, bearded *maghrebin* (the old French slang for a North African) who runs it. We're talking about Marseille and crime. After France lost her North African colonies in the middle of this century, black-marketing, profiteering, organized crime, and drug trafficking eventually took up Marseille's economic slack. *The French Connection,* a classic 1970s film about corruption and drugs, was written about Marseille, and *Borsalino,* the Jean-Paul Belmondo–Alain Delon period piece about gamblers and gangsters in the 1930s, was shot in the city's run-down, pastel-painted immigrant neighborhood Le Panier.

"Ah yes, Marseille," Hassane says, laughing about its image as the vortex of world crime. "Big crime in Marseille is not like that anymore. The great figure of Marseille crime was really Bernard Tapie: a football supporter, a man of culture, a Socialist, a millionaire — and an embezzler. Most people felt terrible when he went down. He was a people's hero." (Tapie's embezzlement conviction in 1997 heralded the end of Socialist hegemony in Marseille. Even so, a recent grafitto outside Marseille read: TAPIE PRESIDENT.) Most Marseillais believe that the period of extreme violence and corruption in the city has come to an end. First of all, Marseille is no longer the best place for drug transshipment. The political changes in Eastern Europe have provided drug traffickers with European entry points that have looser controls and more chaotic governments, places where dirty dealing is simpler than in Marseille, or at least quicker. Second, many of Marseille's gangster figures have been indicted, convicted, and incarcerated. Things seem calmer. You hear about the occasional carjacking—and robberies and burglaries still occur with regularity, especially in the town's more disadvantaged outskirts — but cocaine and heroin are no longer king here. Le Panier is now halfway along toward a gentrified restoration.

Nightlife starts early at Hassane's establishment, with customers hanging out at the bar so soon after sunrise that you can't be sure they are not simply remnants from the night before. They come for a morning drop, stop by after lunch for "*un verre,*" and then spend long postprandial hours there chatting and gossiping and exchanging strongly held opinions about Fabrizio Ravanelli or Titi Camara, two of the most worshiped OM players, or Marseille music, or the new local fashion designers, or any aspect of French politics. On the walls of Le Bar le Maraichers hang black-and-white photos of Jacques Brel, Georges Brassens, and Léo Ferré, the leading musical lights of Paris café life in the 1950s and '60s.

Although Le Procope in Paris is heralded as the first French café, in fact the very first café opened next to Marseille's Hôtel de Ville in 1671, fifteen years before Le Procope was established. And coffee itself, the staple of places like Le Bar le Maraichers, was first brought to France by a Marseillais merchant. Typically, the Marseillais figured out a way to make this luxury item from Istanbul into a drink of the people. In 1730, Marseille began importing coffee from Martinique, and the cheaper cost — made possible by slavery — soon meant that it was available to anyone.

Hassane is drinking an espresso. He's so tall and lanky that he has to hunch over the table to get near his cup. He's from Algeria, but he came to Marseille at a very young and impressionable age. He loves that intellectual-cultural Brel-Brassens thing about France. "Marseille has a culture in common with all ports," says Hassane. "It's open and polyglot. I'm of Muslim origin, but my children consider themselves entirely integrated. Not that they've lost the meaning of their origins, of course, but they feel that to be what they are and to come from where they've come from is essentially a part of what it means to be French today."

This is the optimistic outlook of a first-generation immigrant. In Marseille, however, not far from the surface lurks a suspicion that the rest of France does not regard the more recent immigrants and their children as legitimately French. Bad enough that you're from Marseille, but an immigrant as well! Like the rest of Europe, France is in the throes of deciding what its nationality really means. After all, this is the land where Jean-Marie le Pen of the National Front has made tremendous political inroads on a pointedly racist platform. Marseille itself is sometimes considered a bastion of the Front, because many Marseillais — thousands of whom have foreign roots themselves, many Corsican or Sicilian — do not consider the hundreds of thousands of immigrants who have arrived in the last half century, many from postindependence Algeria, to be really deserving of French nationality. As one taxi driver, Alex, told me, "These people, they don't want to be French, but they want us to welcome them. They want everything from France, but they won't give up anything from their past. Either you are Michel or you are Mohammed, but you can't have it both ways."

Alex is wrong, though. The beauty of Marseille is that you *can* have it both ways: the delicate sautéed seafood with hot sauce, the chili peppers in the rouille for the bouillabaisse. If you go to the Cours Julien, a pretty, gentrifying square in La Plaine, you can find restaurants with names that range from L'Assiette Lyonnaise (the Dishes of Lyon) to Le Palais du Liban (the Palace of Lebanon).

The Cours Julien is Marseilles fashion central, and its ateliers and boutiques similarly display European and North African influences. The doyenne of Marseillais fashion is Mme. Zaza. The designs in her Cours Julien establishment have set the standard for *la mode* marseillaise: rich, brocaded ethnic clothing cut chic and close to the body. Mme. Zaza takes in every cultural accent Marseille has to offer, while paying close attention to what's happening in Paris and Milan. At Diable Noir, another couturier, the dresses are tulle fantasies, and in the back room a designer is putting together a wedding line: muslin and taffeta and satin are wrapped around mannequins and draped from the shelves, and flowers made from silk and chiffon and crinoline droop in wilted heaps from giant hatboxes. Diable Noir, like Mme. Zaza, possesses a certain retro aura that all Marseille designers seem to have, as if they want to express the city's history and specificity in their work.

The Marseillais are wondering what will happen to all of this cultural diversity and fusion gestalt when France becomes part of the new European Union. Jean-Robert thinks it's all to the good; that a European mind-set will stop France from being so Paris-centric and will allow Marseille, one of Europe's great ports, to gain the standing in the world that it has been denied by Paris.

But M. Bertrand is worried. "Our concern is that the center of gravity in the new Europe will be too far north for us, and that Marseille and the area around it will be sort of a rejected outpost on the outskirts of the great economic flow." He's counting on other things to keep Marseille vibrant, and one of these is the tourism that his conservative government has encouraged. "Marseille has outstripped Nice and Genoa economically, because of our new port. For sixty years, American cruise ships went to the Caribbean for the white sands and resorts, but now, with our increased capacity to receive them, they are coming to the Mediterranean, where they can find palm trees *and* gastronomic attractions. You can't get a bouillabaisse in Puerto Rico." M. Bertrand sits back behind the big desk in his crowded office in Marseille's gorgeous Baroque Hôtel de Ville. From the balustraded balcony off the building's vast second-floor reception area, you can see the breadth and length of the Vieux Port.

"Let's be honest," he says, pushing up his glasses. "For years Marseille was perceived as too low-rent, too working class to qualify as a tourist stop. Did you know that this is the only city in France where the city itself is poorer than its suburbs? And the leftist government: for them it was absolute heresy and completely unacceptable

to think about tourism. That image is diminishing. Now we're trying to promote Les Calanques and the forests. Nature. We are also
trying to attract one of the major hotel companies to come and
take the Hôtel Dieu, the former hospital, and turn it into a luxury
hotel, which is one of the few amenities we still cannot provide for
tourists. So tourism, yes, and it may help relieve the economic
problems caused by the Algerian situation. But taking our place in
history?" He gives that French downturned moue of the mouth, at
the same time sending his eyebrows skyward. "Somehow I doubt it."

Les Calanques are magnificent white cliffs that descend along the
coastline directly into the green Mediterranean. Sailing into their
protected lagoons or taking lunch at Le Lunch in Sormiou, among
the high sea cliffs, is a dizzying, unimaginable experience. And
there are other wonders on Marseilles peripheries, in particular
the village of L'Estaque, a seaside hamlet with an arching viaduct
where almost every Cubist and modernist and even some Impres-
sionists stayed and painted, Cézanne, Renoir, Braque, and Dufy
among them.

Jean-Robert's daughter laughs when she hears M. Bertrand's
comments about the comparative wealth of Marseille's suburbs.
"Ah," she says, "*Cagol* city." *Cagol* is derogatory Marseillais slang for
a young suburbanite who lives beyond his means and wears too
much jewelry and drives a car he can't afford. Jean-Robert himself
laughs at M. Bertrand's worries about Marseille's not being in the
center of the new Europe. The region at whose head he sees the
city eventually standing starts in Marseille and extends southward
and eastward, into Africa and the Middle East, into the ancient,
the exotic, the alien, and the unknown. When Jean-Robert thinks
about why he loves Marseille, he is not thinking about the bankers
of Zurich or the corporations of Frankfurt and Neuilly. He is thinking about art and music and culture. M. Bertrand is talking business, about the EU and the euro and European hegemony. Culture
and business: it's hard to say which is more important for Marseille's future right now — although ultimately you probably can't
have one without the other.

The people of Marseille have been characterized in many ways,
not all of them flattering, but common opinion is that they are
tough, quick, proud, volatile, garrulous, and compassionate. "The

only monument to see is its population," according to the writer Henri Bosco, in a pointed assessment of the city's architecture and its people. Caesar is said to have conquered all of Gaul, but in fact he failed for years to conquer Marseille, and when the city finally capitulated, the emperor gave it a special status as an independent city. The usual Roman practice was to massacre those who resisted, but Caesar spared the Marseillais because they were valiant.

But *les gens qui bossent et bouffent* have not always sailed through history valiant and irreproachable. At the Musée des Beaux-Arts at the Palais Longchamp — a folly of fountains built by the city in 1869 to celebrate the completion of the project that first brought a freshwater system to Marseille — the two most riveting canvases in an impressive collection are twin panoramic scenes by Michel Serre from the plague that decimated the city in 1720. In one, you can easily recognize the Hôtel de Ville and the elegant balustraded balcony, as well as the Vieux Port, which in this depiction is a purgatory where bodies line the walkways and poor dying souls reach up toward carriages carrying the wealthy out of town. From one-third to one-half of the city's population was killed by the plague Serre documented.

But Marseille's darkest period — like France's — came during the Nazi occupation. The scars are still visible, if you know what you're looking at. The Nazis, with the complicit Marseille police force, evacuated the city's old neighborhoods, including parts of Le Panier and the Quartier St-Jean near the Vieux Port, which was the working-class heart of the city and also the Jewish quarter. After the evacuation of forty thousand people, the 2,600-year-old area was bombed into oblivion "for reasons of public health and security." Many of the residents were rounded up and sent to the death camps. Anne Sportiello writes of the old quarter in *Thirteen Events from the History of Marseille:* "It was a neighborhood of fishermen, captains, dockers, and sea workers, but artisans and shopkeepers were also numerous. . . . People came from afar and from every neighborhood in town to shop in the great markets of the high street." The area that the old quarter covered now houses the new Marseilles corporate showpiece, the shiny and impressive, but sterile, port business zone.

Today, in spite of Marseille's quickness to destroy and renovate, there are still places where you can recapture what Marseille once had — the long history of the city, the crowds, the verve, and the excitement. One place is the Marché des Capucins. Another is the Arab quarter during the day, a little east and north of the business zone. Colorful banners hang above pedestrians' heads, stretching from one side of a narrow alley to the other, and there is always something to buy — traditional *tajines* with pointed covers, for example — and something to see and something to eat. And then there is the Vieux Port in the evening, perhaps at Le Bar de la Marine, a mahogany-filled Art Deco café-bar that was a favorite of the fabled Marseille director-writer Marcel Pagnol.

There is always plenty of action at Le Bar de la Marine after dusk. A few stylish men stand at one end of the bar, chatting and laughing. Some shopgirls are having after-work drinks at a table near the door. The waiter is busy handing out deep-fried *amuse-gueules* to his patrons. You're so close to the open door that if the patrons weren't making so much noise, you would be able to hear the clanking of the sailboats anchored in the marina. You can see the little harbor ferry scooting back and forth, as people leave the Hôtel de Ville and cross the waterway to entertain themselves here or at any number of bars and restaurants nearby. Sailors from the U.S.S. *Eisenhower* — an aircraft carrier anchored far out, but visible, on the Mediterranean — are busy getting drunker than you imagine a person can be and still remain vertical. Ecstatic to be on shore leave, they allow their spirits to rise higher and higher. The evening has hardly begun, and they are already revealing military secrets.

"Hi," says one inebriated blonde girl, "I'm Erica. I work in weapons sheathing."

Her comrades-at-arms — the men, anyway — look at one another and laugh at a private joke.

"I am drunk," says Erica, weaving slightly and holding on to the back of a chair to steady herself. "But not that drunk, I swear."

"I'm Amy from D.C.," another girl introduces herself. "I swear to God, Girl Scouts' honor. We make the bombs. I put the fans on, I put the fuses in." She looks at the boys, who can barely raise their heads up to return her gaze. "It turns me on."

The waiter shakes his head gently but firmly when the table requests more beer. The sailors try to stumble out but have to sit back down because they just can't get up on their sea legs.

*

Out on the Mediterranean, near the horizon and closer, oil tankers sit waiting to deliver their goods to Europe. The *Eisenhower* gleams eerily on the twilight waves. Lights go on in the string of restaurants that dot the Corniche, the broad road that winds along the coast, taking commuters out of town. THE BEST BOUILLA-BAISSE, boast the signs for one after another.

Night is falling over the Vieux Port, and colossal shadows of evening strollers flicker against the floodlit walls of Fort St-Jean. The double and triple masts sway against the sky as the boats they belong to rise and fall on the windblown surf. Tomorrow morning there will be a regatta. On the sidewalks of the Corniche, mothers are shepherding their children home from school and grocery shopping, and fathers are out walking the dog. Fishermen who have spent the sunny day leaning over the seawall, smoking and casting, are reeling in the day's last catch, cleaning the day's last fish, and packing up their vans. Nearby, a modern obelisk pays tribute to the French Algerians who returned through Marseille in 1962. AUX RAPATRIÉS, it proclaims. Beyond it, the blue and white *Ferryterranée*, a ferry–cruise boat that sails the Mediterranean between France and Corsica, plies the waves.

At the Galerie Marquage, in a pretty stucco building on a picturesque street off the Cours Julien, the owner, who calls himself Age (for no explicable reason), is trying to drum up business as the day ends. His gallery is showing an array of fusion pieces, works that incorporate desert sands and manger straw and Arabic calligraphy along with Marseille newspapers and industrial-strength plastic. "It looks great, doesn't it?" Age asks. "But it's not working." The economy, he says, is in a slump, no matter what M. Bertrand tells you. Age says that the conservative government is trying to drag Marseille into a kind of French touristic modernity with which the city actually has very little in common.

"Marseille has to be appreciated for itself," Age says, flicking his long brown hair back behind his muttonchop sideburns and over his shoulders. "There's a lot of new energy here, a diversity of people, and this diversity works. Marseille is a city to which one grows attached. It has a Provençal mentality. When things are good, they're good! When things are bad, everything is horrible. I'm feeling that it's horrible right now." He looks around the place. "But that could change with one good sale." He smiles at his prospective customers.

That's the spirit of this city of survivors — the refusal to lose hope, and the canny ability to judge the clientele, bargain in the marketplace, grab the chance, make a deal that satisfies both sides, and keep the juices flowing. It is an eternal fisherman's knack that you'll find in Marseille, not only among fishermen but among couturiers, musicians, booksellers, artists, art gallery directors — and politicians.

M. Bertrand is hoping to exploit this innate commercial skill, and Marseille's natural attractions, to make his city a reflexive stop for any tourist, instead of an acquired but addictive taste for the seasoned traveler. "Marseille has character," Jean-Robert concludes. It has character that has endured for its entire long history, from before Caesar's conquest. With any luck, that backbone will never be broken, and this perfectly situated city will gather more aficionados as its reputation grows.

Contributors' Notes
Notable Travel Writing of 1999

Contributors' Notes

William Booth covers the West for the *Washington Post* as bureau chief based in Los Angeles. His journalism has also appeared in numerous magazines. He is working on a book about the California islands.

Bill Buford is the fiction and literary editor of *The New Yorker*. Previously he was the editor of *Granta*. When he took over that magazine, it was a Cambridge University publication with a few hundred readers. Over the next fifteen years, he turned it into a critically acclaimed journal with an international circulation of one hundred thousand. Buford is the author of *Among the Thugs,* a highly personal nonfiction account of British soccer hooliganism and crowd violence, which has been translated into ten languages.

Tim Cahill was one of *Outside*'s founding editors. He is now a contributing editor for *Men's Journal*. His books include *A Wolverine Is Eating My Leg, Jaguars Ripped My Flesh, Pecked to Death by Ducks,* and *Pass the Butterworms: Remote Journeys Oddly Rendered.* Most recently he wrote the text for *Dolphins,* published by the National Geographic Society. He is the coauthor of the IMAX film *Everest* and of the documentary *The Living Sea,* which was nominated for an Academy Award.

Tom Clynes is an author and journalist whose passion for discovery has taken him around the world. He writes about and photographs off-the-beaten-path adventures, cultures, and personalities for publications such as *Outside, Men's Journal,* and the *Washington Post.* He is a contributing editor for *National Geographic Adventure.* His books include *Wild Planet!,* a guide to the world's extraordinary festivals and celebrations, and *Music Festivals from Bach to Blues*. He lives in New York City but continues to wander the world, trying to satisfy "a thirst for spectacle and a fascination with the planet's cultural nooks and crannies."

Dave Eggers is the editor of *McSweeney's*, a quarterly publication and Web site, and the author of *A Heartbreaking Work of Staggering Genius*. He lives in Brooklyn but is moving soon.

David Halberstam has received nearly every major journalistic award, including the Pulitzer Prize in 1964 for his early reports from Vietnam. Among his sixteen books are *Playing for Keeps, The Best and the Brightest, The Powers That Be, The Fifties, The Children,* and *Summer of '49*. He recently edited *The Best American Sports Writing of the Century*.

Mark Hertsgaard is the author of *Earth Odyssey: Around the World in Search of Our Environmental Future*, from which "The Nile at Mile One" is excerpted. He is also a commentator for National Public Radio's *Living on Earth*. He lives near Washington, D.C.

Isabel Hilton is a London-based writer, broadcaster, and documentary filmmaker. She is the author of *The Search for the Panchen Lama*, from which "Spies in the House of Faith" was adapted. She has been a columnist for the *Guardian* since 1996 and is a regular contributor to *The New Yorker,* the *New Statesman, Prospect, El Pais, Time, Granta,* the *New York Times Magazine,* the *Literary Review,* the *Financial Times,* the *Independent,* the *Observer,* and the *Economist*. She also currently presents the BBC radio program *Nightwaves*. Her documentaries include *Petra and the General,* an investigation of the life and death of Petra Kelly; *Kingdom of the Lost Boy,* an account of the search for the eleventh Panchen Lama; *City on the Edge,* a film about economic reforms in China; and *Condemned to Live,* a report on the aftereffects of mass rape and genocide in Rwanda.

Clive Irving was a founding editor of *Condé Nast Traveler* and is currently its senior consulting editor. He writes regularly for that magazine, specializing in pieces about Europe. He is also the author of three novels and four works of nonfiction. He lives in Sag Harbor, New York.

Alden Jones taught English in La Victoria, Costa Rica, in 1995 as a volunteer for WorldTeach, and has returned there so often that her former school director says she is "*como la mala hierba* — like that bad grass you just can't kill." She holds degrees in literature, Hispanic studies, and creative writing from Brown University and New York University. Her work has appeared in the *Iowa Review, Puerto del Sol, Time Out,* the *Barcelona Review,* and elsewhere. She lives in Vermont.

Ryszard Kapuscinski was born in 1932 in the city of Pinsk, in eastern Poland. His many books, including *The Soccer War, Another Day of Life, Imperium,* and *The Emperor,* have been translated into nineteen languages. Writing for the Polish Press Agency from 1958 to 1980, Kapuscinski covered twenty-seven revolutions and coups in Africa, the Middle East, and Latin America.

David Lansing writes a weekly column for the *Los Angeles Times* and is a contributing travel editor at *Sunset* magazine. His book, *Escape to the American Desert,* is forthcoming from Random House.

Jessica Maxwell wrote *Esquire*'s travel column for more than a decade and created *Audubon*'s in-the-field conservation column, "True Nature." She is a contributing editor at *Travel & Leisure Golf* and the author of three books: *I Don't Know Why I Swallowed the Fly: My Fly Fishing Rookie Season; Femme d'Adventure: Travel Tales from Inner Montana to Outer Mongolia;* and *Driving Myself Crazy: Misadventures of a Novice.* Her favorite fishing and golfing destination is Bhutan, because Buddhists aren't allowed to fish so the trout eat anything and because the thin Himalayan air gives duffers an extra fifty yards to their drives. Maxwell is the recipient of a creative writing fellowship for fiction from the National Endowment for the Arts and teaches writing at the University of Oregon between trips.

P. J. O'Rourke is the best-selling author of nine books, including *Holidays in Hell, Parliament of Whores, Give War a Chance,* and most recently *Eat the Rich.* He has written for *Automobile,* the *Weekly Standard, Esquire, Forbes FYI,* the *New Republic,* the *New York Times Book Review, Parade,* the *Wall Street Journal,* and *Rolling Stone,* where he is currently foreign affairs desk chief. He lives in New Hampshire with his wife and daughter.

Tony Perrottet is a freelance travel writer living in the East Village of Manhattan. He started writing as a foreign correspondent in Argentina and traveled extensively throughout South America before settling in New York City ten years ago. His travel writing has appeared in *Outside, Esquire, Civilization,* and the London *Sunday Times,* and he is a contributing editor at both *Escape* and *Islands.* A collection of his travel stories, *Off the Deep End: Travel in Forgotten Frontiers,* was published by HarperCollins/Flamingo in 1997; it describes commuting between an apartment on Tenth Street in

Manhattan to obscure outposts such as Iceland, the Tiwi Islands of Australia, and Tierra del Fuego. He is currently working on a book about following the trail of ancient travelers in the Mediterranean.

Rolf Potts writes "Vagabonding," a biweekly backpacker and adventure travel column on Salon.com. His first book of travel essays, *Marco Polo in Reverse,* will be published late in 2001.

Mark Ross was born in St. Louis, Missouri, and worked as a pilot and forest firefighter before becoming a safari guide based in Kenya. He has been working there for twenty years. He is also a skilled wildlife photographer. His book, *Dangerous Beauty: Life and Death in the Wild, True Stories from a Safari Guide,* will be published by TalkMedia Books in January 2001.

Steve Rushin is a senior writer at *Sports Illustrated.* His book, *Road Swing,* is an account of a year he spent traveling to America's sports shrines. He lives in New York City.

Patrick Symmes fled a career as a daily newspaper reporter to begin writing magazine dispatches about globalization and revolutionary movements in Latin America and Southeast Asia. A contributing editor at *Harper's Magazine,* he is the author of *Chasing Che: A Motorcycle Journey Through the Guevara Legend,* an account of a ten-thousand-mile dirt-bike trip across South America in the tracks of the legendary guerrilla leader.

Jeffrey Tayler is based in Moscow. He is a frequent contributor to the *Atlantic Monthly* and Salon.com, and his work has also appeared in *Harper's Magazine* and *Condé Nast Traveler.* He is a regular commentator on National Public Radio's *All Things Considered.* His first book, *Siberian Dawn,* was published in 1999; his second, an account of his travels on the Congo River, is forthcoming this fall.

Jonathan Tourtellot's first travel story was about the Nairobi-Mombasa train in Kenya, written for the *New York Times.* After three years of freelancing, he joined the staff of the National Geographic Society, becoming a senior editor in the book division and then moving to *National Geographic Traveler.* For *Traveler* and other publications, he has written about such disparate places as the Amazon, Baffin Island, Botswana, Iceland, Maui, the Isle of Man, and (courtesy of NASA hardware) the planet Neptune. In 1995 he launched a series of ecotourism articles in *Traveler* with his report on visitor damage to coral reefs. His subsequent stories for the series covered Atlantic saltmarshes, seal watching in the Magdalen Islands, ecotourism in Costa Rica, and cultural tourism in Samoa. "The Two Faces of Tourism" has won a Lowell Thomas Travel Journalism Award for environmental travel writing.

William T. Vollmann's latest book, *The Royal Family,* was published this summer. His other books include *The Atlas, The Rainbow Stories, Butterfly Stories, Whores for Gloria,* and *The Rifles.* The recipient of a Whiting Award, he lives in California.

David Wallis is a columnist for the *Washington Post* travel section who also contributes articles to *Condé Nast Traveler, The New Yorker,* the *New York Times,* and the *Observer.* In his ongoing quest to cover what he calls the "irony beat," he has traveled to South Africa to ride an ostrich, Costa Rica to crash the president's inauguration, West Virginia to attend sniper school, and Miami, where he scored an exclusive jailhouse interview with the former Panamanian strongman Manuel Noriega. He is based in New York.

Amy Wilentz is the author of *The Rainy Season: Haiti Since Duvalier* (Simon & Schuster, 1989). She writes frequently about the Middle East and is finishing work on a novel about Jerusalem.

Notable Travel Writing of 1999

SELECTED BY JASON WILSON